Eat the Bible

Eat the Bible

Food, Metaphor, and the Nature of Scripture

MICAH E. CHUNG

Foreword by James K. Dew Jr.

☙PICKWICK *Publications* · Eugene, Oregon

EAT THE BIBLE
Food, Metaphor, and the Nature of Scripture

Copyright © 2024 Micah E. Chung. All rights reserved. Except for brief quotations in critical publications or reviews, no part of this book may be reproduced in any manner without prior written permission from the publisher. Write: Permissions, Wipf and Stock Publishers, 199 W. 8th Ave., Suite 3, Eugene, OR 97401.

Pickwick Publications
An Imprint of Wipf and Stock Publishers
199 W. 8th Ave., Suite 3
Eugene, OR 97401

www.wipfandstock.com

PAPERBACK ISBN: 979-8-3852-1148-7
HARDCOVER ISBN: 979-8-3852-1149-4
EBOOK ISBN: 979-8-3852-1150-0

Cataloguing-in-Publication data:

Names: Chung, Micah E. [author]. | Dew, James K., Jr. [foreword writer].

Title: Eat the Bible : food, metaphor, and the nature of Scripture / Micah E. Chung.

Description: Eugene, OR: Pickwick Publications, 2024 | Includes bibliographical references and index.

Identifiers: ISBN 979-8-3852-1148-7 (paperback) | ISBN 979-8-3852-1149-4 (hardcover) | ISBN 979-8-3852-1150-0 (ebook)

Subjects: LCSH: Bible—Inspiration. | Bible—Evidence, authority, etc. | Bible—Criticism, interpretation, etc. | Metaphor—Religious aspects. | Metaphor in the Bible.

Classification: BS480 C486 2024 (paperback) | BS480 (ebook)

VERSION NUMBER 07/02/24

Scripture quotations taken from the (NASB®) New American Standard Bible®, Copyright © 1960, 1971, 1977, 1995 by The Lockman Foundation. Used by permission. All rights reserved. lockman.org

To Alice, my love

But Jesus answered and said,
"It is written, 'Man shall not live on bread alone,
but on every word that proceeds out of the mouth of God.'"

—MATTHEW 4:4

Contents

Foreword by James K. Dew Jr. | ix

Preface | xiii

Acknowledgments | xv

Introduction | xix

1 Setting the Table: Metaphors, Models, and Measures | 1

2 The Appetizers: Three Models of Scripture | 37

3 The Main Course: Scripture Is Food | 85

4 Doing the Dishes: Objections and Rejoinders | 154

Conclusion | 173

Bibliography | 177

Scripture Index | 215

Subject Index | 221

Foreword

St. Thomas Aquinas once said, "It is befitting Holy Writ to put forward divine and spiritual truths by means of comparisons with material things. For God provides for everything according to the capacity of its nature. Now it is natural to man to attain to intellectual truths through sensible objects, because all our knowledge originates from sense. Hence in Holy Writ spiritual truths are fittingly taught under the likeness of material things."[1]

In that spirit, Micah Chung takes up the vital question of how we should understand the Word of God. There is perhaps no greater privilege or responsibility we have as human beings than to partake of God's Word, which he has given to us, preserved for us, and illuminated through the Holy Spirit. These Scriptures are what we base our worldviews and indeed our lives upon. As Christians, then, we (at least we *should*) build our lives around the theological, spiritual, moral, and even practical commands it contains. We structure our churches according to the instructions given in the New Testament, handle our finances according to the wisdom of Proverbs, and strive to follow the Ten Commandments given in the Torah, while resting on the Gospels' account of Jesus' vicarious fulfilment of such commands we could never keep. We are, indeed, people of the book.

But not only do we as Christians believe what is *in* the Scriptures, but we also have beliefs *about* the Scriptures. And, to be sure, what we believe God's Word says is necessarily informed by how we view it and what we understand it to be. And, as with our understanding of anything else, we as fallen and epistemically limited human beings must see through a glass darkly.

---

1. St. Thomas Aquinas, *Summa Theologica* (Green Bay, WI: Aquinas Institute, 2012) 1.1.9.

FOREWORD

One of the principal ways in which we—as humans made in the image of God—attempt to understand that which may be opaque is through the use of metaphor. Not only is metaphor an inextricable part of human language, but it is also a tool and a strategy that can provide us with practical means by which we can understand what was previously unclear or difficult to grasp. Moreover, it can be used to reveal the complex and even beautiful nature of that which was previously unseen or unappreciated without the aid of such a clarifying tool.

This crucial task of better understanding the nature of Scripture—for the purpose of better understanding the *contents* of Scripture—is the one that Chung takes up in this work on Scripture and metaphor. In this work, Chung carefully illuminates the important place that metaphor and models have in human language and interpretation. Beginning with a helpful historical survey of various accounts of metaphor, going back even to Aristotle, he capably establishes the historical backdrop of the issue. Furthermore, he illustrates for the reader the crucial role of metaphor in human language, literature, psychology, and others, while also countenancing other historical detractors of the use of metaphorical language.

After surveying the historical backdrop, Chung introduces his readers to a handful of the most relevant and popular metaphorical models for understanding the Bible. Chung has interacted carefully and deeply with leading scholars on biblical metaphors. He has situated his own position deftly amongst the others by appreciating their contributions, adapting and adopting them when helpful, but nevertheless demonstrating the unique strengths of his own metaphorical system. Chung does all of this while using the Scriptures as his primary justification and source of evidence for his own proposed model. Chung has provided for us a metaphor for the Scriptures that is both biblically grounded and imminently reasonable. It is a metaphor that is widely useful and applicable in the hands of the ministers, scholars, and lay Christians alike.

Chung has creatively constructed this metaphor while remaining grounded in biblical reference. Instead of imagining or fabricating new paradigms that are untethered to how the Bible actually talks about itself, Chung, with great fidelity, employs the whole of Scripture as evidence for the validity of this metaphor. As such, the reader can rest assured of the legitimacy of Chung's "Scripture is food" model because he simply allows the text of the Bible to speak for itself.

FOREWORD

In the end, Chung succeeds in striking that difficult balance that all in Christian scholarship should be pursuing as he provides a unique and creative contribution to the field that is nevertheless rooted in the Scriptures themselves and against the backdrop of historical Christian tradition. As you seek to better understand the Word of God, whether for your own edification or for the sake of pastoral or academic instruction, I'm sure you will find this book, as I have, to be a fresh and helpful source of deeper understanding of the Scriptures. Moreover, you'll walk way with a fully replenished toolbox of helpful illustrations, analogies, and metaphors which are biblically faithful and spiritually potent. And, most importantly, you'll find yourself better equipped to lead the beggar to bread that will never go stale and never leave you hungry.

James K. Dew, Jr., PhD
president, New Orleans Baptist Theological Seminary
professor of Christian philosophy
January, 2024

Preface

PEOPLE LOVE THEIR METAPHORS for the Bible. The Bible is a mirror, a theatrical script, a musical score, a cathedral, a rule book, a user's manual, a lamp, a love letter. But how did metaphor, which in the eighteenth century was seen as a deceptive rhetorical trick, become such a prominent tool for speaking of Scripture? In this book, I explore the theological use of metaphor to describe the nature and interpretation of Scripture. I first trace a history of metaphor—from Aristotle's *Poetics* to Lakoff and Johnson's *Metaphors We Live By*—to show how metaphors become system-shaping models for understanding texts such as Scripture. I survey three such models for Scripture—Anthony Thiselton's "The Bible is a musical score," Kevin Vanhoozer's "The Bible is a theo-dramatic script," and John Feinberg's "The Bible is light"—and evaluate their faithfulness to Scripture and church tradition, fittingness to the subject and current culture, and fruitfulness for understanding and practicing Scripture. Based on these criteria, I argue that the three models, though helpful, fall short of communicating the nature of Scripture adequately. I thus propose a biblically derived model, "Scripture is food," that safeguards more effectively, discloses more comprehensively, and renders more viscerally the nature of Scripture. I develop this food model from the biblical text and historical theology, specifically drawing from the works of Athanasius, Origen, Gregory the Great, Eugene Peterson, Norman Wirzba, and John Feinberg. I then evaluate the food model over against the other three models to demonstrate that the food model better communicates the nature of Scripture. I also defend the food model against general, theological, and practical objections, and I employ the model to outline practical implications for the nature and function of Scripture today.

Acknowledgments

"The Lord has done great things for us; we are glad" (Ps 126:3). First and foremost, I praise God for his faithfulness and provision throughout this amazing journey of writing this book. My deepest appreciation goes to my wife, Alice, who has loved and supported me steadfastly throughout this process of writing for these past six years, during which we've had two beautiful children, Evelyn and Elijah.

I wholeheartedly thank my parents, Wilfred and Sharon Chung, who brought me up in the fear of the Lord and modeled for me how to love God and his Word, the Bible. I thank them especially for watching Evie weekly this past year so that I could complete this book. I also thank my brother, Caleb, his wife, Jenny, and my niece, Kira, for their love and prayers for me. My thanks also go to David and Tsui Lai, my parents-in-law, who also watched over Evie on countless occasions and kept me well fed so that I could think and write.

Evie taking my advice a little too literally (2024)

I praise God for the churches who have nurtured me throughout my life and especially during this season of study: Chinese Community Baptist Church (Lake Forest, CA), Brooklyn Chinese Baptist Church (Brooklyn, NY), and Metairie Church (Metairie, LA). Specifically, I thank Augustine Hui, who has served as my faithful pastor, friend, and groomsman for my wedding. I also owe a great debt of gratitude to his parents, Pastor Mark and Florence Hui, who have taken me under their wing and loved me as their own son. I also thank the New Orleans Baptist Association, especially Jack Hunter, Alex Brian, and Leroy Fountain, who supported me with a job as administrative assistant for three years and provided me with steadfast encouragement along the way.

My immense gratitude goes to the faculty and staff of the New Orleans Baptist Theological Seminary, which has proven a place of healing, nurture, and growth for me during six years of PhD study, especially through the Leeke Magee Christian Counseling Center. I specifically thank the professors who led my seminars and colloquia: Jeffrey Riley, Page Brooks, Rhyne Putman, Jamie Dew, Larry Lyon, Mike Edens, Adam Harwood, Steve Lemke, Rex Butler, Robert Stewart, Lloyd Harsch, and Tyler Wittman. This book would not have been possible without their wise guidance, constant encouragement, academic excellence, and Christlike example both in and out of class. I especially thank Dr. Stewart for entrusting me with a job as his research assistant for four years. My deepest thanks go to Dr. Riley, who not only served as Guidance Committee Chairperson for my PhD dissertation but met with me weekly for four years to provide academic and spiritual guidance. He went above and beyond to nurture and encourage me through this process of writing. I also thank Dr. Putman, who served as Second Chair of my Guidance Committee and pastored me through some of the most difficult moments of my journey toward the PhD. Dr. Putman's seminar on the theological interpretation of Scripture provided the fruitful context in which the initial ideas for this book germinated. I thank Dr. Harwood, who served as third reader for my dissertation and provided invaluable comments and insights. I am deeply grateful to Pam Cole, who edited this work for form and style. I also appreciate Zach Bruketta, who led the office of financial aid at NOBTS and secured for me an emergency scholarship during a particularly trying semester.

I owe thanks to Joe Waller, who has shared countless meals with me discussing the contents of this work, and to Chuck Anderson, who first broached the subject of completing my PhD while I lived in New York City. Thanks also to Dr. Greg Woodward, who welcomed me to New Orleans with his characteristic enthusiasm and hospitality, and to my fellow classmates, who have sharpened me as I hope to have sharpened them (cf. Prov 27:17).

My deep gratitude goes to Dr. Robin Parry, who reached out to meet with me during the 2023 annual meeting of the Evangelical Theological

Society. He served as managing editor for this book. Without his initiative, interest, and partnership, this book would not exist. Thanks also to Wipf and Stock for publishing my work.

May God be glorified in this work, through which I hope many will "taste and see that the Lord is good" (Ps 34:8). I dedicate this work to my wife, Alice, my partner in the grace of life. I pray that we will never cease to eat and share God's Word as a joy and delight to our hearts (cf. Jer 15:16).

Introduction

ASK CONTEMPORARY SCHOLARS, "WHAT is a text?" and their answer will likely come in a metaphor. For instance, Dale Martin writes, "Is [a text] like a box containing something we call 'meaning'? Is it a puzzle we must figure out? Is it an opportunity for creating something, like the raw material for the production of meaning?"[1] Such metaphors carry far-reaching implications for how one might interpret a text, especially a text like the Bible, which evangelicals regard as authoritative Scripture and the written word of God.[2] Unsurprisingly, then, theologians use metaphors to describe the ontology of Scripture: "What is the nature of Scripture? Should we understand it as a

---

1. Martin, *Pedagogy of the Bible*, 17. These metaphors correlate with Stephen Fowl's conception of texts being either determinate, anti-determinate, or underdeterminate. If texts have determinate meaning, they are a "puzzle" the reader must figure out. If texts have anti-determinate meaning, they are "raw material" merely serving the aims and purposes of the reader. If texts have underdeterminate meaning, they are an "opportunity" for meaningful interaction between text and reader. See Fowl, *Engaging Scripture*, 32–61. Eugene Peterson recommends metaphor as the starting point for interpreting Scripture, claiming that misunderstanding metaphor will lead to misunderstanding most of the Bible. See Peterson, *Eat This Book*, 93.

2. Much debate surrounds the meaning of the authority of Scripture. Martin distinguishes between authorities such as governmental, scientific, and even culinary. Cf. Martin, *Pedagogy of the Bible*, 80. For the purposes of this book, calling the Bible authoritative means that it has come from God and thus has the right to command belief and obedience. In Fowl's words, "The Bible, for Christians, is their scripture. As scripture, the Bible provides a normative standard for the faith, practice, and worship of Christian communities." Fowl, *Engaging Scripture*, 2. Putman highlights how the authority of the Bible comes from God, not from the Bible itself: "evangelicals, with the consensus of Christian believers for the past two millennia, recognize that biblical authority is God's authority. The divinely inspired and human words of Scripture serve as the primary instrument or vehicle of divine authority in the world today." Putman, *In Defense of Doctrine*, 6.

INTRODUCTION

rule book? a constitution? a foundational document? a 'space' we occupy?"[3] These questions are not trivial; they highlight how metaphor can form the basis for one's understanding of the ontology of the Bible, and there "are many different conceptions or assumptions about what sort of thing the Bible is. How one interprets Scripture, though, depends a great deal on what one thinks the Bible is. Most people . . . are tacitly working with implicit—almost never explicit—models of Scripture."[4] These models of Scripture are metaphors that have become system-shaping and central to one's understanding of the nature of Scripture. Yet not all metaphors are created equal, and one cannot simply choose whatever metaphor one wants. The choice of wrong metaphor can reduce, distort, or even conceal attributes of Scripture, such as its authority, necessity, sufficiency, and clarity.

In this book, I will argue that metaphorical models play an essential role in conveying the nature of Scripture but that current models, though helpful, fall short of communicating that nature adequately. I propose a biblically derived model, "Scripture is food," that safeguards more effectively, discloses more comprehensively, and renders more viscerally the nature of Scripture. My argument will proceed in two stages. By tracing a history of metaphor to show how metaphors become powerful models that shape one's view of reality, I will gather criteria for evaluating models. I will use these criteria to critique three current models of Scripture—Anthony Thiselton's "Scripture is a musical score," Kevin Vanhoozer's "Scripture is a theo-dramatic script," and John Feinberg's "Scripture is light"—over against the model of "Scripture is food" to demonstrate how the food model conveys the nature of Scripture better than the other models. I will conclude by answering possible objections to the model and suggesting areas for further study.

---

3. Martin, *Pedagogy of the Bible*, 21. Martin places the question of the nature of Scripture at the root of theological interpretation: "The different questions raised by issues of theological hermeneutics are many and could be multiplied ad infinitum. But they all basically come down to the central issues concerning the nature of Scripture and how it should be interpreted in the life of the church and in the lives of individual Christians." Martin, *Pedagogy of the Bible*, 22. Martin criticizes fundamentalism for its model of Scripture as "a machine for generating truths and rehearsing known truths." Martin, *Pedagogy of the Bible*, 60. Peterson adds the fortune cookie or astrological chart as illegitimate metaphors for Scripture. Cf. Peterson, *Eat This Book*, 101.

4. Martin, *Pedagogy of the Bible*, 74.

Importance of the Study

Metaphor harnesses the power of language to describe and shape the world people live in, and some metaphors not only shape systems but become new systems, or models, for experiencing the world.[5] The metaphorical models one uses to describe the Bible, therefore, really matter in shaping one's understanding of the nature of Scripture.[6] Though models such as Vanhoozer's theo-dramatic script, Thiselton's musical score, and Feinberg's light have important insights to add to one's understanding of the nature of Scripture, the intra-biblical model of food offers a more real, universal, vital, and comprehensive vision of the nature of Scripture.

Definitions of Terms

The following terms figure prominently in this book and impact its thesis: food, metaphor, model, nature, and Scripture. Unless otherwise specified, they carry these definitions.

Food

One might define food as simply "something fit to eat," but food also carries complex social, psychological, political, and cultural meaning.[7] As "the first of the essentials of life, the world's largest industry, and our most frequently

---

5. Fiumara suggests that the ability of metaphor to promote new social structures may have influenced Aristotle to prohibit slaves from using metaphor. Perhaps he did not want slaves to change the structure of Greek society, and granting "permission to address their 'superiors' metaphorically would be comparable to recognizing slaves' capacity to migrate from one epistemic context to another." Fiumara, *Metaphoric*, 2. When metaphors solidify into models, they can enhance or subvert current social structures. As Boersma notes, "Metaphors take words out of their original contexts and use them in new, *seemingly inappropriate* ways." Boersma, *Violence, Hospitality, and the Cross*, 101, emphasis mine.

6. Metaphor involves both "coming up with new definitions for things" and "discovering everything that can be said about a given subject." Eco, *From the Tree to the Labyrinth*, 41. Thus George Lakoff and Mark Johnson can say that "the human conceptual system is metaphorically structured and defined." Lakoff and Johnson, *Metaphors We Live By*, 6. Gemma Fiumara considers metaphor an "indicator of our cultural metabolism . . . the use of one part of experience to illuminate another." Fiumara, *The Metaphoric Process*, 26. Metaphors have "transformative power" in that they allow people "to influence and shape [their] environment." Boersma, *Violence, Hospitality, and the Cross*, 103.

7. Hung, "The Original Taste of Real Food," 149.

indulged pleasure," food brings with it "considerable concern and dread."[8] Highlighting these complexities, David Kaplan lists no less than thirteen conceptions of what food can be: nature, nutrition, fuel, medicine, diet, pleasure, taboo, commodity, goods, meaning, spirituality, recipe, and art.[9] Given these sociocultural factors, food researchers customarily distinguish between "feeding" (what all animals do by intaking food) and "dining" (what only humans do by attaching cultural significance to food).[10] Norman Wirzba even points out that food connects profoundly to death and sacrifice, and probably "nothing is more frightening than the prospect of running out of food."[11]

For the purposes of this book, I adopt Kaplan's definition of food as "a substance or material that originates in the environment in plants, animals, or water. It is made up of naturally occurring nutrients metabolized by an organism to sustain, grow, and repair vital life processes. The primary function of food is to provide nourishment to an organism."[12] This definition highlights that food is fundamental to survival and includes both solid and liquid nutriment, which subsumes drink under the category of food. Yet one must keep in mind that food comprises much more than ingested material but also has theological, social, psychological, political, and cultural aspects, many of which this book will explore in chapter 3.

Metaphor

Historically, two major views of metaphor have prevailed: the classical "substitution" view and the more recent "interaction" view. An original proponent of what is now called the "substitution" view, Aristotle defines the Greek word *metaphora* as "giving a thing a name that belongs to something else."[13] In other words, to make a metaphor means to substitute one thing's name for another's to enhance one's speech.

---

8. Belasco, "Future of Food: A History," 676.
9. Kaplan, *Food Philosophy*, 19.
10. Belasco, *Food: The Key Concepts*, 15.
11. Belasco, "Future of Food," 676; cf. Wirzba, *Food and Faith*, 40, 93–94, 156–62. Daily, humans remain painfully aware that they "must eat or somehow take in nutrients. This makes eating one of a remarkably short list of 'vitals' without which human life cannot be sustained." Boisvert and Heldke, *Philosophers at Table*, 126.
12. Kaplan, "Introduction," 3.
13. Aristotle, *Poetics*, 1457b6.

Since I. A. Richards's *The Philosophy of Rhetoric* in 1936, however, the "interaction" view has gained prominence, which defines metaphor as the union of two halves: a tenor (or principle subject) and a vehicle (an idea or object from which attributes are borrowed to describe the tenor). Richards thus recognizes metaphor as more than a displacement of names but "a borrowing between and intercourse of thoughts, a transaction between contexts."[14] This view has given rise to Janet Soskice's definition of metaphor, which I adopt in this book: "speaking about one thing in terms which are seen to be suggestive of another."[15] This definition captures that metaphor involves not only names or objects but also thoughts and ideas, which do not collapse together but remain "in permanent tension with one another" in a complex interplay of similarity and difference between the tenor and vehicle.[16]

Soskice's definition also highlights that metaphors are not neutral but *suggestive*, seeking to direct or affect the hearer to think or feel a certain way. Thus, metaphors can result in vital shifts in meaning and "in this sense are seen as "rule-changing" and not just "rule-governed" aspects of language. They do not follow established conventions but break new ground in creating a dialectic between literal and figurative truth as one's perspective on 'the way things are' (God and the world) is transformed."[17] In other words, metaphors have "structural as well as affective power," able to structure and even change how people view reality.[18]

14. Richards, *The Philosophy of Rhetoric*, 94.
15. Soskice, *Metaphor and Religious Language*, 49.
16. McFague, *Metaphorical Theology*, 42.
17. Osborne, *The Hermeneutical Spiral*, 388.
18. McFague, *Metaphorical Theology*, 42. One should distinguish what a metaphor is not. It is not symbol, analogy, allegory, satire, synecdoche, metonymy, or simile. It is not a symbol because a symbol need not be linguistic (like the cross in Christianity). It is not an analogy because analogy only speaks of positive comparison, whereas metaphor can cover negative contrasts as well; metaphor "involves two terms which are contrasted *and* compared." Soskice, *Metaphor and Religious Language*, 20. Allegory and satire differ from metaphor in scope and intention, since their scope is usually much longer than a single statement and their intention is often to disguise rather than to clarify. Synecdoche and metonymy resemble metaphor but differ in that they make one term "stand in" for another, while metaphor does not include this "standing in" but rather "interaction" of its two terms. Simile differs from metaphor in that simile creates "epistemic distance" by its use of "like" or "as." See Soskice, *Metaphor and Religious Language*, 56–60. Aristotle calls simile "less attractive" than metaphor since it is longer and "does not say outright that 'this' *is* 'that', and therefore the hearer is less interested in the idea." Aristotle, *The Rhetoric and the Poetics of Aristotle*, 1410b18–19; cf. 1406b20–26.

INTRODUCTION

Model

A model is "a representation of the real or imaginary thing for which it stands."[19] Max Black distinguishes between four types of models: scale (as in a model plane), analogue (as in economic systems or electrical circuits), mathematical (as in the analytical equations that represent empirical data), and theoretical (those that constitute systems of thought).[20] In this book, the term *models* refers to theoretical models, which derive from metaphor and constitute "metaphysical systems" of thought.[21] Such models are thus "*systematically-developed metaphors*" that suggest "new ways of looking at a problematical situation by transferring some of the features of another situation which is better understood."[22] As "imaginative mental constructs invented to account for observed phenomena,"[23] theoretical models are "dominant metaphors" that play an influential role in sustaining progress and constituting coherent systems of thought in both science and theology, as will be shown in chapter 1. Such models even become "major ways of structuring and ordering experience."[24]

Nature

I understand *nature* to include not just essential characteristics or attributes but also how something behaves, functions, and accomplishes its goals. *Nature* thus carries implicit assumptions about function, interpretation, and application, which become subsumed under the category "nature."[25] Regarding the nature of Scripture, then, *nature* refers to what Scripture is, what it does, and how it is to be interpreted and applied, thus encompassing

---

19. Black, *Models and Metaphors*, 220.
20. Black, *Models and Metaphors*, 219–43.
21. Black, *Models and Metaphors*, 240.
22. Barbour, *Myths, Models and Paradigms*, 43.
23. Barbour, *Myths, Models and Paradigms*, 30.
24. McFague, *Metaphorical Theology*, 23.
25. Hans Georg Gadamer also rejects any hard-and-fast distinction between nature, interpretation, and function. He questions the longstanding division between understanding (*subtilitas intelligendi*), interpretation (*subtilitas explicandi*), and application (*subtilitas applicandi*), arguing that these cannot exist in isolation from one another but inform one another inseparably. Gadamer, *Truth and Method*, 308–11; cf. Thiselton, *The Hermeneutics of Doctrine*, 91.

its essence, function, effect, and goals.[26] Distinguishing between these facets of the nature of Scripture can prove helpful and necessary, but one cannot understand the nature of Scripture apart from its interpretation since God's communication "is bound up with our interpretation of the Bible as 'Holy Scripture.'"[27] Nature and interpretation inextricably inform one another, and one's understanding of the nature of Scripture in many ways predetermines and conditions how one interprets it. As Dale Martin puts it, "How one interprets Scripture . . . depends a great deal on what one thinks the Bible is."[28] So even if one were to try to develop a model for only the interpretation of Scripture, that model nonetheless carries implications for the nature of Scripture. The interpretation of Scripture, therefore, fits under the category of its nature.

Scripture

Writing from an evangelical perspective, I define Scripture as the sixty-six-book canon of the Bible, identifying that Bible as the written Word of God. Rhyne Putman summarizes this evangelical perspective: "Evangelicals contend that the biblical canon is the written word of God and the supreme and unrivaled authority in matters of faith and practice."[29] Evangelicals thus equate the Bible, the Word of God, and Scripture, and this equating makes biblical interpretation distinctly theological: "'Theological interpretation' means simply interpreting the text of the Bible *as Scripture*, the 'word of God.'"[30] This identification of Scripture, or the Bible, as the written Word of God implicitly assumes the supreme authority of Scripture as the "primary and governing source" of evangelical theology, which evangelicals term *sola scriptura*.[31]

---

26. See Webster, *The Domain of the Word*, 3–19.
27. Allen, *Theological Method*, 13.
28. Martin, *Pedagogy of the Bible*, 74.
29. Putman, *In Defense of Doctrine*, 4–5.
30. Martin, *Pedagogy of the Bible*, 21. Havilah Dharamraj thus calls the Bible the Word of God "inscripturate." Dharamraj, "On the Doctrine of Scripture," 56.
31. Feinberg, *No One Like Him*, 26–27.

INTRODUCTION

Delimitations

I cannot address every work on metaphors or models but will cover the major ones to get a sense of historical context and helpful criteria for evaluating models. I also cannot list all types of models in science and theology but will focus on metaphorical, or theoretical, models.

Being a human eater is a theological, philosophical, and social concept. Speaking biblico-theologically, food spans the entirety of redemptive history, from the fall to the marriage supper of the Lamb. Since the data on food is overwhelming in amount and scope, I limit the number of works addressing food and Scripture. Though many church fathers mention food, I draw insights only from select fathers, such as Athanasius, Origen, and Gregory the Great. I also limit the biblical and theological works to major ones needed to present the food model of Scripture.

This book does not present an exhaustive doctrine of Scripture. Not every detail of the doctrine will receive in-depth treatment but only those details that show how food can influence one's understanding of the doctrine and its categories. For example, I concentrate on how food can help to communicate the way Scripture nurtures, gives life, and demands surrender. These kinds of insights remain the focus of this book. I also do not address every reference to food in Scripture but will concentrate specifically on passages that link food to the Word of God, especially the Word of God as written document.

Outline

This book will proceed in four chapters. Chapter 1, "Setting the Table: Metaphors, Models, and Measures," traces a brief history of metaphor to demonstrate how metaphors turn into system-shaping models and to glean criteria to evaluate models. Chapter 2, "The Appetizers: Three Models of Scripture," uses the criteria gathered from chapter 1 to evaluate three helpful models—Anthony Thiselton's "Scripture is a musical score," Kevin Vanhoozer's "Scripture is a theo-dramatic script," and John Feinberg's "Scripture is light." Chapter 3, "The Main Course: Scripture Is Food," queries Scripture and theology to substantiate and develop the model "Scripture is food," and I evaluate this model over and against the other three to show how the food model better conveys the nature of Scripture. Chapter 4, "Doing the Dishes: Objections and Rejoinders," answers objections to the food model. A brief conclusion sums up main points and suggests areas of further research.

I

Setting the Table

Metaphors, Models, and Measures

TRACING A HISTORY OF metaphors demonstrates how they become system-shaping, reality-depicting models. This history also supplies criteria by which to evaluate models.

Metaphor: A Brief History

Aristotle: Metaphor as Sign of Genius

The first known analysis of metaphor comes from Aristotle in his *Poetics* and *Rhetoric* (c. 330 BCE).[1] He defines the Greek word *metaphora* as "giving a thing a name that belongs to something else."[2] This name transfer-

---

1. See Soskice, *Metaphor and Religious Language*, 1.

2. Aristotle, *Poetics*, 1457b6. Aristotle divides metaphor into four types: genus to species, species to genus, species to species, and analogy. Only the last, analogy, is considered metaphor today. Cf. Aristotle, *Poetics*, 1457b6. The Greek *metaphora* means "to transfer" (*meta* "trans" + *pherein* "to carry"). Soskice, *Metaphor and Religious Language*, 1. George Kennedy adds, "*Metaphor* is itself a metaphor and literally means 'carrying something from one place to another' . . . 'a movement [*epiphora*] of an alien [*allotrios*] name.'" Kennedy, *Aristotle on Rhetoric*, 222. As for the term *allotrios* ("alien"), Paul Ricoeur contends that Aristotle uses it "to assimilate three distinct ideas: *deviation* from ordinary usage, *borrowing* from an original usage, and *substitution* for an absent word by an available ordinary word." Ricoeur, *The Rule of Metaphor*, 303.

ence enhances speech with liveliness, beauty, clarity, persuasiveness, and extension of knowledge.³ Since such benefits come from using metaphor,

> 3. Aristotle, *Rhetoric*, 1411a1–b29. Liveliness results from "being graphic (i.e. making your hearers *see* things). . . . By 'making them see things' I mean using expressions that represent things as in a state of activity." Aristotle, 1411b22. A prime example is "Homer's common practice of giving metaphorical life to lifeless things. . . . [Homer] represents everything as moving and living; and activity is movement." Aristotle, *Rhetoric*, 1411b32, 1412a8–23.
>
> By beauty, Aristotle means that metaphors must both sound and mean beautiful things. See Aristotle, *Rhetoric*, 1405b6. For instance, Aristotle recommends using "rosy-fingered morn" instead of "crimson-fingered" or, even worse, "red-fingered." Aristotle, *Rhetoric*, 1405b19. This beauty includes appropriateness to the subject discussed, as when "one word is more proper than another and more like the object signified and more adapted to making the thing appear 'before the eyes.'" Kennedy, *Aristotle on Rhetoric*, 225. Metaphors "are inappropriate if they are ridiculous or overly dignified, and so they fail to persuade." Austin, *Plant Metaphors*, 25.
>
> Clarity means that the metaphor is immediately grasped by the audience. Cf. Aristotle, *Rhetoric*, 1410b34. For Aristotle, "the virtue of style is clarity. . . . Metaphors are important to good style because they help people understand things clearly." Aristotle, 1411b22. In Eco's words, metaphors must "'put the thing before our eyes.' . . . Aristotle appears to insist on it with conviction: a metaphor is not a mere transfer but a transfer that is immediate in its evidence—but clearly unfamiliar, unexpected, thanks to which things are seen in action (1410b34), or better, signified in action." Eco, *From the Tree*, 64.
>
> For more on persuasiveness, see Aristotle, *Rhetoric*, 1405a3–19. In Austin's words, "Metaphors push thinking in certain directions. [Aristotle] says metaphors need to be appropriate; if one wishes to honor something, one uses metaphors that come from something higher (like saying a beggar prays instead of begs), and to insult, one uses something worse" Austin, *Plant Metaphors*, 24; cf. Aristotle, *Rhetoric*, 1410b21–25. For instance, Aristotle notes that calling someone a "mother-slayer" provokes people to think negatively of a person, while calling someone "his father's avenger" does the opposite. Aristotle, *Rhetoric*, 1405b23. Drawing from Aristotle, Gemma Fiumara calls metaphors "mediating instruments" for "sharpening thought." Fiumara, *The Metaphoric Process*, 116. In contrast to the clarity of metaphor, "Words of ambiguous meaning are chiefly useful to enable the sophist to mislead his hearers." Aristotle, *Rhetoric*, 1404b32. Aristotle warns against such ambiguity: "Metaphors must not be far-fetched, or they will be difficult to grasp, nor obvious, or they will have no effect." Aristotle, *Rhetoric*, 1410b31–34.
>
> By "extension of knowledge," Aristotle means that metaphors aid in learning new ideas by helping hearers "to get hold of new ideas easily. . . . It is from metaphor that we can best get hold of something fresh." Aristotle, *Rhetoric*, 1410b10–15. In *Poetics*, Aristotle suggests that metaphor has the capacity to "name the unnamed." Aristotle, *Poetics*, 1457b. Thus, metaphor can "fill what linguists now call lexical gaps," and thus "metaphor may be active in the extension of our understanding." Soskice, *Metaphor*, 9. Paul Ricoeur draws out implications for interpretation: "Metaphor . . . introduces the spark of imagination into a 'thinking more' at the conceptual level. This struggle to 'think more' . . . is the soul of interpretation." Ricoeur, *Rule of Metaphor*, 303. Eco notes how metaphor can work to change one's mind entirely: "When the metaphor makes us see things the opposite from the way we thought they were, it becomes evident that we have learned

Aristotle calls metaphor "a sign of genius" that cannot be taught, so that "the greatest thing by far is to be a master of metaphor."[4]

One reason Aristotle's study remains fascinating today is "that this first theorization of metaphor does not consider it as a mere ornament of discourse but assigns it a cognitive function."[5] In other words, metaphors do something to the mind: they cause the mind to reach "beyond" the metaphor's naming function and begin to see new meanings, new horizons, new ways of understanding the world.[6] For example, Aristotle observes that pirates like to refer to themselves as *purveyors*, a positive term borrowed from the mercantile realm.[7] By calling themselves *purveyors* instead of *pirates*, pirates thus insinuate "that the plunderer and the merchant share a characteristic in common, since both of them facilitate the transfer of goods from a source to the consumer," and this linguistic shift subtly encourages the society of their day "to reconsider the role of the pirate in the economy of the Mediterranean."[8] Metaphors suggest new attitudes, new mindsets, and even new models for seeing reality.

Aristotle also recommends using solemn metaphors for solemn matters and trivial metaphors for trivial matters. To suggest outrage, one should use the language of anger. To suggest celebration, one should use the language of exultation.[9] In other words, metaphors must be "fitting," which means that "they must fairly correspond to the thing signified."[10] Aristotle likens this "fittingness" to putting a red cloak on a young man while putting

---

something, and our mind seems to say: 'That's the way it was, and I was mistaken about it.'" Eco, *From the Tree*, 64.

4. Aristotle, *Poetics*, 1459a6. Metaphor reveals genius because "a good metaphor implies an intuitive perception of the similarity in dissimilars" and because it "is the one thing that cannot be learnt from others." Aristotle, 1459a6. Eco reasons that since metaphor cannot be learned from others, Aristotle implies that "therefore it is not a matter of mere imitation but of invention." Eco, *From the Tree*, 63.

5. Eco, *From the Tree*, 62.

6. Peterson calls this ability of metaphor to suggest new meanings as its "beyond": "the 'beyond' extends and brightens our comprehension rather than confusing it." Peterson, *Eat This Book*, 96.

7. Aristotle, *Rhetoric*, 1405a20–33. Aristotle explains that "two different words will represent a thing in two different lights; so on this ground also one term must be held fairer or fouler than another. For both of two terms will indicate what *is* fair, or what *is* foul." Aristotle, *Rhetoric*, 1405b8–10.

8. Eco, *From the Tree*, 63.

9. Aristotle, *Rhetoric*, 1408a10–19.

10. Aristotle, *Rhetoric*, 1405a3–5.

a dignified coat on an old man. Saying that a begging man is "praying" suggests a positive attitude, while saying that a praying man is "begging" suggests the opposite.[11] So metaphors are not "neutral" but suggest certain attitudes and actions, like loving and hating, "nurturing and nourishing, ... caring and tolerating, improving and preserving."[12] Aristotle thus sets the tone for all subsequent treatments of metaphor.

Quintilian: Metaphor as Beautiful Substitution

Quintilian, in *Institutio Oratoria*, calls metaphor "the commonest and by far the most beautiful of tropes."[13] Agreeing with Aristotle that metaphor transfers a noun or verb "from the place to which it properly belongs to another," Quintilian clarifies how metaphor can extend knowledge by giving a name "where there is either no literal term or the transferred is better than the literal."[14] Some metaphors merely "produce a decorative effect," but in some cases metaphor proves necessary to clarify the meanings of things that otherwise cannot be communicated.[15]

Contrasting metaphor to simile, Quintilian emphasizes how metaphor moves beyond comparison to actual substitution of two things, creating "effects of extraordinary sublimity" and rendering some metaphors "almost hazardous."[16] For example, to say that a man does something "like a lion" suggests a looser comparison, but to say that a man "is a lion" produces a much closer and more provocative association between the two.[17]

To use metaphor too frequently, however, serves not to beautify or clarify but "merely to obscure our language and weary our audience."[18] Quintilian thus warns against overusing metaphor unless the moment proves "temperate and timely."[19] One misuses metaphor if it appears too far-fetched or employed simply for metrical necessity, as in poetry.[20] Like

11. Aristotle, *Rhetoric*, 1405a5–19.
12. Fiumara, *Metaphoric*, 37.
13. Quintilian, *Institutio Oratoria*, 8.6.4.
14. Quintilian, *Institutio Oratoria*, 8.6.5.
15. Quintilian, *Institutio Oratoria*, 8.6.6.
16. Quintilian, *Institutio Oratoria*, 8.6.11, 14.
17. Quintilian, *Institutio Oratoria*, 8.6.9.
18. Quintilian, *Institutio Oratoria*, 8.6.14.
19. Quintilian, *Institutio Oratoria*, 8.6.14, 16–17.
20. Quintilian, *Institutio Oratoria*, 8.6.17.

Aristotle, Quintilian recognizes metaphor's ability not only to place a thing "vividly before the eye" but to serve a cognitive function: to "move the feelings, [and] give special distinction to things."[21] In other words, metaphors not only help hearers see but shape how they see, evoking particular emotions and drawing attention to certain distinctions.

Thomas Hobbes and John Locke: Metaphor as Deceptive Trick

Despite the Greeks' high regard, metaphor remains an almost entirely neglected topic in philosophy from Aristotle's time to the seventeenth and eighteenth centuries. Even then, philosophers prefer the literal language of math and science.[22] Thomas Hobbes's *Leviathan* and John Locke's *An Essay Concerning Human Understanding* both disparage the use of metaphor, Locke even calling the use of figurative language like metaphor a "fault" and an "abuse of language."[23] Locke writes that metaphors "are for nothing else but to insinuate wrong ideas, move the passions, and thereby mislead the judgment; and so indeed are perfect cheats ... wholly to be avoided."[24] The British empiricists despise metaphor as that which stirs the emotions toward illusion, and later the Romantics reinforce the dichotomy between rational truth and imaginative art by embracing subjectivism.[25] Metaphor thus comes to be regarded as a mere ornament of style, "a sort of happy extra trick with words," while the literal propositions of math and science come to be seen as the only true descriptors of reality.[26] To call a state-

---

21. Quintilian, *Institutio Oratoria*, 8.6.19.

22. Such tension partly results from the fact that "metaphor is literally a lie. A metaphor states as true something that is literally not true." Peterson, *Eat This Book*, 94; cf. Eco, *From the Tree*, 133; Aaron, *Biblical Ambiguities*, 36; and Putti, *Theology as Hermeneutics*, 192.

23. Locke, *Essay Concerning Human Understanding*, 372; cf. Hobbes, *Leviathan*, 29. Ironically, despite Hobbes's antagonism toward metaphor, he "extensively employs metaphors in his writing." Cantalupo, "Hobbes' Use of Metaphor," 20.

24. Locke, *Essay Concerning Human Understanding*, 372–73.

25. Lakoff and Johnson, *Metaphors We Live By*, 192.

26. Richards, *Philosophy of Rhetoric*, 90. Cf. Soskice, *Metaphor and Religious Language*, 12–13. These attitudes toward literal vs. metaphorical language have come to be reflected in biblical interpretation. Peterson notes that "there is the assumption that what we are reading is the 'word of God,' which means that it absolutely must be taken seriously. But 'seriously' in our present-day reading culture very often means literally." Peterson, *Eat This Book*, 94; cf. Putman, *In Defense of Doctrine*, 302; Fiumara, *Metaphoric*, 77; Lakoff and Johnson, *Metaphors We Live By*, 159, 190; Boersma, *Violence, Hospitality, and*

ment "simply metaphorical" comes to mean that the statement is at best not really true, and at worst, deliberately aiming to deceive.[27] Such negative attitudes toward metaphor endure to this day.

I. A. Richards: Metaphor as Cognitive Interaction

A turning point comes in 1936 with I. A. Richards's *The Philosophy of Rhetoric*, which moves away from the perception of metaphors as "mere language" and begins to retrieve their "conceptual nature, their contribution to understanding, [and] their function in cultural reality."[28] Taking issue with Aristotle's notion that metaphor is unteachable and reserved only for geniuses, Richards explains how to understand and use metaphor. He defines metaphor as the union of two halves: a tenor and a vehicle.[29] The tenor is the "underlying idea or principal subject," and the vehicle is

---

the Cross, 104. This dismissive attitude reflects even in biblical commentaries, where a phrase can be called "simply a metaphorical term," implying that a metaphor is somehow inferior to a literal term. See Seitz, *Colossians*, 186.

Eco notes that even medieval writers mistakenly confine metaphor to "a merely ornamental function and fail to recognize, at least on the theoretical level, its cognitive possibilities." Eco, *From the Tree*, 129. How could medieval writers have failed to give metaphor its due, especially given Aristotle's view? Eco explains that they had very late access to Aristotle's writings and, even then, only bad translations of those writings. Eco, *From the Tree*, 95–115. However, Thomas Aquinas does support the use of metaphor to explain abstract truths in concrete ways. Cf. Aquinas, *Summa of the Summa*, 47.

27. Fiumara observes that literal language tends to be "generally regarded as primary and proper, while any propensity for metaphoric usage is deemed parasitic and deviant, alien to 'normal' communication and only acceptable to the extent that it can be paraphrased into the standard vocabulary of the dominant context." Fiumara, *Metaphoric*, 52. Lakoff and Johnson add that "metaphor is typically viewed as characteristic of language alone, a matter of words rather than thought or action. For this reason, most people think they can get along perfectly well without metaphor." Lakoff and Johnson, *Metaphors We Live By*, 3; cf. 190.

28. Richards, *Philosophy of Rhetoric*, 159; cf. Van Hecke, *Metaphor in the Hebrew Bible*, 3. In Soskice's estimation, "I. A. Richards has come nearest to providing a satisfactory account" of metaphor in that he emphasizes "that metaphor is an intercourse of thoughts, as opposed to a mere shifting of words or a substitution of term for term." Soskice, *Metaphor and Religious Language*, 44, 45.

29. Richards lists some "clumsy" ways to describe these two halves of a metaphor: "the original idea and the borrowed one," "the underlying idea and the imagined nature," "the principal subject and what it resembles," or "the idea and its image." Richards, *Philosophy of Rhetoric*, 96. The word *metaphor* refers to the union of both halves. Max Black calls these two components the "focus" and the "frame." Black, *Models and Metaphors*, 28.

"an image or object" from which attributes are borrowed to describe the tenor.[30] For example, in the metaphor "man is a wolf," "man" is the tenor (the principal subject) and "wolf" is the vehicle from which attributes are borrowed to describe "man."[31]

By defining metaphor in this way, Richards recognizes metaphor as much more than merely "a verbal matter, a shifting and displacement of words"; rather, metaphor is "a borrowing between and intercourse of *thoughts*, a transaction between contexts."[32] Metaphor is not merely verbal but conceptual, not just a matter of words but a meaning-making meeting of mindsets. Richards exposes what Aristotle and Quintilian only hint at: that metaphors serve a cognitive function. They do something to the mind; they provoke the mind to make new thought connections based on the interaction of tenor and vehicle.[33] As the tenor and vehicle interact, they change the way one thinks of both.

Richards argues further that metaphor constitutes the very principle of thought and language: "*Thought* is metaphoric, and proceeds by comparison, and the metaphors of language derive therefrom."[34] Metaphors thus describe not just what the mind thinks about but even how the mind

---

30. Richards, *Philosophy of Rhetoric*, 96.

31. Metaphors can work backward, borrowing the tenor's attributes to describe the vehicle. "Man is a wolf" can thus give both wolf-like characteristics to man and also man-like characteristics to wolves. See Richards, *Philosophy*, 119; cf. MacCormac, *Metaphor and Myth in Science and Religion*, 74.

32. Richards, *Philosophy of Rhetoric*, 94.

33. Richards, *Philosophy of Rhetoric*, 100. Richards describes metaphor as learning to "perceive or think of or feel about one thing in terms of another—as when looking at a building it seems to have a face and to confront us with a peculiar expression. I want to insist that this sort of thing is normal." Richards, *Philosophy of Rhetoric*, 116–17. Black terms this the "interaction view" of metaphor, wherein metaphors filter an interaction of ideas. Max Black, *Models and Metaphors*, 33–44; cf. Austin, *Plant Metaphors*, 14. MacCormac refers to this interaction as a "tension" between a tenor and vehicle. MacCormac, *Metaphor*, xi.

34. Richards, *Philosophy of Rhetoric*, 116–17. Richards realizes the widespread implications of his theory, thus calling command of metaphor "a command of life." Richards, *Philosophy of Rhetoric*, 95. Conley agrees with Richards and calls metaphor "the very essence of language, which continually calls up borrowed and related missing contexts. Metaphor is, in fact, the essence of thought itself, since thought is also a transaction between contexts as thought works about its activities of sorting, comparing, and abstracting." Conley, *Rhetoric in the European Tradition*, 265–66. Richards, however, does not call metaphor the "essence" of language but rather the "omnipresent principle" of language, which raises the question of whether Conley has misunderstood Richards here.

thinks.[35] Richards challenges philosophers to observe how they "cannot get through three sentences of ordinary fluid discourse without [using metaphor].... Even in the rigid language of the settled sciences we do not eliminate or prevent it without great difficulty."[36] In short, metaphors describe reality, even the reality of the sciences. Far from being imaginary flights of rhetorical fancy, metaphors describe realities of the mind and of language.

George Lakoff and Mark Johnson: Metaphor as Everyday Function

George Lakoff and Mark Johnson's *Metaphors We Live By* has demonstrated abundantly the reality-describing character of metaphor. Lakoff and Johnson make an extensive list of metaphors that pervade virtually every activity of life, such as referring ("a beautiful catch"), quantifying ("so much hatred"), identifying aspects ("ugly side of his personality"), identifying causes ("pressure of his responsibilities"), and setting goals ("seek fame and fortune").[37] Metaphor is thus "as much a part of our functioning as our sense of touch, and as precious."[38]

Lakoff and Johnson even explore how metaphors influence a cultural system. For example, the metaphor "argument is war" promotes "a systematic way of talking about the battling aspects of arguing,"[39] influencing a culture to conceive of argument in this way. For example, a culture that believes that "argument is war" will use aggressive terms like "attack a

---

35. Vincent Brümmer calls this "the fundamentally *metaphorical* nature of all human thought and experience ... a basic characteristic of all our thinking." Brümmer, *The Model of Love*, 8.

36. Richards, *Philosophy of Rhetoric*, 92. Austin observes that since Richards, metaphor is no longer considered a merely verbal matter; metaphor is now "widely recognized as an integral part of how we communicate and how we understand the world around us." Austin, *Plant Metaphors*, 14.

37. Lakoff and Johnson, *Metaphors We Live By*, 26.

38. Lakoff and Johnson, *Metaphors We Live By*, 239. At the same time, they come to a fascinating conclusion that "is fundamentally at odds with certain key tenets of postmodernist thought, especially those that claim that meaning is ungrounded and simply an arbitrary cultural construction. What has been discovered about primary metaphor, for example, simply does not bear this out. There appear to be *both* universal metaphors *and* cultural variation." Lakoff and Johnson, 274. Boersma mentions theological implications of this view of metaphor since "the metaphorical character of all language in no way precludes the possibility of divine revelation and is as such a dependable way of interpreting the world and also a trustworthy way of speaking about God and about his actions in the world." Boersma, *Violence Hospitality, and the Cross*, 107.

39. Lakoff and Johnson, *Metaphors We Live By*, 7.

position," "indefensible," "strategy," "line of attack," "win," "gain ground," and so forth, which affects how people would engage in argument. A different metaphor, however, would yield different results. Instead of "argument is war," consider the metaphor "argument is dance," wherein "the participants are seen as performers, and the goal is to perform in a balanced and aesthetically pleasing way. In such a culture, people would view arguments differently."[40] Metaphor thus does more than pass on information; rather, "it conveys an atmosphere."[41]

Another example of a culture-shaping metaphor is "Time is money." This connection goes beyond mere wordplay; it encourages people within a culture to "*conceive of* time that way. Thus we understand time as the kind of thing that can be spent, wasted, budgeted, invested wisely or poorly, saved, or squandered."[42] Moreover, "time is money" "isn't a necessary way for human beings to conceptualize time; it is tied to our culture."[43] No longer seen as a mere trick of rhetoric, metaphor has come to be regarded as a descriptor of reality, something that shapes culture and influences how people actually think and behave in everyday life. Metaphor is thus "ubiquitous, an everyday phenomenon in the lives of ordinary men, women, and perhaps especially, children."[44] It describes and shapes how people see their world.

Not only does metaphor become regarded as "absolutely central to ordinary natural language semantics," but metaphor comes to mean

---

40. Lakoff and Johnson, *Metaphors We Live By*, 5. Fiumara adds other metaphors such as "argument is agriculture," "argument is therapy," and "argument is development," suggesting that "such alternative paradigms might significantly influence our practices and enhance the search for greater scope in exhibiting the reasons for accepting or refusing an argument." Fiumara, *Metaphoric*, 43.

41. Boersma, *Violence, Hospitality, and the Cross*, 102.

42. Lakoff and Johnson, *Metaphors We Live By*, 8.

43. Lakoff and Johnson, *Metaphors We Live By*, 9. As metaphors shape social realities, they form "a guide for future action. Such actions will, of course, fit the metaphor." Lakoff and Johnson, *Metaphors We Live By*, 156.

44. Ortony, "Metaphor, Language, and Thought," 15. This insight also carries profound implications for the study of history. Since metaphors "disclose a way of looking at the world, a way of understanding the world," Louth suggests that understanding how the ancients understood their world means to "pay heed to their use of metaphors." Louth, *Discerning the Mystery*, 19. Drawing from Giambattista Vico, Louth views metaphors not as "ingenious conceits" but rather reflections of the common sense, or *sensus communis*, of a given society. Metaphors thus give clues to the basic presuppositions of any culture and expose the common assumptions that define the ways people think within that culture. Louth, 19–20; cf. Vico, *The New Science of Giambattista Vico*, 170.

"a cross-domain mapping in the conceptual system."[45] Metaphors link together conceptual domains, resulting in new ways to see the concepts involved and thus new matrixes or worlds that reflect and shape people's culture and everyday experience. This now dominant view of metaphor has come to be known as the "cognitive linguistic view,"[46] which emphasizes metaphor as "a major means for constituting reality. . . . [Metaphor] serves as a structuring principle, focusing on particular aspects of a phenomenon and hiding others; thus, each metaphor produces a different description of the 'same' reality."[47] Metaphors carry implicit assumptions, attitudes, and perspectives regarding the things they describe, which then influence how people behave.[48]

This brief foray into the reality-depicting, culture-shaping, and behavior-influencing power of metaphor suggests that metaphor proves not only "constitutive of our cognitive efforts but, indeed, of our whole [social] being."[49] We might even describe society itself as metaphorical since humans live within a metaphorical matrix of complex interactions, not only "in terms of telematics and currencies, in terms of the air we breathe and the water we drink, but we are even more subtly and profoundly linked by the language we create and live by."[50] Metaphor harnesses this power of language to describe and shape the world.[51]

45. Lakoff, "The Contemporary Theory of Metaphor," 203.
46. Kövecses, *Metaphor: A Practical Introduction*, x.
47. Foss, *Rhetorical Criticism: Exploration and Practice*, 286–87.
48. Foss, *Rhetorical Criticism*, 287.
49. Fiumara, *Metaphoric*, 6; cf. Peterson, *Eat This Book*, 97. McFague thus calls metaphor "the *way* we think." McFague, *Metaphorical Theology*, 16.
50. Fiumara, *Metaphoric*, 3. Thus, Fiumara encourages "life-enhancing engagement in metaphoric talk." Fiumara, 60. Lakoff and Johnson call metaphor "not just a matter of language"; rather, "human *thought processes* are largely metaphorical." Lakoff and Johnson, *Metaphors We Live By*, 6. As McFague puts it, "Whether consciously or unconsciously, all people live by metaphors." McFague, *Metaphorical Theology*, 55.
51. Kövecses calls models "constitutive" metaphors that "create an understanding of much of the world for ourselves." Kövecses, *Metaphor in Culture*, 198, 228. Metaphor involves both "coming up with new definitions for things" and "discovering everything that can be said about a given subject." Eco, *From the Tree*, 41. Lakoff and Johnson thus say that "the human conceptual system is metaphorically structured and defined." Lakoff and Johnson, *Metaphors We Live By*, 6. For more on current research regarding the cognitive linguistic theory of metaphor, see Kövecses, *Metaphor in Culture*; Kövecses, *Where Metaphors Come From*; Kövecses, *Extended Conceptual Metaphor Theory*; Prandi, *Conceptual Conflicts in Metaphors and Figurative Language*; and Littlemore, *Metaphors in the Mind*. The transformative power of metaphor has entered popular culture in works

From Metaphors to Models

Some metaphors not only shape systems but *become* new systems, or models, for experiencing the world. These models come to define how scientists and theologians do their work.

Max Black: Metaphor as System-Shaping Model

Drawing from I. A. Richards's "interaction" view of metaphor, Max Black provides a foundational account of how metaphors turn into models in his *Models and Metaphors*, in which he suggests calling theoretical models "a sustained and systematic metaphor."[52] Returning to Richards's metaphor "Man is a wolf," Black points out that the vehicle, wolf, "suppresses some details, emphasizes others—in short, *organizes* our view of man."[53] This organizational ability in metaphor gives rise to new systems from which new implications can arise.[54] Metaphors thus become new models, or systems of thought, and these models function not only descriptively but also speculatively, provoking new insights or ways of conceiving reality.[55] Black thus likens a model to a wedding, a new connection of "disparate subjects" that becomes a wholly new system, replete with unpredictable connections, implications, and outcomes.[56]

---

like Cohen's *Thinking of Others: On the Talent for Metaphor* and Geary's *I Is an Other: The Secret Life of Metaphor and How It Shapes the Way We See the World*.

52. Black, *Models and Metaphors*, 236. Barbour calls such theoretical models "*systematically-developed metaphors*" that suggest "new ways of looking at a problematical situation by transferring some of the features of another situation which is better understood." Barbour, *Myths, Models and Paradigms*, 43, emphasis his.

53. Black, *Models and Metaphors*, 41, emphasis his.

54. Black, *Models and Metaphors*, 237.

55. Based on Black's account, Ricoeur argues that models belong "not to the logic of justification or proof, but to the logic of discovery," by which he means that models constitute a new cognitive process or rational method to arrive at new insights. Ricoeur thus calls for "an examination of the constitution of the metaphoric universe as a network." Ricoeur, *Rule of Metaphor*, 240, 243.

56. Black, *Models and Metaphors*, 237. Soskice argues that Black, and later Paul Ricoeur, misunderstand Richards here in thinking that the tenor and vehicle are actually two interacting subjects, whereas Richards's original idea concerns two interacting *ideas* concerning one subject. Cf. Soskice, *Metaphor and Religious Language*, 46–49. According to Soskice, Richards holds that "a metaphor has one true subject which tenor and vehicle conjointly depict and illumine." Soskice, *Metaphor and Religious Language*, 47. However, this misunderstanding, though limiting to Black's concept of metaphor, does not render

Black argues such models pervade science and have generated breakthroughs in physics, such as Rutherford's solar system and Bohr's atom, pointing out that these scientists "worked not *by* analogy, but *through* and by means of an underlying analogy. Their models were conceived to be more than expository or heuristic devices."[57] So metaphorical models not only describe theories but even form the systematic frames of reference necessary for such theories to arise.[58] A model not only explains but also conditions possible explanations and even gives rise to new explanations. This realization leads Black to state provocatively, "Perhaps every science must start with a metaphor and end with algebra; and perhaps without the metaphor there would never have been an algebra."[59] Black thus argues that such "root metaphors" wield organizational, systematic, and perspective-shaping faculties and can survive rigorous critical examination into their "appropriateness, faithfulness, partiality, superficiality, and the like. . . . In this way, they can, and sometimes do, generate insight about 'how things are' in reality."[60]

To the question "Why use models at all?" Black offers four reasons: (1) use of models brings results; (2) models offer a more readily visualized picture; (3) models enable an intuitive grasp of implications for a given domain; and (4) research often requires a model to proceed in the first place.[61] So according to Black, models play an essential role in science by forming new conceptual landscapes that foster insights, imagination, and the possibility for new discovery.[62]

Black's account of metaphorical models unhelpful, nor does it keep Black's account from being "the most satisfactory contemporary philosophical account of metaphor, and certainly the most often cited." Soskice, *Metaphor and Religious Language*, 38.

57. Black, *Models and Metaphors*, 228–29.
58. See Black, "More about Metaphor," 38.
59. Black, *Models and Metaphors*, 242.
60. Black, "More about Metaphor," 39. Seeking to improve on Stephen C. Pepper's term "root-metaphors," Black prefers to call models "conceptual archetypes," which he defines as "a systematic repertoire of ideas by means of which a given thinker describes, by *analogical extension*, some domain to which those ideas do not immediately and literally apply." Black, *Models and Metaphors*, 241, emphasis his; cf. Pepper, *World Hypotheses*, 91–93; and Ricoeur, *Rule of Metaphor*, 244.
61. Black, *Models and Metaphors*, 231–33.
62. Black, *Models and Metaphors*, 234. One thinker whose work relates significantly but tangentially to this book is Thomas S. Kuhn, whose book *The Structure of Scientific Revolutions* envisions scientific progress as "paradigm shifts," which are in essence changes in models or patterns shared by a group of scientists. Kuhn admits in the second

Ian T. Ramsey: Models as Essential in Science and Theology

Ian T. Ramsey argues that models play a definitive role not only in science but also in religion, which Ramsey hopes can help to bridge the widening gap between the two. In his pioneering work *Models and Mystery*, Ramsey draws three parallels between their use of models: (1) models build discourse by "giving rise to large-scale interpretations of phenomena"; (2) models help to discuss subjects that have a perplexing logical structure, such as grace and atonement, thus making "visible" what remains largely invisible; and (3) models help to talk about subjects that elude or surpass literal description, such as the nature of God.[63] Models thus allow for "disclosures," or genuine insights, into the nature of what the model models by allowing for articulation of what would remain indescribable otherwise.[64] Models thus succeed in giving describable structure to both scientific and religious phenomena. As an example of such a success story in science, Ramsey points to a case in which "the mathematics of the electronic computer or calculating machine is taken as a model of the brain and can certainly lead to experimental verifications of the highest usefulness and significance."[65] In religion, models like God as Judge, King, Father, Shepherd, and so on employ human and visible phenomena "to understand what [is] divine and largely invisible."[66] So models render difficult, perplexing realities in clearer, more accessible ways and thus constitute "a bridge between theory and fact."[67] Yet one must use models carefully because they

---

edition of his book that were he to write it again, he would use the term "model": "Rewriting the book now I would describe such commitments as beliefs in particular models, and I would expand the category models to include also the relatively heuristic variety. ... All models have similar functions. Among other things they supply the group with preferred or permissible analogies and metaphors. By doing so they help to determine what will be accepted as an explanation and as a puzzle-solution; conversely, they assist in the determination of the roster of unsolved puzzles and in the evaluation of the importance of each." Kuhn, *The Structure of Scientific Revolutions*, 184.

63. Ramsey, *Models and Mystery*, 14–15.
64. Ramsey, *Models and Mystery*, 10–13.
65. Ramsey, *Models and Mystery*, 28.
66. Ramsey, *Models and Mystery*, 5. For further development of Ramsey's work on theological models and his categorization of specific models into those of activity, economy, and presence, see Ramsey, *Models for Divine Activity*. Ramsey demonstrates that models not only pervade Scripture but that they consistently imply the nearness and conceptual accessibility of God to humanity.
67. Ramsey, *Models and Mystery*, 13.

guide the mind toward a certain way of thinking about the phenomena modeled, and models often become representative of, or a proxy for, such phenomena. Models also tend to emphasize or deemphasize phenomena "by singling out 'fundamental notions' which again it echoes in the disclosure which brings it to birth."[68] This tendency in models necessitates a critical attitude toward one's choice of model.

Ramsey holds that models reveal truths about the actual universe: "Models in science not only enable us to generate verifiable deductions, and models in theology not only make possible empirical fit. They each arise out of, and in this way become currency for, a universe that discloses itself to us in a moment of insight."[69] Models thus reflect and articulate not imagined insights but actual truths about the universe that makes itself known to us through such models in a way much akin to divine revelation since a kind of "cosmic disclosure" authenticates and reveals these models.[70] Models thus enable people to be articulate about reality and yet arise mysteriously from revelation-like insights.

For theology in particular, Ramsey goes so far as to say that models constitute the very nature of theological understanding because they combine disclosure and mystery. For example, the model "God is a loving father" articulates truths about God but still requires qualifying statements so as to preserve both disclosure and mystery: "God is a loving father" discloses God's love but maintains mystery by not entailing finiteness or limitedness of human fathers.[71] To preserve such mysterious disclosures, Ramsey recommends using multiple models and a critical approach that clarifies explicitly "where the essential emphasis is to be placed."[72]

Ramsey provides clear examples of this critical approach in *Models for Divine Activity*, in which he explores scriptural models of divine activity, economy, and presence to demonstrate how models "point to the cosmic disclosures which are the empirical anchorage for all our talk about God."[73] Starting with the doctrine of the Holy Spirit, Ramsey traces the scriptural models of the Spirit as wind, fire, anointing oil, rain, and dew, finding that each conveys profound revelations of God's activity both individually and

---

68. Ramsey, *Models and Mystery*, 12.
69. Ramsey, *Models and Mystery*, 19–20.
70. Ramsey, *Models and Mystery*, 58; cf. Ramsey, *Models for Divine Activity*, 13.
71. Ramsey, *Models and Mystery*, 58–61.
72. Ramsey, *Models and Mystery*, 61.
73. Ramsey, *Models for Divine Activity*, 13.

in conversation with one another. For instance, wind communicates not only the Spirit's power as a gale but also the Spirit's kindness as relief from the heat of day, the Spirit's vitality as breath of life, the Spirit's indwelling as the one whom the believer breathes in, and the Spirit's mystery since wind remains elusive. Wind as breath even points to the Spirit as Creator, since breath gives life to every living being.[74] Combined with the model of fire, the Spirit must be terrifying and all consuming, and some Scriptures interweave wind and fire to describe the Spirit.[75] So these models combine for richer revelation: "The activity of God can be spoken of in terms of wind and breath and life, telling of mystery and power; it can be said, like water and rain and dew, to refresh and cleanse and purify and revive; like oil, it can soothe and illuminate: and some words, e.g., 'revive', occur in more than one strand of discourse."[76] Drawing all of his models from Scripture, Ramsey demonstrates how their interaction leads to fruitful discourse.

Such discourse does not manifest in "word-spinning, airborne theology" but remains firmly accessible and experiential, "appealing to situations recognizable in principle by the secular world."[77] Models must not be built out of thin air or mere imagination but stay true to life, anchored in real-world experience.[78] By "cosmic disclosures," Ramsey means those moments in which God reveals himself in real-world situations as identified by Scripture.[79] These disclosures go beyond mere subjective experiences and must include an objective reference.[80] Therefore, models must remain accessibly rooted in and applicable to the real world, thereby enabling people

---

74. Ramsey, *Models for Divine Activity*, 4–9.

75. Ramsey, *Models for Divine Activity*, 10; cf. Isa 4:4 and Ps 104:4.

76. Ramsey, *Models for Divine Activity*, 11. Ramsey treats "Spirit" itself as a model that includes all of these insights into God's activity.

77. Ramsey, *Models for Divine Activity*, 8.

78. Ramsey, *Models for Divine Activity*, 13.

79. Tellingly, all of Ramsey's models come from "cosmic disclosures" found in Scripture. After all, one would be hard pressed to know how to identify a "cosmic disclosure" apart from the revealed statements of Scripture. Ramsey seems thus to be implying a criterion for models in which models must have "empirical fit" with the "cosmic disclosures" revealed in Scripture. In the next chapter, Ramsey traces a scriptural term, *oikonomia*, through its use in historical theology, thus implying that models should prove faithful not only to Scripture but to church tradition. Ramsey, *Models for Divine Activity*, 15–27. Peacocke points out that a big part of Ramsey's pioneering work on theological models is his recognition that much of the language used in Scripture and theology "utilizes models over a wide range of its discourse." Peacocke, *Intimations of Reality*, 29–30.

80. Ramsey, *Models for Divine Activity*, 64.

to be more theologically articulate and fruitful.[81] In Ramsey's words, "the world must be such as to bear the discourse to which the model leads."[82] Models must ring true to experienced reality.

As for criteria, Ramsey recommends preferring models that provide "the most simple, coherent, comprehensive and consistent" discourse and that have "the best empirical fit" to the divine disclosures described in Scripture and corroborated by Christian experience.[83] Ramsey thus insists his use of models does not aim "to invent new discourse but to trace logical paths through long-flourishing theological discourse" by recognizing use of models as a longstanding practice that gives rise to faithful and fruitful discourse firmly rooted in real-world experience.[84]

Ian G. Barbour: Models as Reality-Depicting Systems

Ian Graeme Barbour, like Ramsey, draws his theological models from Scripture but develops in a much more systematic fashion how models operate in science and religion. He argues that models go beyond mere disclosures to constitute "organizing images" that "restructure one's perception of the world."[85] Models thus carry profoundly system-shaping implications that require explicit criteria to test their validity and the beliefs derived from them.

Barbour criticizes Ramsey for rooting models in self-authenticating moments of "divine self-disclosure" since doing so "bypasses the problem of their relation to each other and to anything outside man."[86] Barbour finds Ramsey's construal of models too subjective in that it runs the risk of losing any positive analogy with reality. He finds unsettling that Ramsey ignores that some models contradict others and that models must correspond to some objective reality outside a person's psychology to remain helpful. Barbour thus asks, "Are there *criteria* for evaluating religious models themselves, or are they to be judged solely by their psychological effectiveness for particular individuals in evoking disclosures?"[87]

---

81. Ramsey, *Models for Divine Activity*, 17–19.
82. Ramsey, *Models for Divine Activity*, 20.
83. Ramsey, *Models for Divine Activity*, 62–63.
84. Ramsey, *Models for Divine Activity*, 6.
85. Barbour, *Myths, Models and Paradigms*, 49.
86. Barbour, *Myths, Models and Paradigms*, 63.
87. Barbour, *Myths, Models and Paradigms*, 63.

To shore up these weaknesses in Ramsey's proposal, Barbour develops a much more systematic account of models. He addresses four proposed functions of religious models: they (1) help interpret experience, (2) express certain attitudes, (3) evoke disclosures, and (4) construct metaphysical systems.[88] He does not disagree with these but moves beyond them, espousing that "a religious model may also direct attention to particular patterns in events. It provides a perspective on the world and an *interpretation of history and human experience*."[89] In other words, models serve as "organizing images" that draw attention to particular patterns, integrate diverse areas of experience, and thus alter ways that individuals and communities see and interpret the world.[90] For example, images of God as King, Judge, Shepherd, Husband, and Father "form a model of God as a personal being, which is used in interpreting corporate as well as individual experience."[91] These models suggest beliefs that correlate with these kinds of human relationships and also provide the framework to integrate and interpret one's relationship with God. Such models thus encourage one "to interpret *his whole life* as lived in the presence of God."[92] So models carry prescriptive and not only descriptive force, and they move beyond subjective experience to "represent the enduring structures of the cosmic order," shaping the way people perceive and interpret the world.[93] Models emphasize certain features of the world and restructure the way people perceive reality. They also unify diverse experiences of God since many models refer to the same God.[94]

Both metaphors and models influence attitudes, behavior, and conceptions of the world, but metaphors become models when used repeatedly and systematically. For instance, "the LORD is my shepherd" stays a metaphor as it appears infrequently, while "God is a father to his children"

---

88. Barbour, *Myths, Models and Paradigms*, 51–67. Barbour distinguishes between experimental models (physical constructs to run experiments), mathematical models (equations make quantitative predictions), computer models (programs that run scenarios), and theoretical models (imaginative mental constructs that systematize, explain, and predict phenomena). Theoretical models are those that make up religious models. See Barbour, *Myths, Models and Paradigms*, 30–31, 36, 45.

89. Barbour, *Myths, Models and Paradigms*, 51, emphasis his.

90. See Barbour, *Myths, Models and Paradigms*, 16, 49–50.

91. Barbour, *Myths, Models and Paradigms*, 56.

92. Barbour, *Myths, Models and Paradigms*, 56, emphasis added.

93. Barbour, *Myths, Models and Paradigms*, 49; cf. 57.

94. Barbour, *Myths, Models and Paradigms*, 56.

forms a model because of its dominant, repetitive emphasis in Scripture.[95] A model, then, is "*systematically developed*, and the positive and negative analogy are specified," such that models come to represent a much larger scope and more comprehensive system.[96]

This system-building quality means that models do more than provoke distinctive attitudes or recommend a way of life; they make ontological claims about the nature of the real world. In Barbour's words, "these *non-cognitive uses* presuppose *cognitive beliefs*. . . . It would be unreasonable to adopt or recommend a way of life unless one believes that the universe is of such a character that this way of life is appropriate."[97] Both scientists and theologians believe that their models feature "some isomorphism between the model and the real structures of the world."[98] So models assume nonliteral correspondence with objective reality. Models pull together reality and imagination, objective truth and subjective construct, making them apt tools for the approach to science and theology known as critical realism.[99]

Critical realism, to be truly critical and not merely subjective, requires criteria. Since models make serious ontological claims about reality and influence how people understand that reality by linking integrated systems

---

95. Barbour, *Myths, Models and Paradigms*, 16.
96. Barbour, *Myths, Models and Paradigms*, 44.
97. Barbour, *Myths, Models and Paradigms*, 58.
98. Barbour, *Myths, Models and Paradigms*, 42.
99. Critical realism is a philosophical approach to science developed by Roy Bhaskar, though Barbour uses the term before Bhaskar; cf. Bhaskar, *Reclaiming Reality*. Critical realism "retains the direct-realist commonsense belief in independent physical things, but in the face of the verification problem inherent in correspondence theories of truth, admits that these are not directly and homogeneously presented to us in perceptual situations. It concedes to idealism that whenever something is perceived it is an object for a mind, but insists that it does not follow from this that a given 'something' has no existence except in its being perceived." Patterson, *Realist Christian Theology*, 13–14. So critical realists, like Patterson and Barbour, seek through models a middle way between the extremes of literalism and fictionalism, between naïve positivism and mere instrumentalism. Since models reflect objective reality yet remain a human, mental construct (they are neither literal pictures of reality nor "useful fictions" that have no correlation to reality outside the mind), Barbour finds models helpful vehicles for making humble and yet truthful claims that seriously, though not literally, describe the nature of things. Cf. Barbour, *Myths, Models and Paradigms*, 34–38. Osborne concurs that critical realism best fits the use of models: "Models do not observe reality (the positivistic approach) or relate exact descriptions (the naïve realist approach) or provide dispensable approximations of a theory (the instrumentalist approach). Rather, models suggest and explore patterns that potentially depict the reality envisions (the critical realist approach)." Osborne, *The Hermeneutical Spiral*, 391–92.

from widely divergent domains, Barbour insists on the need for criteria to measure the validity of any given model. He suggests five such criteria: (1) simplicity; (2) coherence; (3) correlation with external data; (4) extensibility of application, or fruitfulness; and (5) comprehensiveness.[100] Simplicity means that the model requires the least number of independent assumptions or conceptual categories. Coherence means that the model exhibits logical soundness as a system and does not contradict itself. Correlation with external data, which Barbour deems "the most important criterion," requires that the model correspond accurately to and convey faithfully the significant historical events and experiences that give rise to the model.[101] Extensibility of application, or fruitfulness, entails that the model holds relevance for the way people interpret and live their lives today. Comprehensiveness means that the model helpfully orders "diverse types of experience within a systematic metaphysics."[102]

In his most famous work, *Religion in an Age of Science*, Barbour consolidates his criteria to four: (1) agreement with data; (2) coherence; (3) scope, or comprehensiveness; and (4) fertility, or fruitfulness.[103] He elaborates that scope includes the ability to interpret other kinds of experience, not just religious, and that fertility regards not only applicability to contemporary life on a personal level but also "future promise in providing the framework for an ongoing research program."[104] In other words, models must prove fruitful not only at the personal but also at the systemic level, offering potential for future progress and discovery.

Arthur Peacocke: Models as Ubiquitous in Theology

Like Ramsey and Barbour before him, Arthur Peacocke recognizes that models pervade scriptural and theological language. Taking Barbour's systematic treatment of religious models even further, Peacocke lists models in theology proper (God as Father, Creator, Maker, King, Sovereign, Shepherd, Judge), Christology (Christ as Second Adam, Son of God, Redeemer, Savior), pneumatology (the Spirit as Holy Ghost, Comforter), and

---

100. Barbour, *Myths, Models and Paradigms*, 143.
101. Barbour, *Myths, Models and Paradigms*, 143.
102. Barbour, *Myths, Models and Paradigms*, 143.
103. Barbour, *Religion in an Age of Science*, 34, 38–39. This work has been revised and expanded into *Religion and Science: Historical and Contemporary Issues*.
104. Barbour, *Religion in an Age of Science*, 34.

soteriology (i.e., atonement theories, which depict salvation as sacrifice, redemption, ransom, substitution, and moral example). Scripture even communicates God's relationship to humanity through various models: "father-son, lord-servant, mother-child, hen-chickens, lover-beloved, husband-wife, master-slave, etc."[105] Peacocke thus argues that such models "are so deeply embedded in Christian language that it is extremely difficult to frame theories and concepts entirely devoid of metaphor, for even abstract words like 'transcendent,' 'immanent,' and 'pan-en-theism' partake of spatial metaphors."[106] For Peacocke, models are everywhere; and unlike Ramsey and Barbour, Peacocke explicitly recognizes models outside of Scripture drawn from Christian tradition.

Such models are also indispensable, as such "root-metaphors" for God claim much more comprehensive control than scientific models do.[107] For example, not only do theological models claim to speak accurately of reality, but they wield more "personal" and "participatory" force; they call people to action and carry a "strong affective function evoking moral and spiritual response" such as total "commitment and self-involvement," whereas models in science tend to be "observer" models that only explain, represent, and predict.[108] The ability of theological models to evoke response and stir affections, however, should not detract from their aim also to explain, describe, and represent reality since "Christian believers take their models to depict reality; otherwise they would be affectively and personally ineffectual and inoperative."[109] Thus Peacocke, like Barbour, champions critical realism wherein models depict reality without being naively or unrevisably descriptive. Theologians thus "speak realistically of God through revisable metaphor and model."[110]

---

105. Peacocke, *Intimations of Reality*, 41.

106. Peacocke, *Intimations of Reality*, 41.

107. The term "root-metaphor" comes from Pepper, *World Hypotheses*, 93. Despite this difference between theological and scientific models, Peacocke insists that both rely heavily on analogy, even to the point that scientific theories cannot hold explanatory power apart from a good model. For example, the billiard ball model for gases allows for the development of theories involving gaseous velocity, impact, reflection, and so forth. Peacocke, *Intimations of Reality*, 31.

108. Peacocke, *Intimations of Reality*, 43–44. Janet Soskice takes issue with this claim and argues that scientific and theological models do not differ much. Cf. Soskice, *Metaphor and Religious Language*, 108–17.

109. Peacocke, *Intimations of Reality*, 44.

110. Peacocke, *Intimations of Reality*, 46.

As for criteria for models, Peacocke addresses three: explanatory value, fruitfulness, and ability to unify a community in communication. By explanatory value, he means that a model can explain data, structures, and experience within a current field, which in theology means that the model accurately communicates the experiences of God in the actual lives of flesh-and-blood persons.[111] Fruitfulness means that the model not only explains current data, structures, and experiences but also opens up vistas to discover new data and structures. Such a model suggests "new possibilities for investigation . . . to predict and accommodate new observations . . . throwing light 'forward,' as it were, into new areas of investigation and by raising previously unformulable questions about those new domains."[112] So a good model "throws light forward," providing a framework from which new questions, observations, and insights can emerge.

Sallie McFague: Models as Ordering Networks

Sallie McFague sees the theological task itself as model-making, defining a model as "a dominant metaphor, a metaphor with staying power . . . [as when] some metaphors gain wide appeal and become major ways of structuring and ordering experience."[113] So models organize and systematize theological thought around a dominant root-metaphor that reflects one's basic assumptions about the nature of the world, or "a way of seeing 'all that is' through a particular key concept."[114] McFague suggests, as examples, that Paul's root-metaphor is justification by grace through faith; Augustine's is radical dependence of all on God; Aquinas's is the analogy of being; Schleiermacher's is the feeling of absolute dependence, and Barth's is the election

---

111. Peacocke, *Intimations of Reality*, 32, 39.

112. Peacocke, *Intimations of Reality*, 31.

113. McFague, *Metaphorical Theology*, 23. When metaphors solidify into models, they can enhance as well as subvert current social structures. Fiumara notes how metaphors create subliminal anxiety within a society: "Metaphor frequently inhabits the margins of discourse and its potential incivility generates concern for its management. There is a subliminal anxiety which results from the difficulty of maintaining the boundary between 'proper' terminology in the face of metaphorical boundary-crossers." Fiumara, *Metaphoric*, 3. Boersma also notices "impropriety" inherent in metaphor: "Metaphors take words out of their original contexts and use them in new, seemingly inappropriate ways." Boersma, *Violence, Hospitality, and the Cross*, 101.

114. McFague, *Metaphorical Theology*, 28.

of all to salvation through Christ.[115] These root-metaphors frame how people experience the world and interpret reality, each model claiming to be the most comprehensive and fundamental description of that reality.[116] So models set priorities within religious traditions; provide an expandable network of language to speak intelligibly about the unfamiliar; and even control how people understand the nature of God, human beings, and the world.[117] For instance, the model "God is father" serves "as a grid or screen through which to see not only the nature of God but also our relations to the divine and with one another."[118]

---

115. McFague, *Metaphorical Theology*, 28. One might take issue with whether McFague's examples here are actually metaphors. In her view, all language is at least somewhat metaphorical, and she argues that these examples at least become used metaphorically to represent entire systems of theology. McFague's tendency to treat so much of theology as metaphor, however, becomes problematic regarding her view of the authority of the Bible. Treating the Bible as merely "the premier metaphor" and "the classic model" for theology, McFague claims that "the Bible 'is and is not' the word of God. The Bible is a metaphor of the word or ways of God, but as metaphor it is a relative, open-ended, secular, tensive judgment. . . . As a metaphor it cannot be absolute, 'divinely inspired,' or final. . . . The Bible can never *be* the word of God, can never capture the ways of God. . . . The Bible as *model* underscores the relative, groping character of this very human work." McFague, *Metaphorical Theology*, 54, 62. This "metaphorical" view essentially denies the Bible's inspiration and authority by overly relativizing its interpretation. Likening the Bible to the US Constitution or the Greek Parthenon, McFague claims, "The richness of the metaphorical quality of a great work means that it will not only bear many interpretations but also demands them. It is not a travesty, then, to interpret the Bible in many different ways, but precisely what should occur given the nature of the text." McFague, *Metaphorical Theology*, 60.

116. To be clear, McFague sees models not as actual representations of reality but as mostly fictional frameworks that people choose for themselves. McFague, *Models of God*, 192, 196. Still, McFague admits that "all serious users of models believe, at least to some degree, that their models refer to reality, . . . something *new* is being said about reality which the user of the model believes describes it better, more appropriately, than the accepted views." McFague, *Metaphorical Theology*, 133–34. Putman affirms that models are "illustrative devices" that depict reality in both science and theology. Cf. Putman, *In Defense of Doctrine*, 304. Since metaphors do describe reality, "Let us never conclude that because it is a metaphor, it is only an illustration and not 'true.'" Sumner, "Theory and Metaphor in Calvin's Doctrine of the Atonement," 50.

117. McFague, *Metaphorical Theology*, 25. Metaphorical models are not simply fictions but "have the power to define reality. They do this through a coherent network of entailments that highlight some features of reality and hide others. . . . In all aspects of life, not just in politics or in love, we define our reality in terms of metaphors and then proceed to act on the basis of the metaphors." Lakoff and Johnson, *Metaphors We Live By*, 157–58.

118. McFague, *Metaphorical Theology*, 9.

[It] suggests a comprehensive, ordering structure with impressive interpretive potential. As a rich model with many associated commonplaces as well as a host of supporting metaphors, an entire theology can be worked out from this model. Thus, if God is understood on the model of "father," human beings are understood as "children," sin is rebellion against the "father," redemption is sacrifice by the "elder son" on behalf of his "brothers and sisters" for the guilt against the "father" and so on.[119]

So each model comes with its own system for organizing and interpreting the world.

Though models like "God is Father" carry such impressive interpretive potential, McFague warns that models also come with dangers. Unlike other metaphors, models tend to "lock in" meaning in one direction to the exclusion of other models.[120] This tendency excludes "other ways of thinking and talking, and in so doing [a model] can easily become ... identified as *the* one and only way of understanding a subject."[121] McFague thus laments that the model "God the Father" tends "to militate against a model like 'God the Mother.'"[122] This tendency of models to oppose one another poses "the single greatest risk in their use," which hints at a disturbing truth about models: they can not only reveal but also conceal aspects of reality by blinding their adherents to insights that other models might offer.[123]

119. McFague, *Metaphorical Theology*, 23.

120. This tendency makes models much more dangerous than metaphors "because models have a wider range and are more permanent; they tend to object to competition in ways that metaphors do not." McFague, *Metaphorical Theology*, 24; cf. Brümmer, *Model of Love*, 21.

121. McFague, *Metaphorical Theology*, 24. Thus Fiumara comments that the human propensity toward metaphors (and hence models) "entails in fact a potential to enlighten and blind, to nourish and poison," carrying both "formative and damaging effects." Fiumara, *Metaphoric*, 133, 136. Brümmer points out that this privileging of a single model yields "a very one-sided theology in which many other essential features of the Christian understanding of life and the world would be filtered out and ignored." Brümmer, *Model of Love*, 21.

122. McFague, *Metaphorical Theology*, 24. Soskice has written a whole chapter discussing the feminist aversion to the model of God as Father. She finds that "the symbolism is ineradicably masculine," and she points out two further reasons to continue calling God "Father": that Jesus's calling God "Father" would have been just as offensive and surprising within his cultural context, and that calling God "Father" highlights Jesus as the only Son who "can show us the Father. Without the Son, 'the Father' is not God, but an idol." Soskice, *The Kindness of God*, 81, 83.

123. McFague, *Metaphorical Theology*, 24. MacCormac describes how one model can completely conceal the truth of another: "At the time that men believe the world to be in

Another danger involves "inversion," where models become inverted with their subjects and come to stand in for them. This occurs in science when, for example, a computer models the brain but leads to scientists regarding the brain merely as a computer. Theological models "are especially prone to inversion, for the human features chosen to provide models of God are raised to divine status and become 'godlike,'" which idolatrously conflates the human and the divine.[124]

Given these dangers, McFague insists "that *many* metaphors and models are necessary, that a piling up of images is essential, both to avoid idolatry and to attempt to express the richness and variety of the divine-human relationship."[125] Despite these drawbacks and limitations, models remain unavoidable and necessary, since humans inevitably think by metaphors and models. In fact, the human mind cannot help but make models "as comprehensive ways of envisioning reality, . . . as metaphors that control the ways people envision both human and divine reality."[126] Moreover, some models achieve a "godlike" status as they become idolatrously dominant in ways that exclude other models.

Such far-reaching consequences make paramount the question of criteria. McFague suggests several. First, models must be simple, concrete, and well known while providing sufficient complexity to suggest many new connections and hypotheses. Good models exhibit "a *dialectic* of simplicity and detail," such as "body," "machine," and "person."[127] Second, models must explain coherently its subject's systematic structure and behavior.[128] Third, the model must remain "*both true and untrue*; they invite existential commitment but in a qualified manner; while believed to be appropriate,

---

actuality the way that the root-metaphor describes it, few even doubt that it could be any other way. Only later when a new theory supplants the old one do men recognize that what had been held earlier to be literal truth was really a myth." MacCormac, *Metaphor*, 141.

124. McFague, *Metaphorical Theology*, 73. Given this concern, Osborne affirms that no model "should have permanent status in and of itself, although those that have stood the test of time (such as the creeds) come close. Even these, however, are subject to further insight and restatement, as seen in the growing number of evangelical studies on cardinal doctrines like the Trinity or christology." Osborne, *The Hermeneutical Spiral*, 393.

125. McFague, *Metaphorical Theology*, 20; cf. 144.

126. McFague, *Metaphorical Theology*, 25.

127. McFague, *Metaphorical Theology*, 73–74, emphasis hers.

128. McFague, *Metaphorical Theology*, 92.

they are also held to be partial and inadequate."[129] Models thus aid in discovery and explanation of truth while humbly maintaining necessary epistemic distance based on the limits of human subjectivity and language.[130]

Furthermore, models must interact coherently with one another within a theological system. They must exhibit similarity with and complement other models within the system. In McFague's words, they must belong "to the same syndrome."[131] For example, models in the Western tradition emphasize personal and positive traits, such as healing, restoration, guidance, protection, and liberation, thus depicting God as father, protector, healer, and savior. These models all "fit together" in such a way that renders impossible models such as God as jailer, destroyer, or devil.[132] Such diametrically opposed models would face disqualification based on lack of fit with other models in the system. Moreover, a good model should cope with anomalies, or "contra-factors," such as events or experiences that strain the model beyond its limit.[133] For example, the fact that not all people respond to salvation strains the model of election, leading Calvin to develop his doctrine of double predestination. Also, the Jewish Holocaust puts strain on traditional models of evil, as does the feminist critique on traditional models of God.[134] For McFague, the ability to deal with such anomalies constitutes perhaps the most serious criterion for assessing a system or model, and better models handle contra-factors more adequately.[135]

Finally, McFague repeats Ramsey's criterion of "empirical fit."[136] Models must fit with the human data of lived experience, not only in limited cases but for an entire system: "Such illumination in theology is not just a

---

129. McFague, *Metaphorical Theology*, 92, emphasis hers.

130. According to Soskice, models allow theists to talk rationally and truthfully about God while acknowledging the inherent inadequacy of human language. Soskice, *Metaphor and Religious Language*, 141.

131. McFague, *Metaphorical Theology*, 140. I take McFague's use of "syndrome" as identical with "system."

132. McFague, *Metaphorical Theology*, 140.

133. McFague, *Metaphorical Theology*, 139.

134. McFague, *Metaphorical Theology*, 139–40.

135. McFague, *Metaphorical Theology*, 140–41. This criterion of contra-factors also calls for what Osborne calls a "pluralistic or humble attitude" toward opposing viewpoints, since the "best way to attain truth is to allow the opposing side to challenge our basic beliefs and then to seek to learn from it and be driven back to the text so that we might see anew what Scripture really teaches." Osborne, *The Hermeneutical Spiral*, 393–94.

136. McFague, *Metaphorical Theology*, 141.

passing insight, as, for instance, one may derive from a good poetic metaphor. Rather, [a model] provides opportunity for an illuminating system, a pattern of increasing insight that makes sense out of life as a whole."[137] In other words, good models must have a kind of systematic illuminative potential, helping people make more or less comprehensive sense out of life. More importantly, these models make sense out of life "*because* they refer to reality, because in their own way—that is, partially and indirectly—they are a redescription of it."[138] Models must correlate with reality to be truly helpful, corresponding with actual lived experience. Such correspondence with reality makes choosing models "neither arbitrary nor absolute; models are selected and survive because they make sense out of human experience," which means that the scope of theological models moves far beyond religion to "encompass all dimensions of life in the world ... and illuminate all ways of looking at the world and all 'truths' about life we hold to be significant."[139]

McFague even argues that people tend to live within their models as fish in water; subtly and often imperceptibly, models influence how people think and feel about their world, and new models can result in shifts of meaning or a new set of conventions.[140] So models, as metaphors, can offer "basically a new or unconventional interpretation of reality, whether that interpretation refers to a limited aspect of reality or to the totality of it."[141] Models not only follow the rules but also change them, shifting the

---

137. McFague, *Metaphorical Theology*, 141.

138. McFague, *Metaphorical Theology*, 142, emphasis hers.

139. McFague, *Metaphorical Theology*, 143. According to McFague, "all serious users of models believe, at least to some degree, that their models refer to reality." McFague, 133. However, McFague distinguishes between how models in science and theology refer to reality. Unlike scientific models, theological models (1) seek comprehensive ordering rather than singular discovery; (2) push more toward ultimate meaning; (3) are indispensable, ubiquitous, and hierarchical; and (4) carry a valuational component that affects feelings and actions. McFague, *Metaphorical Theology*, 107.

140. In McFague's own words, "good metaphors shock, they bring unlikes together, they upset conventions, they involve tension, and they are implicitly revolutionary. The parables of Jesus are typically metaphorical in this regard, for they bring together dissimilars (lost coins, wayward children, buried treasure, and tardy laborers with the kingdom of God); they shock and disturb; they upset conventions and expectations and in so doing have revolutionary potential." McFague, *Metaphorical Theology*, 17.

141. McFague, *Metaphorical Theology*, 40. According to Soskice, these metaphors and models "become not only part of our language but also part of the way in which we interpret our world, and the implications of one metaphor are very different from those of another." Soskice, *Metaphor and Religious Language*, 62.

way people conceive of God, themselves, and the world.[142] Models wield worldview-shaping and perspective-shifting influence.

Avery Dulles: Models as Faithfulness to Revelation

In *Models of Revelation*, Avery Dulles follows Barbour's view that models "yield limited but valid knowledge concerning the reality itself."[143] Theological models present a limited yet accurate organization of what Christians believe about a certain topic, although such models inevitably fail at fully encompassing the divine being or activity. Still, models pull together a system of theologically relevant data and suggest provocative hypotheses for solving certain sets of problems.[144]

Models, however, cannot themselves guarantee the truth of their hypotheses, so Dulles suggests seven criteria to judge the validity of these models and their hypotheses: (1) faithfulness to the Bible and Christian tradition, (2) internal coherence, (3) plausibility, (4) adequacy to experience, (5) practical fruitfulness, (6) theoretical fruitfulness, and (7) value for dialogue.[145] Dulles argues that these criteria stay mostly neutral and objective, though he admits that they remain rather ambiguous in that disagreements may arise over their exact meaning. Yet he argues that this ambiguity does not leave the criteria vacuous since they serve to focus the discussion of truth in models without committing one outright to any presupposed theory of theology. Most helpfully, however, Dulles's first criterion, that of

---

142. For more on how metaphors and models transform perspectives, see Osborne, *The Hermeneutical Spiral*, 387–94.

143. Dulles, *Models of Revelation*, 32.

144. Though drawing helpful insights from Dulles's conception of models, John Feinberg takes issue with Dulles's definition of a model as that which "explains, and in some degree conditions, the characteristic theses of the theologians who rely on it." Dulles, *Models of Revelation*, 31. Feinberg finds this definition wanting, adding that a model does much more. A model identifies the source of its subject, discloses the contents and boundaries of its subject, and explains transmission of those contents from sender to recipient and how to know that the contents have been sent and received. Regarding revelation, a model implies whether revelation is now complete or one should expect more to come. Models of revelation also imply criteria to decide "whether a new claim of divine revelation should be believed." Feinberg, *Light in a Dark Place*, 40. For instance, "a biblical model of revelation should include many different things as the content of revelation, and it will likely propose that revelation comes in various forms. It should also distinguish different forms in which revelation comes." Feinberg, *Light in a Dark Place*, 45.

145. Dulles, *Models of Revelation*, 16–17.

faithfulness to the Bible and church tradition, reminds all model-users that worthwhile models in Christian theology should exhibit fidelity to the authority of Scripture and the church's theological heritage.[146]

Janet M. Soskice: Models as Determinative Frames

Janet Martin Soskice, in *Metaphor and Religious Language*, has offered the most comprehensive and incisive account of theological metaphors and models to date. Like those who have come before, Soskice agrees that metaphor "forms the implicit and unrecognized structure of most human life" and that a metaphor becomes a model when it envisions one state of affairs in terms of another.[147] Soskice takes issue, however, with the tendency to conflate metaphors and models; rather, she suggests the need for stronger distinction between the two: models establish the *frame* by which metaphorical discourse arises.[148] For example, the model "God is father" makes fatherhood the model that frames a certain understanding of God, and based on this fatherhood model, one can speak metaphorically of "God's loving concern for his children." So models enable and form the foundation for metaphorical discourse, and "the latter is what we have when we speak on the basis of the former."[149]

A model, then, is not simply a kind of metaphor or a metaphor taken to a higher degree but an entirely separate category. Models constitute the fundamental basis or frame from which one can speak intelligibly by metaphors. As frames for how people experience and speak of the world, models thus play a determinative role in "not only what sort of answers we get,

---

146. This criterion of faithfulness to Scripture and tradition appears also in other theologians' works. John Sanders includes the two criteria of conceptual intelligibility and adequacy for the demands of life, but he prioritizes consonance with tradition. Cf. Sanders, *The God Who Risks*, 16–19. Putman argues that theological metaphors "need to be *faithful* to Scripture and *fitting* to context. Because of our commitment to the material and formal sufficiency of Scripture, evangelicals will always approach theological metaphor making cautiously." Putman, *In Defense of Doctrine*, 305, emphasis his. Brümmer puts consonance with tradition at the forefront of his four criteria, followed by comprehensive coherence, adequacy for the demands of life, and personal authenticity. Brümmer, *Model of Love*, 22–29.

147. Soskice, *Metaphor and Religious Language*, 81, 55.

148. See Soskice, *Metaphor and Religious Language*, 101. Soskice specifically criticizes Black and Barbour, who tend to conflate metaphor and model. Cf. Soskice, 101.

149. Soskice, *Metaphor and Religious Language*, 55.

but what kind of questions we ask."[150] Much more than proposing analogies to certain contexts or systems of thought, models themselves become the contexts and systems of thought that determine what people consider important or relevant. Metaphors propose analogies, but models determine what even counts as a metaphor or an analogy. Metaphors suggest connections, but models establish the reality-depicting systems that allow those connections to make sense in the first place.[151]

Against the notion that scientific models are explanatory while religious models merely affective, Soskice argues that all models, to be affective, must prove at least somewhat explanatory of reality. A model that fails to explain real-world systems would fail to be a model at all. Rather, "Christians respond to the models of their religious tradition not because they take them to be elegant and compelling means of describing the human condition, but because they believe them in some way to depict states and relations of a transcendent kind."[152] In other words, Christians must believe their models depict reality for such models to guide affections and actions, not the other way around.

As concerns criteria for models, then, Soskice insists firmly on the criterion of reality-depiction: that models represent real states of affairs and not simply emotive values or evocative affections. At the same time, models must prove fruitful in providing "the matrix for the descriptive vocabulary which Christians continue to employ in attempts to describe their experience."[153] Moreover, Christian models must display faithfulness to Scripture and Christian tradition, as numerous models, such as "God is a rock," are "embedded in Scripture and tradition, and the subject of innumerable glosses and reinterpretations."[154] Finally, good models open possi-

---

150. Soskice, *Metaphor and Religious Language*, 63.

151. Van Huyssteen describes models as "comprehensive interpretive frameworks" that "*control* and *regulate* the way we reflect on God and humanity." Van Huyssteen, *Theology and the Justification of Faith*, 139, emphasis mine. In Dulles's words, a model "explains, and in some degree conditions, the characteristic theses of the theologians who rely on it." Dulles, *Models of Revelation*, 31.

152. Soskice, *Metaphor and Religious Language*, 112. Osborne concurs that "models are primarily 'reality depicting' in purpose and only secondarily evocative or action-guiding. Thus to speak of God as 'our Father' is first of all to tell us who he is and on that basis to guide our response to him." Osborne, *The Hermeneutical Spiral*, 392.

153. Soskice, *Metaphor and Religious Language*, 153.

154. Soskice, *Metaphor and Religious Language*, 115–16. Osborne observes that the Bible itself supports the use of metaphorical models since it "tends to use metaphors to describe the reality of God and his relation to this world. Therefore, most biblical models are metaphorical at the core." Osborne, *Hermeneutical Spiral*, 391.

bilities for "a new vision, the birth of a new understanding, a new referential access."[155] Models must demonstrate conceptual fruitfulness, enabling discourse to "go on" and develop a more comprehensive understanding of the subject modeled.

Criteria for Evaluating Models

Heeding Barbour's wisdom that one best acquires criteria "from studying past exemplars,"[156] I integrate the insights above to yield three overarching criteria, each with two sub-criteria, or qualifications. The three overarching criteria are faithfulness, fittingness, and fruitfulness. Faithfulness includes two sub-criteria of faithfulness to Scripture and faithfulness to church tradition. For fittingness (or appropriateness), two sub-criteria include fittingness to the subject and fittingness to current culture. As for fruitfulness, the two sub-criteria involve conceptual fruitfulness and practical fruitfulness. I explain each below.

Criterion #1: Faithfulness

FAITHFULNESS TO SCRIPTURE

Given *sola scriptura*, evangelical theology presupposes the supreme authority of Scripture.[157] Its authority, therefore, must reign over and temper all theological models and play the defining role in choosing which models to adopt. Models must either arise from or remain consonant with Scripture, and any model that contradicts Scripture falls out of bounds.[158] In other words, the Bible should be the main source for model making, as it is for doctrine forming. Though Ramsey and Barbour do not state this

---

155. Soskice, *Metaphor and Religious Language*, 58. Since models transform mindsets, Lawley and Tompkins apply models toward counseling in *Metaphors in Mind*. Cohen also commends the social uses of metaphor in *Thinking of Others: On the Talent for Metaphor*.

156. Barbour, *Myths, Models and Paradigms*, 115.

157. See Putman, *In Defense of Doctrine*, 4–5.

158. In Osborne's words, the most helpful theological model "best restates the eternal truths of Scripture." Osborne, *Hermeneutical Spiral*, 391. Osborne thus privileges models found in Scripture because, in his view, models lose reference to literal truth and reality the more one shifts from scriptural models to biblical-theological ones and finally to systematic-theological ones. Osborne, 391.

criterion explicitly, they affirm it in practice since both draw their models exclusively from Scripture. For example, Barbour lists his models for God as King, Judge, Shepherd, Husband, and Father, all of which stem directly from Scripture and together "form a model of God as a personal being."[159] Soskice also acknowledges this criterion by saying that many Christian "traditionalists" would argue "that no individual nor even the Church has the right to dispense with the models given to us by the biblical writings."[160] So drawing models from Scripture reflects faithfulness to Scripture.

Faithfulness to Scripture, however, does not mean that all models must come directly out of the pages of Scripture or that those developed from metaphors outside of Scripture are illegitimate. On the contrary, theologians often formulate legitimate and helpful extrabiblical models for doctrine, a case in point being the Trinity, a term not explicitly stated in the Bible but abundantly implied in the biblical text. As Putman says, faithfulness to Scripture simply means to "ask whether new metaphors utilized in theology are ways of contemporizing biblical judgments or concepts or ways of introducing notions and concepts alien or contrary to Scripture. The ultimate norm in these creative metaphors is neither experience nor utility, but God's self-revelation in the Bible."[161] So theologians must measure all models by the words of Scripture, to see whether Scripture would affirm or deny their legitimacy.

Faithfulness to Tradition

Though Scripture takes priority as Christians' ultimate authority for making and evaluating models, the church's theological tradition can serve as a secondary indicator of a model's faithfulness to God's revelation. While Scripture remains "of course the fundamental Tradition that tradition transmits,"[162] viewing a model in light of church tradition can offer a historical perspective on whether a model fits within the boundaries of orthodox belief and takes seriously McFague's insight that models must belong "to the same syndrome."[163] In other words, a model must interact coherently with other faithful models within the church's theological tradition. Good

---

159. Barbour, *Myths, Models and Paradigms*, 56.
160. Soskice, *Metaphor and Religious Language*, 116.
161. Putman, *In Defense of Doctrine*, 306–7, emphasis mine.
162. Work, *Living and Active*, 261.
163. McFague, *Metaphorical Theology*, 140.

models complement and do not contradict other faithful models within the tradition. As examples, tradition would disqualify a contradictory model such as "God is the devil" and would "make it absurd to extend the model of God's fatherhood so far as to say that he has a wife."[164] In ways like these, appealing to tradition helps to safeguard the truth content of models while warning against their misuses or faulty implications.

Expanding on this criterion, Vincent Brümmer offers two reasons why theological models must stay consonant with church tradition. First, theologians do not operate independently but as part of a communal and cumulative tradition. That tradition, therefore, should determine "the range of models which are acceptable within the community of believers."[165] Of course, theologians should innovate and develop new models to reinterpret the faith, but the cumulative tradition helps weed out those models that prove too remote or even opposed to the community's belief system. Second, appealing to tradition "enables theologians to learn from the efforts and the mistakes of their predecessors"; for better or worse, many theologians of the past have developed their own metaphorical models, and tradition reveals "which conceptual models have proved their staying power and systematic potential and have gained recognition as viable alternatives within the community of faith."[166] Though Scripture takes precedence over such "staying power," "systematic potential," and even tradition itself, anyone "who intends to do Christian theology will seek to stand in continuity with what believers of previous generations have recognized as compatible with faith."[167] Tradition thus helps to set certain guidelines or boundaries for discerning legitimate versus illegitimate models, and models that fall outside these limits should arouse suspicion or face outright rejection.

Criterion #2: Fittingness

FITTINGNESS TO THE SUBJECT

For Ramsey, the articulation or disclosure of a subject forms the whole point of using a model since models allow people to speak about subjects

---

164. Soskice, *Metaphor and Religious Language*, 116.

165. Brümmer, *Model of Love*, 23.

166. Brümmer, *Model of Love*, 24.

167. Dulles, *Models of Revelation*, 16–17. In fact, a model "is always constrained by received experience and theoretical assumption or bias in science as well as in religion." Soskice, *Metaphor and Religious Language*, 116.

that would remain indescribable otherwise.[168] Ramsey calls this articulateness "empirical fit" and likens it to a well-fitting shoe that matches the foot comfortably and does not "pinch."[169] So a model should fit its subject well, articulating as much as possible without too many anomalies—which McFague would call "contra-factors"—that would strain the model beyond its ability to cope.[170] Both Barbour and McFague concur with Ramsey's criterion of "empirical fit," which Barbour calls "agreement with data" and "the most important criterion."[171] "Empirical fit" also reflects Soskice's concern that models depict reality, since such fit involves objective reference to a subject outside the model itself.[172] In short, models must tell the truth about their subject.

Returning to Ramsey's metaphor, a shoe should fit comfortably around the *entire* foot, so fittingness entails comprehensiveness and coherence: a model should articulate its subject completely and cogently with few internal difficulties and no logical contradictions.[173] In other words, a model is "judged by its stability over the widest possible range of phenomena, by its ability to incorporate the most diverse phenomena not inconsistently."[174] Using Barbour's terms, a good model provides "systemic interrelatedness (the presence of connections and implications between statements)" in that it organizes "diverse types of experience within a systematic metaphysics."[175]

---

168. See Ramsey, *Models and Mystery*, 12–13, 20–21.

169. Ramsey, *Models and Mystery*, 17.

170. See McFague, *Metaphorical Theology*, 139.

171. See Barbour, *Myths, Models, and Paradigms*, 143; *Religion in an Age of Science*, 34, 38.

172. See Soskice, *Metaphors and Religious Language*, 112.

173. See Barbour, *Myths, Models and Paradigms*, 143. Brümmer terms this criterion "comprehensive coherence." Brümmer, *Model of Love*, 25–26.

174. Ramsey, *Models and Mystery*, 17.

175. Barbour, *Myths, Models and Paradigms*, 143. Black affirms the need for a model to encapsulate a comprehensive system: "Systematic complexity of the source of the model and capacity for analogical development are of the essence." Black, *Models and Metaphors*, 239. Systematic comprehensiveness also figures prominently in John Feinberg's definition in which a model "capture[s] a whole metaphysical conception of all that God is and does in our universe ... much as scientists do when they talk about a theoretical construct for organizing and explaining as much data as possible." Feinberg, *No One Like Him*, 55. Osborne concurs that a model "is a more permanent and comprehensive description that becomes a pattern for belief." Osborne, *Hermeneutical Spiral*, 391; cf. Soskice, *Metaphor and Religious Language*, 51.

So the best model offers the most comprehensive, systematic, and coherent presentation of the subject with as few inconsistencies as possible.

Fittingness to Current Culture

Aristotle and Quintilian attest that good metaphors exhibit clarity, which means that an audience easily and immediately grasps them.[176] To repeat Quintilian's phrase, a metaphor must place a subject "vividly before the eye," and Quintilian warns against using obscure or numerous metaphors since metaphors should clarify and not confuse.[177] As good metaphors, then, models should speak with immediate clarity to their audience, communicating in a way that fits, or speaks directly to, their current culture. As Lakoff and Johnson have shown, metaphors reflect and shape the everyday language of a cultural system, so metaphorical models should prove immediately accessible to their audience within a given culture.[178] Better yet are models that speak to many cultures, manifesting cross-cultural accessibility and more universal clarity.

Such immediate accessibility or clarity to an audience also includes what Barbour calls "simplicity," wherein a model requires the "minimum number of independent assumptions and conceptual categories" to remain intelligible.[179] In terms of fittingness to culture, simplicity means that people within a culture should grasp the meaning of a model without an excessive number of extra explanations, qualifications, or complications.

Criterion #3: Fruitfulness

Conceptual Fruitfulness

Conceptual fruitfulness involves what Black calls a model's "implicative power" or what Peacocke describes as a model's ability to "throw light

---

176. See Aristotle, *Rhetoric*, 1411b22; Quintilian, *Institutio Oratoria*, 8.6.14, 19.

177. Quintilian, *Institutio Oratoria*, 8.6.19; cf. 8.14, 16–17.

178. See Lakoff and Johnson, *Metaphors We Live By*, 26. Andrew Louth argues that knowing a culture's metaphors brings profound insight into how that culture thinks and understands the world since metaphors reveal that culture's commonsense assumptions. Cf. Louth, *Discerning the Mystery*, 19–20. Good models, therefore, reveal what a culture takes for granted or finds patently obvious or clear. Models reveal what a culture takes to be reality.

179. Barbour, *Myths, Models, and Paradigms*, 143.

forward."[180] In short, a "good model suggests possibilities."[181] As Soskice says, models make way for "a new vision, the birth of a new understanding, a new referential access," illuminating "areas where work might continue."[182] Barbour terms this criterion "fertility," wherein a model expands the scope of research and thus offers "future promise in providing the framework for an ongoing research program."[183] Good models prove fruitful regarding the subject itself and even at the systemic level, generating potential for future progress and discovery. They have "theoretical fruitfulness," suggesting new questions, hypotheses, speculations, and ways of observing data that may not have arisen without the model.[184] Such a conceptually fruitful model advances research and insight regarding both its subject and other related subjects while hiding as little as possible from view.

Practical Fruitfulness

Fruitfulness also has a practical and applicatory side, wherein "the model holds relevance for the way people interpret and live their lives today."[185] McFague calls such fruitfulness "fit with lived data" and likens it to the "shock of recognition" one might get while reading poetry.[186] To use Peacocke's metaphor again, apt models "throw light forward" not only cognitively but experientially, providing new awareness and application for daily, embodied life.[187] Dulles terms this "practical fruitfulness," in which a model offers new possibilities of pragmatic applications in the real world, not just in theory.[188] In the words of Erin Heim, good models "provide 'thick' and multifaceted epistemic access into the metaphor-maker's view of the world. Moreover, the 'shared vision' that metaphors create must be thought of holistically,

---

180. Black, *Models and Metaphors*, 242; Peacocke, *Intimations of Reality*, 31.
181. Soskice, *Metaphor and Religious Language*, 114.
182. Soskice, *Metaphor and Religious Language*, 58, 114.
183. Barbour, *Religion in an Age of Science*, 34.
184. Dulles, *Models of Revelation*, 17; cf. Black, *Models and Metaphors*, 239. Barbour calls such fruitfulness "extensibility of application." Barbour, *Myths, Models, and Paradigms*, 143.
185. Barbour, *Myths, Models and Paradigms*, 143.
186. See McFague, *Metaphorical Theology*, 141.
187. See Peacocke, *Intimations of Reality*, 31.
188. Dulles, *Models of Revelation*, 17.

encompassing cognitive and affective/emotive attributes."[189] A good model not only creates room for progress by providing a framework from which new questions, observations, and insights can emerge, but it also draws together a community that interacts around and through the model.

Summary and Disclaimer

Drawn from this history of metaphors and models, these three criteria of faithfulness to Scripture and tradition, fittingness to the subject and current culture, and fruitfulness conceptually and practically enable evaluation of the models to follow. Though not exhaustive, these three criteria prove relatively neutral in that none presupposes or obligates acceptance of any particular model. I admit that they remain somewhat ambiguous and arguable. For example, one's definition of "fruitfulness" may differ from another's, and disagreements can arise. Despite these ambiguities, these criteria have received sufficient definition above to proceed as viable categories by which to critique models and to weigh the data pointedly while allowing room for needed "*self-criticism* of one's own basic beliefs."[190] So while these criteria do not remain entirely objective and are open to critique themselves, they allow for more focused analysis and some semblance of objectivity in evaluating the models to follow.

---

189. Heim, "Paths Beyond Tracing Out, 118.

190. Barbour, *Myths, Models, and Paradigms*, 145; cf. Dulles, *Models of Revelation*, 17–18.

2

The Appetizers

Three Models of Scripture

As "COMPREHENSIVE WAYS OF envisioning reality," models carry weighty implications when applied to Scripture.[1] As Martin states, "People work with different models of Scripture, and how they interpret the Bible depends greatly on what sort of thing they take Scripture to be. . . . In fact, it may affect what we will eventually consider a 'good' interpretation as opposed to a 'bad' interpretation."[2] With so much at stake, Christians have developed several models to "think critically, self-consciously, and creatively about what sort of thing Scripture is—in their own assumptions and in the history and practices of their communities."[3]

---

1. McFague, *Metaphorical Theology*, 25.
2. Martin, *Pedagogy*, 79–80.
3. Martin, *Pedagogy*, 80. Examples of models include Martin's "Scripture is a museum"; Stephen E. Fowl's "Scripture is an underdeterminate voice"; John Goldingay's "Scripture is a witnessing tradition, authoritative canon, inspired word, and experienced revelation"; Telford Work's "Scripture is an icon"; John D. Morrison's "Scripture is a hierarchical, interactive disclosure"; Jeannine K. Brown's "Scripture is communication"; Kevin J. Vanhoozer and Daniel Treier's "Scripture is a mirror"; Hans Boersma's "Scripture is a sacrament"; Mark Reasoner's "Scripture is a plurality of documents, stories, prayers, laws, and oracles"; and Eugene H. Peterson's "Scripture is food." Peterson's book comes closest to this book's subject, though he writes for a lay audience and aims more to promote the spiritual practice of *lectio divina* than to develop a systematic model of Scripture. For a practical guide to *lectio divina*, see Magrassi, *Praying the Bible*. Cf. Fowl, *Engaging*

Three models have arisen in evangelical circles: Anthony Thiselton's "Scripture is a musical score," Kevin Vanhoozer's "Scripture is a theo-dramatic script," and John Feinberg's "Scripture is light."[4] The first two constitute "performance metaphors" drawing from the insights of Hans-Georg Gadamer in *Truth and Method*,[5] and the third draws from a prominent, intra-biblical motif. Each model comes from a highly respected scholar in Christian academia and invites people to "perform our construal—by participating in its vision."[6] Each also forwards a particular vision that influences how believers see and interpret Scripture, and each proves sufficiently comprehensive to employ the criteria of faithfulness, fittingness, and fruitfulness to evaluate their strengths and weaknesses in communicating the nature of Scripture. Their weaknesses, however, expose the need for a more adequate model, "Scripture is food."

Scripture Is a Musical Score

Anthony Thiselton envisions Scripture as a musical score, which has a set structure, melody, and notation that control and limit the score's performance. Every performance of a piece of music must correlate with its score, or else the performance would not be a faithful representation of that piece of music. Yet each performance proves unique and gives space to the performer to express creative imagination, whereas wooden adherence to the score may "turn out to be less faithful to the score" by lacking improvised creativity.[7] Still, each creative expression must occur within the clear limits set by the score.

Similarly, the structure and text of Scripture set clear limits to its interpretation.[8] Yet Scripture allows for creative performances and fresh

---

Scripture; Goldingay, *Models for Scripture* and *Models for the Interpretation of Scripture*; Work, *Living and Active*; Morrison, *Has God Said?*; Brown, *Scripture as Communication*; Vanhoozer and Treier, *Theology and the Mirror of Scripture*; Boersma, *Scripture as Real Presence*; Reasoner, *Five Models of Scripture*; and Peterson, *Eat This Book*.

4. See Thiselton, "Knowledge, Myth and Corporate Memory," 74–76; Vanhoozer, *Drama of Doctrine*, 115–242; and Feinberg, *Light in a Dark Place*, 1–770.

5. See Gadamer, *Truth and Method*, 106–7, 130.

6. Fiumara, *Metaphoric*, 133.

7. Thiselton, "Knowledge, Myth and Corporate Memory," 74.

8. Paul Ricoeur speaks of staying close to the "logic of the explication" to give "a correct performance, even though every performance is *individual* and stands alone." Ricoeur, *The Rule of Metaphor*, 96; cf. Putman, *In Defense of Doctrine*, 246.

interpretations of its text, leaving room for "new performances of the same work, sometimes with different tempos, additional improvisation, different performers, or slightly modified arrangements."[9] Such room for newness and diversity also suggests that Scripture has a corporate dimension: the church community, past and present, helps to safeguard its message through faithful listening and performing of its text, which provides a rich breadth and range of corporate memory in exchange for a narrow, individualistic viewpoint.[10]

Yet the individual and community do not stand at odds with one another but interact in a mutually reinforcing way. Scripture does not advocate group-think but rather calls individuals "to ways of understanding and acting towards God and others which transcend the limits of a strictly 'private' or individual world."[11] Scripture calls for self-involvement and engagement in the practical dimensions of faith and community, with shared commitments, attitudes, and patterns of behavior. As a musical score, then, Scripture tunes the community in shared performance, making belief much more than a cognitive or private endeavor but rather an active and public one. The Christian must act according to Scripture, much like a musician must stay faithful to the score's notation yet exercise creative expression for the good and delight of God and others who witness the performance.[12]

The transformative potential of Scripture thus awaits performance to be actualized.[13] Just as the notes of a musical score "become actualized only in the temporal flow of the performance, or when a skilled musician 'reads' the score in his or her head," the transformative effects of Scripture lie dormant until the community perceives and interprets its text, actualizing "an event of communication [that] takes place *within the temporal flow of the reader's life and experience.*"[14] Since performance actualizes the power of the text, the interpretation of Scripture exists not in some disembodied, abstract, or merely cognitive realm. Rather, its interpretation necessarily comes with application as an essential part. Scripture requires performance in time and space to consummate its life-changing potential.[15] Just as a mu-

---

9. Putman, *In Defense of Doctrine*, 245–46.
10. Thiselton, "Knowledge, Myth and Corporate Memory," 74.
11. Thiselton, "Knowledge, Myth and Corporate Memory," 74–75.
12. Thiselton, "Knowledge, Myth and Corporate Memory, 76.
13. Cf. Thiselton, *New Horizons in Hermeneutics*, 31.
14. Thiselton, *New Horizons in Hermeneutics*, 31.
15. Thiselton, *New Horizons in Hermeneutics*, 320.

sical score "has been encoded by a composer, and waits to be de-coded by an orchestra or singers in a musical event,"[16] Scripture has been encoded by its divine Author and awaits decoding by the church to perform its words. Thiselton even suggests that readers become "co-authors" of the text, as a musician becomes the "co-author" of a score by performing it and actualizing the music.[17]

Texts not only transform readers, however; readers also transform texts, for better or worse. Readers may misuse texts by domesticating them merely to maintain or confirm prejudices imposed upon others.[18] Thiselton hints at ways readers misuse Scripture for self-serving ends, much like one might exploit music for the purpose of political propaganda. On the other hand, readers may imbue texts with new life through fresh interpretations and improvisations on familiar themes. Still, Thiselton warns against misusing the musical model to extricate biblical texts from their historical contexts: "Music can be endlessly played and enjoyed, without our necessarily asking about the conscious horizons and situation of the composer. . . . But it becomes an entirely different matter if we place biblical texts (or at least the overwhelming majority of biblical texts) within the boundaries of this model."[19] So Thiselton recognizes when his model goes too far and includes this disclaimer.

A musical score also captures the complexity of Scripture. Just as a musical score contains a complex code of bars, notes, and "the physical-spatial shapes of crotchets and quavers,"[20] Scripture comprises a complex text that presupposes "several layers of code."[21] For example, John's Apocalypse uses several levels of linguistic code, at one level presupposing the linguistic conventions of Hellenistic Greek, yet on another operating on a system of conventions established by earlier apocalyptic. Furthermore, its allusions to OT texts like Ezekiel, Zechariah, and Daniel "are not merely reminders about earlier traditions. Sometimes they perform not a stylistic but a *semiotic* function, providing yet another level of encoding in terms of which a message is to be read."[22] This intertextual transposition of linguistic

16. Thiselton, *New Horizons in Hermeneutics*, 80.
17. Thiselton, *New Horizons in Hermeneutics*, 99.
18. Thiselton, *New Horizons in Hermeneutics*, 31.
19. Thiselton, *New Horizons in Hermeneutics*, 129.
20. Thiselton, *New Horizons in Hermeneutics*, 31.
21. Thiselton, *New Horizons in Hermeneutics*, 80.
22. Thiselton, *New Horizons in Hermeneutics*, 80–81.

conventions parallels the way musical code borrows from many layers of previous convention, which enables the composer and orchestra to decode the score's meaning. After all, music illustrates the complex interplay of linguistic presuppositions, systems, and conventions that come together to enable a text like Scripture to communicate effectively.[23] Musicians may understand the structure of a musical score even when they have never seen a particular melody before. In this way, a score expands the musicians' horizon to make room for new melodies. Music thus provides a way to speak of how Scripture operates on a network of textual conventions yet expands its readers' horizons with God's life-changing, often surprising words.

Scripture Is a Theo-Dramatic Script

Seeking to replace an older model of Scripture as merely "a handbook of propositional truths," Kevin Vanhoozer views Scripture as "a script that calls for faithful yet creative performance" in God's theo-drama.[24] As a script, Scripture not only constitutes "the supreme norm for Christian doctrine" but calls for "responsive action and embodiment. *The script demands to be played out.*"[25]

---

23. Thiselton, *New Horizons in Hermeneutics*, 80. To allow for this complex interplay, Thiselton prefers the term "horizons" over "presuppositions." To Thiselton, a presupposition tends to refer to an overly cognitive, arbitrary belief that only changes with difficulty, a horizon implies the capability "of movement and expansion as the subject of perception moves focusses [sic] the dual element of the strange and the familiar in processes of seeking to understand texts." Thiselton, *New Horizons in Hermeneutics*, 44.

24. Vanhoozer, *Drama of Doctrine*, 31. Seeking to move away from what he sees as dry, propositional doctrines that convey merely cognitive information, Vanhoozer recommends dramas, since they "*are not devised primarily to convey information but to move us, to persuade us, to delight us, to purge us of unwanted feelings.*" Vanhoozer, *Drama of Doctrine*, 182, emphasis his. Dramas promote response and action. By "theo-drama," Vanhoozer means "a series of divine entrances and exits, especially as these pertain to what God has done in Jesus Christ . . . the Trinitarian economy of divine self-communicative action." Vanhoozer, *Drama of Doctrine*, 31. So "theo-dramatic" acts refer to God's communicative words and deeds throughout redemptive history. Vanhoozer also draws this term from Hans Urs von Balthasar, whose massive, five-volume *Theo-Drama: Theological Dramatic Theory* retells the gospel through the model of theater. Cf. Balthasar, *Theo-Drama*. Vanhoozer often employs "theo-dramatic" as synonymous with *theological*. Cf. Vanhoozer, *Drama of Doctrine*, 30–31.

25. Vanhoozer, *Drama of Doctrine*, 113, 115.

This theatrical model reenvisions the doctrine of *sola scriptura* as "not only a principle but a *practice*,"[26] pushing toward participation in the world created by the biblical text. Human beings become "walk-on" actors on God's stage, God becomes the playwright and director, and the script becomes the directions and lines for the actors to play out.[27] The Bible is seen as more than a history book but as directions for today's speech and action.[28] Scripture both witnesses to what God has done and "*summons the reader rightly to participate,*"[29] addressing both God's agency and humanity's response. Scripture is thus "divine communicative action, *a divine canonical practice,*" and wields God's authoritative agency; Scripture "is the vehicle of Word and Spirit. In the context of the divine drama, the canon is the external means by which Christ exercises his authority over the church," not just how the church regulates itself.[30] For this reason, "Scripture as Script" safeguards *sola scriptura* as more than a principle but ultimately "a practice to be performed by the church in the power of the Spirit."[31]

Yet the church does offer the interpretive guardrails of theological tradition to ensure faithful exegesis of the text, since "*exegesis without tradition—apart from participation in the history of a text's reception—is impossible.*"[32] Just as previous acting troupes offer precedents for how to act out a script, church tradition offers faithful direction for how to receive and enact Scripture, similar to how Philip guides the Ethiopian eunuch in Acts 8 to understand better the Scripture he reads.[33] Thus "*formed and transformed by the ensemble of canonical practices that constitute Scripture,*"[34] Christians serve their role in God's theo-drama. Meanwhile,

---

26. Vanhoozer, *Drama of Doctrine*, 32.
27. Vanhoozer, *Drama of Doctrine*, 212, 177, 237.
28. Vanhoozer, *Drama of Doctrine*, 237, 295.
29. Vanhoozer, *Drama of Doctrine*, 181, emphasis his.
30. Vanhoozer, *Drama of Doctrine*, 114, emphasis his.
31. Vanhoozer, *Drama of Doctrine*, 115.
32. Vanhoozer, *Drama of Doctrine*, 113, emphasis his.
33. Vanhoozer, *Drama of Doctrine*, 116–20. Vanhoozer draws out two salient points from this episode in Acts 8: (1) that genuine understanding leads to action and not just intellectual assent; and (2) Philip's interpretive structure does not start with Philip but reflects the interpretive practice of Jesus back in Luke 24:27.
34. Vanhoozer, *Drama of Doctrine*, 331, emphasis his. By "ensemble," I take Vanhoozer to mean a collection of performances by various actors that work together in harmony.

God is the playwright and main actor who, through Scripture, "has an ongoing speaking part."[35]

Like Thiselton's musical score, Vanhoozer's theatrical script emphasizes improvisation. In fact, Vanhoozer suggests that improvisation proves obligatory to the theological task since "the Christian theologian can be responsible both to the action of the drama (whose principal acts have now been scripted) and to the present situation *only* as a faithful improviser."[36] As a dramatic script, Scripture not only encourages but requires improvisation. Theatrical improvisation thus becomes Vanhoozer's metaphor for practical wisdom.[37]

To improvise well, one must acquire two skills and avoid two pitfalls. The two skills are training and discernment, both of which enable improvisers "to act from instinct, yet with imagination."[38] Both also come largely, though not exclusively, through *"being apprenticed to the canon: of having one's capacity for judging (a capacity that involves imagination, reason, emotion, and volition alike) formed and transformed by the ensemble of canonical practices that constitute Scripture."*[39] In other words, the canon of Scripture forms believers in sufficient training and discernment so that believers can incorporate their lives into the canon's *"larger interpretive framework"* appropriately and spontaneously, as through improvisation.[40]

Though good improvisation appears reflexive and effortless, it actually comes from "years of disciplined preparation. The improviser is ready both because of her prior training and because she is alert and attentive to her environment."[41] Similarly, a wise Christian is a good improviser, trained to read both Scripture and the current culture to apply Scripture appropriately

---

35. Vanhoozer, *Drama of Doctrine*, 177, emphasis his. Critiquing what he sees as George Lindbeck's overemphasis on the community's authority, Vanhoozer places firm emphasis on God as the ultimate communicative agent: "Lindbeck rightly sees that language is a means of navigating the social world, yet he fails to see that *God, too, is a member of the linguistic community.* . . . *God is the ultimate agent of canonical discourse.* . . . In sum: it is the divine illocutions—God's use—that constitute biblical authority. . . . The divine author is not merely a teacher who passes on propositional truths or a narrator who conveys the discourse of others but a dramatist who does things in and through the dialogical action of others." Vanhoozer, *Drama of Doctrine*, 177–79, emphasis his.

36. Vanhoozer, *Drama of Doctrine*, 341.
37. Vanhoozer, *Drama of Doctrine*, 336–41.
38. Vanhoozer, *Drama of Doctrine*, 337.
39. Vanhoozer, *Drama of Doctrine*, 331, emphasis his.
40. Vanhoozer, *Drama of Doctrine*, 201, emphasis his.
41. Vanhoozer, *Drama of Doctrine*, 338.

to the contemporary situation. As Vanhoozer says, "Our spontaneity reveals our spirituality."[42] Spiritual reasoning becomes "improvisatory reasoning" or "improvisatory judgments."[43]

Vanhoozer further develops his model to encapsulate the inspiration, canonization, literary structure, and doctrines of Scripture. Inspiration refers to *"the Spirit's prompting the human authors to say just what the divine playwright intended."*[44] Canonization involves the church's acknowledgment of Scripture as its authoritative script, and its genres comprise strategies for social action and participation in particular social situations.[45] Doctrines function as "improvised judgments" and "intellectual habits" consistent with the canonical script and fitting to communicate with the current culture. As "indispensable imaginative habits" for playing the proper roles in God's theo-drama, doctrines *"draw upon the synthetic power of the imagination to enable us to see this world in otherworldly—which is to say, eschatological—terms."*[46] According to Vanhoozer, the script model encapsulates these key elements of the nature of Scripture while necessitating performance of God's words.

In fact, God's words constitute his action, according to speech-act theory, a linguistic philosophy that Vanhoozer regards as the "great discovery of twentieth-century philosophy of language" developed first by J. L. Austin and later by John Searle.[47] Speech-act theory holds that any sentence performs three acts: (1) the locutionary act, or the speaking of the words; (2) the illocutionary act, or the intended action performed by speaking the locutionary act; and (3) the perlocutionary act, or the intended effect of the

---

42. Vanhoozer, *Drama of Doctrine*, 338.

43. Vanhoozer, *Drama of Doctrine*, 336. Vanhoozer also draws on the model of music, specifically jazz improvisation, to elaborate on how a Christian should stay near the core theme of the gospel in community and yet express that theme in fresh ways: "As in ensemble acting, so in jazz improvisation: the jazz musician is responsible both to the core idea of the music and to the other players. Indeed, the jazz performer is 'more responsible to the score-reader, not less, to the unfolding continuities and structures of the work.' One jazz pianist comments that 'soloists elaborate upon what the structure of the piece has to say.' The theme and structure of the Christian play is, of course, the theo-drama. Christian theology is a matter of faithful improvisation on a theo-dramatic theme." Vanhoozer, *Drama of Doctrine*, 338.

44. Vanhoozer, *Drama of Doctrine*, 227, emphasis his.

45. Vanhoozer, *Drama of Doctrine*, 229, 215.

46. Vanhoozer, *Drama of Doctrine*, 335, 337, 378, emphasis his.

47. Vanhoozer, *Drama of Doctrine*, 63; cf. Austin, *How to Do Things with Words*; and Searle, *Speech Acts*.

locutionary act on the hearer.[48] Applying speech-act theory to Scripture, Vanhoozer hopes to render Scripture "as performative rather than simply informative discourse ... [as God] *doing* something in *saying* something."[49] In other words, he proposes viewing Scripture as "*a divine communicative act that exists for the sake of covenantal relations*."[50] Speech-act theory thus reconceives Scripture as much more than information or "a deposit of revealed truths."[51] Rather, Scripture is a "triune speech-act" wherein God performs his authoritative locutions, illocutions, and perlocutions "to Israel, to the church, and to the world as both playwright and player."[52] Scripture performs God's speech-acts, such as creating, promising, commanding, warning, judging, and comforting his creatures.

Scripture Is Light

In *Light in a Dark Place*, John Feinberg develops a comprehensive model of Scripture using the metaphor of light. Emphasizing "the need to reflect accurately what Scripture teaches about itself, lest we misrepresent God and what he has said about this book,"[53] much of Feinberg's work consists of in-depth expositions of Scripture so as to walk by the "light" of the biblical text.[54] Feinberg thus seeks to see Scripture through the light of Scripture itself, and his method consists of answering the question "What, then, does Scripture tell us about its own nature?"[55]

Feinberg argues that Scripture speaks of three kinds of light: creation light, redemption light, and revelation light. God gives these "three special expressions of light to meet life's most pressing needs."[56] Creation light includes the sun, moon, and stars (Gen 1:17), without which natural life

48. Vanhoozer, *Drama of Doctrine*, 63–68.
49. Vanhoozer, *Drama of Doctrine*, 64.
50. Vanhoozer, *Drama of Doctrine*, 68, emphasis his.
51. Vanhoozer, *Drama of Doctrine*, 67.
52. Vanhoozer, *Drama of Doctrine*, 64.
53. Feinberg, *Light in a Dark Place*, 18.
54. For example, Feinberg treats natural revelation by expositing Rom 1:16–32; 2:11–16; Acts 14:15–17; 17:16–29; and Ps 19:1–6. Cf. Feinberg, *Light in a Dark Place*, 48–66. He also points out that many of the Hebrew and Greek words for "reveal" include perceiving and seeing, which support the model of light. Cf. Feinberg, *Light in a Dark Place*, 79.
55. Feinberg, *Light in a Dark Place*, 17.
56. Feinberg, *Light in a Dark Place*, 23.

could not exist. Redemption light involves God sending his Son, Jesus, as "Light of the world" (John 8:12) to restore fellowship between God and humanity.[57] Revelation light refers to Scripture, which 2 Pet 1:19 calls "a lamp shining in a dark place." Feinberg thus categorizes Scripture as "the third form of light" to guide humans out of moral and spiritual darkness.[58] Moreover, light describes God's own nature (1 John 1:5; 1 Tim 6:16), making the model of light both appropriate and consequential: to try to live without Scripture means to choose moral and spiritual blindness rather than sight.[59] One lives tragically in spiritual darkness without the light of God's written Word.

Feinberg organizes his presentation into four parts: the creation of Scripture (revelation and inspiration), attributes of Scripture (inerrancy and authority), boundaries of Scripture (canonicity), and usefulness of Scripture (clarity, power, and sufficiency).[60] In "Part One: Creating Scripture," Feinberg immediately builds his model and begins to lay out implications. Like light, Scripture warms from the cold, discloses the concealed, and protects those who pay attention to it from stumbling over obstacles. Just as daylight makes the physical challenges of life more manageable, the light of Scripture makes the spiritual and moral challenges of life more navigable. In fact, the apostle John divides all people into two moral groups: those of light and those of darkness (1 John 2:8–11).[61] Jesus, the light of the world, shines in the darkness, though the darkness rejects him; those who believe in him, however, have the light of life (cf. John 1:1–5; 8:12).[62]

The transmission of spiritual light is called revelation, which itself means "to unveil, uncover, [or] bring to light."[63] Such light remains needful

---

57. See Feinberg, *Light in a Dark Place*, 24.

58. Feinberg, *Light in a Dark Place*, 25.

59. See Feinberg, *Light in a Dark Place*, 23.

60. This last section includes a chapter on the Holy Spirit's illumination, in which the Spirit also serves as light to illuminate "the minds and hearts of Scripture's readers to Scripture's message." Feinberg, *Light in a Dark Place*, 28. Interestingly, the fourth section on the usefulness of Scripture somewhat conflates the boundaries of the nature and function of Scripture, which Feinberg admits. See Feinberg, *Light in a Dark Place*, 27–28.

61. See Feinberg, *Light in a Dark Place*, 31–32.

62. See Feinberg, *Light in a Dark Place*, 31–32. Feinberg distinguishes between Jesus and Scripture as God's Word: "Jesus is the highest form of divine revelation we have. But probably *Scripture* is the largest *amount* of divine revelation available." Feinberg, *Light in a Dark Place*, 109, emphasis his.

63. Feinberg, *Light in a Dark Place*, 38.

even in Eden to Adam and Eve because of their intellectual, moral, and spiritual finitude. Yet this light becomes ever more needful after they break God's law, stand condemned, and yet remain woefully in the dark about how to remedy their predicament.[64] Thankfully, God continues to unveil the light of his Word to offer hope and salvation. God gives special revelation through divine acts, speech, dreams, visions, symbolic acts, theophanies, and the incarnate Word, Jesus Christ; but the "final form of special revelation is Scripture."[65] More than a mere "record" or "witness," Scripture is God's Word in written form, all of it the product of God's breath (cf. 2 Tim 3:16; 2 Pet 1:21). So Scripture affirms itself as God's inspired Word, revealing what God wants humanity to know.

Feinberg maintains that scriptural "revelation can and does occur even if the recipient rejects it and lives a different way than the revelation requires," arguing from 2 Tim 3:16 that "Paul doesn't say that all Scripture is the product of God's breath (revelation) if you obey it. God spoke all of it and it is his word—period! . . . Some will say that, unless we obey what we read, no revelation occurs, but this is wrong, because it demands appropriation of what God said for there even to be revelation."[66] Scripture remains fully sufficient and effective even when readers reject it or fail to enact it.[67]

In "Part Two: Scripture's Characteristics," Feinberg treats the inerrancy of Scripture as "true light" and its authority as "commanding light." As "true light," Scripture speaks only the truth that diametrically opposes the darkness of falsehood or lies. Light thus serves as an apt metaphor for the inerrancy (or infallibility) of Scripture, meaning its inability to lie or speak falsely. Everything Scripture says corresponds to reality and describes the actual world.[68]

---

64. See Feinberg, *Light in a Dark Place*, 32–33.

65. Feinberg, *Light in a Dark Place*, 105.

66. Feinberg, *Light in a Dark Place*, 107.

67. Feinberg reasons from the inspiration of Scripture that Scripture itself is "God's word, not just a witness or signpost pointing to the word"; and though Scripture does witness to many forms in which revelation came, "*Scripture itself is a distinct form of revelation.*" Feinberg, *Light in a Dark Place*, 216–17, emphasis his.

68. See Feinberg, *Light in a Dark Place*, 232, 252–56. Based on 2 Pet 1:16–18 and 1 John 1:1–3, Feinberg argues that the "biblical writers clearly intended to report what they saw, heard, and knew to be true of the life they lived and the events they witnessed." Feinberg, 254–55. Feinberg stresses this point on inerrancy more than any other topic in his book, devoting more than a hundred pages to refuting common arguments against it. See Feinberg, *Light in a Dark Place*, 287–386. As for the term *infallibility*, Feinberg discusses the differing views on the term (cf. 264–73) to conclude that it "only muddies

Stretching the metaphor, Feinberg titles his chapter on the authority of Scripture "Commanding Light." As God's Word, Scripture derives its authority from God himself, who is the supreme authority over all creation and "has the right to command thought and behavior, and its divine author has the right and power to enforce compliance."[69] Feinberg argues that Scripture carries not only functional but ontological authority since its author is God.[70] The ontological authority of Scripture carries two implications: (1) all doctrinal formulations should start from and "fit" with scriptural teaching; and (2) in cases where Scripture and tradition conflict, Scripture takes precedence.[71] Church tradition should not form a second locus of authority but bow to the supreme authority of Scripture.

In "Part Three: Setting the Boundaries," Feinberg addresses the canonization of Scripture as "Light Canonized." Just as Feinberg rejects the notion that the revelation of Scripture depends on its reception by the community, he also rejects "a community's *perception of* or *recognition of* a book as authoritative (and hence allowing the book to *function* authoritatively in the community) as having anything to do with what makes a book in and of itself canonical."[72] So light remains light whether a community perceives or recognizes it or not. Likewise, canonicity involves whether a text shows evidence of God as its ultimate author.[73] A text belongs in the canon of Scripture if it gives evidence of being divinely inspired, evidence such as God's revelation, inerrancy, and authority.[74] One could say that these books have evidence of being light coming from the One who is Light, though Feinberg does not make this statement explicitly. Other than the chapter titles, light receives little mention in this section.

In "Part Four: The Usefulness of Scripture," Feinberg discusses the illumination of Scripture as "Light Embraced," its clarity as "Clear, Understandable Light," its animation as "Living, Powerful Light," its sufficiency as "Light Enough," and its preservation as "Enduring Light." For illumination, Feinberg expands the light metaphor to include the Holy Spirit, who not only

---

the waters needlessly.... If infallibility must be used, I prefer to use it synonymously with inerrancy." Feinberg, *Light in a Dark Place*, 273.

69. Feinberg, *Light in a Dark Place*, 393.
70. Feinberg, *Light in a Dark Place*, 394–97.
71. Feinberg, *Light in a Dark Place*, 404.
72. Feinberg, *Light in a Dark Place*, 451.
73. See Feinberg, *Light in a Dark Place*, 455.
74. See Feinberg, *Light in a Dark Place*, 453.

supervises the transmission of Scripture but also "illumines human minds and hearts to understand intellectually and to live God's truth!"[75] Light thus covers not only the Revealer and his revelation but also his Spirit to understand that revelation.[76] With regard to the clarity of Scripture, the Spirit imparts a volitional understanding of Scripture, the willingness to obey it.[77]

As for the animation of Scripture, light emphasizes the power of Scripture to produce, correct, sustain, and guide spiritual life. Feinberg argues that Heb 4:12 refers to Scripture and thus teaches that God's Word "is so powerful that it is able to penetrate to the very core of one's soul, the very center of one's spirit.... Because Scripture can probe to the core of our spirit and our bodies, nothing of who we actually are and of what we are thinking in our innermost being can escape the power of Scripture."[78] Light makes good sense of this "bringing to light" of people's innermost being, penetrating their darkness and exposing religious phoniness.[79] God's Word also serves as the guide to life (Ps 119:105), a "lamp to our feet and light to our path. Such light shows us where it is safe to walk, and where it is unsafe."[80]

As for the sufficiency of Scripture as "light enough" and its preservation as "enduring light," Scripture proves adequate to meet all spiritual needs and will persist in its entirety to meet those needs in the indefinite future.[81] Since Scripture "will be preserved in written language that will be available to humans until the end of world history on the current earth and under the current heavens," people should receive that Word and submit to its light so that it informs their lives and decisions.[82] Closing with a personal testimony to how Scripture has served as light in his life—including when his wife battled Huntington's Disease—Feinberg presents Scripture as much more than an academic interest but rather "an ever-present, unrelenting source of light and life . . . for all of the places of our life—the dark ones, the light ones, and everything in between."[83]

---

75. Feinberg, *Light in a Dark Place*, 619.
76. See Feinberg, *Light in a Dark Place*, 660.
77. See Feinberg, *Light in a Dark Place*, 624.
78. Feinberg, *Light in a Dark Place*, 670.
79. See Feinberg, *Light in a Dark Place*, 668.
80. Feinberg, *Light in a Dark Place*, 673.
81. See Feinberg, *Light in a Dark Place*, 707, 717, 747.
82. Feinberg, *Light in a Dark Place*, 708–9.
83. Feinberg, *Light in a Dark Place*, 769–70.

Evaluating the Models

Feinberg, Vanhoozer, and Thiselton all express confidence that their models render the nature of Scripture legitimately and helpfully. Even so, models are not self-validating. To validate their legitimacy and helpfulness, I will evaluate them by the criteria of faithfulness, fittingness, and fruitfulness from chapter 1. This evaluation highlights strengths but also exposes weaknesses that the food model addresses more adequately.

Evaluating Faithfulness

Faithfulness to Scripture

Faithfulness to Scripture means loyalty to its authoritative dictates, treating Scripture as the ultimate source and guide for one's model making. Questioning the source of a model for Scripture proves especially important to evangelicals, who treat Scripture as their authority and hold to *sola scriptura*. Thus *sola scriptura*, not human experience or utility, should guide one's choice of model, especially for Scripture itself. As Putman puts it,

> Because of our commitment to the material and formal sufficiency of Scripture, evangelicals will always approach theological metaphor making cautiously. In contrast with other postmodern approaches to metaphorical theology that *reduce the Bible's role* in doctrinal formation to the way it "models" metaphor making in the Christian experience, evangelicals will ask whether new metaphors utilized in theology are ways of *contemporizing biblical judgments or concepts* or ways of introducing notions and concepts alien or contrary to Scripture. The ultimate norm in these creative metaphors is neither experience nor utility, *but God's self-revelation in the Bible.*[84]

In other words, Scripture should be the main source for model making, as it is for doctrine forming. Scriptural judgments and concepts should stand in judgment over any metaphors or models employed by Christian theology.

Since Scripture should be the main source and "ultimate norm" in creating theological models, one may question why the Bible does not describe itself explicitly as a musical score or a theatrical script. Stanley Porter criticizes the script model for relying more on speech-act theory than biblical exegesis since the "relation of speech-act theory to the writings of the Bible

---

84. Putman, *In Defense of Doctrine*, 306–7, emphasis mine.

THE APPETIZERS

is unclear. This perhaps accounts for the fact that so little actual analysis of Scripture has taken place using this model."[85] Rather than relying on how the Bible describes itself, these two models of "Scripture is a musical score" and "Scripture is a theo-dramatic script" instead seem to rely more on J. L. Austin's *How to Do Things with Words* and Hans-Georg Gadamer's *Truth and Method* as their source, which may imply that the real authority behind these models are these extrabiblical sources rather than the Bible. These models are not unhelpful, but they should not take priority over models that the Bible gives for itself. Intra-biblical models drawn explicitly from the biblical text should take precedence over extra-biblical models drawn from implications based loosely on the biblical text.

Scripture makes one metaphorical reference to theater when Paul states in 1 Cor 4:9, "For, I think, God has exhibited us apostles last of all, as men condemned to death; because we have become a spectacle to the world, both to angels and to men." Here, the Greek word for "spectacle" is "theater" (*theatron*), and Paul may have in mind his harrowing experience when an angry mob of Artemis worshipers dragged him and his companions into a literal theater in Ephesus, seeking to do them harm (cf. Acts 19:29–31). These references to theater, however, seem more to highlight Paul's hardships rather than to form the basis of a model for Scripture. The immediate context of *theatron* seems far removed from the modern, aesthetic context of theatergoing, with its comforts and high-culture terminology. Instead, *theatron* here seems more to highlight the gladiator-level suffering endured by Paul and the other apostles "as men condemned to death." Although Vanhoozer acknowledges this weakness to his model and admits that the scarcity of biblical references makes it "easy to see why the church has been ambivalent about the theater," he nonetheless maintains that theater remains helpful for seeing doctrine not statically but "theatrically: a *lived performance*."[86] For Vanhoozer, the benefit of this action-oriented understanding of doctrine outweighs the lack of biblical data for the model.

Regarding *sola scriptura* and the Bible as the source of a model, Feinberg's light shines brilliantly. Not only does Feinberg derive his model directly out of Scripture, but Feinberg's method reflects the biblical faithfulness of his model since he uses the light of Scripture to illuminate the nature of Scripture by asking repeatedly, "What does Scripture have to say

---

85. Porter, "Hermeneutics, Biblical Interpretation, and Theology," 117–18.
86. Vanhoozer, *Drama of Doctrine*, 17.

about Scripture?"[87] Such obsessive repetition highlights Feinberg's conviction that "by [God's] light do we see light" (Ps 36:9). Through and through, Feinberg's light model refers to Scripture as its exegetical and theological source, which proves an immense strength of the model. Whereas the score and script models do stay faithful to key tenets of the nature of Scripture—namely, its instructional and performative force—the light model more comprehensively demonstrates unquestionable fidelity to the teaching of Scripture about itself using its own language, as Ps 119:105 affirms, "Your word is a lamp to my feet and a light to my path."[88]

Of these three models, then, light most faithfully reflects Scripture as its main source by relying on the words, concepts, and judgments found in Scripture to shape the model. The score and script models are not unfaithful models since they too reflect true theological concepts and judgments about Scripture, but their lack of explicit support from the words of Scripture leaves a question mark as to the strength of their fidelity to Scripture when other models, such as light, come directly out of Scripture and thus demonstrate the direct sanction of Scripture for their use.

Faithfulness to Tradition

All three models draw from faithful strands of the church's theological tradition. In *Drama of the Divine Economy*, Paul M. Blowers argues that the theatrical model runs as far back as the church fathers, including Irenaeus, Tertullian, Origen, and Dionysius the Areopagite.[89] In fact, one cannot escape the "implicitly, sometimes explicitly, dramatic character of patristic theological reflection on Creator and creation" such that the framework of drama broadly "provided early Christian theologians a way to hold together the many aspects and intricacies of the doctrine of creation while still privileging the 'play within the play,' the Christo-drama of the Creator's self-revelation in Jesus Christ, as the key to the whole."[90] Carefully tracing

---

87. See Feinberg, *Light in a Dark Place*, 17–18, 26, 40, 112–13, 114, 433, 708.

88. See Feinberg, *Light in a Dark Place*, 673.

89. Blowers, *Drama of the Divine Economy*, 375–80; cf. Irenaeus, *Against Heresies*, 1.10.3; 3.16.6–7; 3.23.1–8; 5.36.1; Tertullian, *Against Praxeas*, 12.3; Tertullian, *Against Marcion*, 1.15.4–6; 2.2.4–7; 5.5.9–5.6.2; Origen, *De Principiis*, 1.2.10; 1.4.1–5; 1.5.1–5; 1.6.1–4; 1.8.1–4; 2.1.1–5; 2.3.1–5; 2.9.1–8; 3.1.1–24; 3.5.1–3.6.9; Origen, *Against Celsus*, 4.67–68; 5.20; 6.53–56; and Dionysius the Areopagite, *On Divine Names*, 4.10–17; and Dionysius the Areopagite, *Ecclesiastical Hierarchy*, 2–7.

90. Blowers, *Drama of the Divine Economy*, 373.

the theological works of these early church fathers, Blowers finds consistent elements of theater, such as the "*personae dramatis* of salvation, and its internal dialectics of prophecy and fulfillment, mystery and disclosure, suspense and resolution, desire and satisfaction, and its relentlessly teleological orientation."[91] According to Blowers, then, the dramatic, theatrical model stays faithful to even the oldest forms of Christian theological reflection.

The theatrical model features even more explicitly in John Calvin, who also includes the model of musical score. He writes in his *Commentary on the Psalms*, "The whole world is a theatre for the display of the divine goodness, wisdom, justice, and power, but the Church is the orchestra, as it were—the most conspicuous part of it; and the nearer the approaches are that God makes to us, the more intimate and condescending the communication of his benefits, the more attentively are we called to consider them."[92] Here Calvin has in mind both theater and music, calling the world a theater and the church an orchestra meant to display God's glory. From this setup, one can reason theologically to conceive of Scripture as the musical score that the orchestra performs to display "conspicuously" God's "intimate and condescending . . . communication of his benefits" to humanity, communication that humanity must "more attentively" consider. Expanding upon Calvin's metaphor, John Piper and David Matthis have edited *With Calvin in the Theater of God*, a volume of essays that develop implications for anthropology, hamartiology, bibliology, sociology, and eschatology based on the theatrical model. Piper even calls eschatology the *dénouement*, or "final part of a play, movie, or narrative in which the strands of the plot are drawn together and matters are explained or resolved."[93] So Calvin provides a theological precedent that implicitly testifies to the faithfulness to church tradition of the script and score models, though Calvin falls short of explicitly calling Scripture a score or script.

Another theological precedent for the theatrical model comes from Hans Urs von Balthasar's five-volume *Theo-Drama: Theological Dramatic Theory*,[94] to which Vanhoozer refers extensively.[95] Balthasar renders the entirety of redemptive history as theater wherein God plays the lead role

---

91. Blowers, *Drama of the Divine Economy*, 374.
92. Calvin, *Commentary on the Book of Psalms*, 5:178.
93. Piper and Mathis, eds., *With Calvin in the Theater of God*, 133.
94. See Balthasar, *Theo-Drama*.
95. Cf. Vanhoozer, *Drama of Doctrine*, 17, 30, 38, 47–50, 84, 106–7, 359, 383–84, 390, 395.

but "does not play the world drama all on his own; he makes room for man to join in the acting."[96] Following in Balthasar's footsteps, Vanhoozer holds that "what lies at the heart of the gospel is not an idea or an ideal or an experience, but an action."[97] Just as Balthasar's theater model faithfully prioritizes God's action and his call for humanity's action, Vanhoozer's script model frames Scripture as more than a set of propositions but a prompt for personal action within God's theo-drama.[98] So Balthasar stands as another witness to the faithfulness of the script model to church tradition, though, like Calvin, he does not explicitly call Scripture a script.

The musical score model seems the weakest in terms of support from church tradition. Outside of Calvin's oblique reference to the "orchestra" of the church, no theologians until Thiselton have modeled Scripture as a musical score. Martin Luther does say that "next to the word of God, music deserves the highest praise," but this high praise of music juxtaposed to God's Word still falls short of explicitly comparing God's Word to a musical score.[99] This dearth of theological support leaves one to wonder why this model has not occurred to the church until the twentieth century. Of course, the newness of the model does not automatically discount its faithfulness to church tradition, but Feinberg rightly asks that "if the new way of thinking and/or acting is so valuable, why has no one ever thought of it before? And, if it is really what we most need, surely God, who knows everything, would know that we need this novel approach. As a good God, why would he withhold this information?"[100] Such lack of corroboration in historical theology thus raises concerns as to the faithfulness of the score model to tradition.

In contrast, Feinberg's light model enjoys overwhelming support from church tradition. Given prominent verses like Gen 1:3 ("And God said, 'Let there be light'"), Ps 4:7 ("Lift up the light of your countenance upon us, O LORD"), Ps. 35:10 ("In your light we see light"), and 1 John 1:5 ("God is light and in him there is no darkness at all"), virtually every theologian refers to God and his revelation in terms of light. The use of light to describe God's Word—both Scripture and Christ himself—proves so ubiquitous that "the theological language of light is mostly a dead metaphor in contemporary

---

96. Balthasar, *Theo-Drama*, 91.
97. Vanhoozer, *Drama of Doctrine*, 50.
98. See Vanhoozer, *Drama of Doctrine*, 107.
99. Luther, "Preface to Georg Rhau's *Symphoniae iucundae*," 321–22.
100. Feinberg, *Light in a Dark Place*, 707.

Christianity."[101] Overuse of light in theology threatens to hamper the metaphor from conveying the awe of the connections between light, God, and God's Word.

This threat has prompted David L. Whidden III to seek to recapture the theological awe associated with light. Tracing the theme of light through Pseudo-Dyonysius, Augustine, the Cappadocians, Anselm, Bonaventure, and Aquinas, Whidden argues that "the very nature of scripture itself . . . serve[s] to support the light language. . . . For Aquinas and those who came before him, scripture by its very nature and content brings light into human darkness."[102] Feinberg thus has strong support from tradition for his model of Scripture as light in a dark place.

Evaluating Fittingness

FITTINGNESS TO THE SUBJECT

Since evaluating fittingness to Scripture presupposes some grasp of the nature of Scripture as a whole, I will use six common categories in systematic theology to focus the discussion on the nature of Scripture: inspiration, authority, necessity, sufficiency, clarity, and inerrancy.[103] A good model elucidates all six without raising insurmountable problems.

Inspiration

The inspiration of Scripture points to its being *theopneustos* (cf. 2 Tim 3:16), meaning "breathed out by God" or "the product of God's breath."[104]

---

101. Whidden, *Christ the Light*, 2.

102. Whidden, *Christ the Light*, 3, 17.

103. Though not exhaustive, these six categories enjoy longstanding support in systematic theology, though Scripture does not bind Christians to these specific terms. According to Timothy Ward, the four terms of authority, necessity, sufficiency, and clarity "have historically been the attributes most commonly cited" when evangelicals speak of their fundamental beliefs about Scripture. Ward thus calls these four "the traditional evangelical doctrinal headings for Scripture." Ward, *Words of Life*, 96–97; cf. Bavinck, *Reformed Dogmatics*, 1.449–94; Grudem, *Systematic Theology*, 62–168. I add the other two—inspiration and inerrancy—since they also often appear as major categories in evangelical and reformed treatments of the doctrine of Scripture; cf. Erickson, *Christian Theology*, 168–209; Ward, *Words of Life*, 78–89; Bavinck, *Reformed Dogmatics*, 1.387–448; and Feinberg, *Light in a Dark Place*, 111–228.

104. Feinberg, *Light in a Dark Place*, 182; cf. Vanhoozer, *Drama of Doctrine*, 226–31.

In short, inspiration means that God has spoken all the words of Scripture; they all proceed "out of the mouth of God" (Matt 4:4). Such divine inspiration, however, does not entail rote memorization and inscription of God's words but rather the Holy Spirit's movement within the hearts of men such that they write exactly what God intends while speaking authentically from their own unique personalities and agency (cf. 2 Pet 1:20–21).

The script model readily depicts this interactive process. As Vanhoozer says, inspiration "*is a matter of the Spirit's prompting the human authors to say just what the divine playwright intended.... Inspiration is about God entering into real human communicative practices in order to say and do things with words on the stage of world history.*"[105] This "entering" by God "enables prophets, apostles, and others to participate in the theo-drama by writing its authoritative script."[106] Vanhoozer goes so far as to say that the Spirit sits not on the stage but "hidden beneath it, well out of the footlights, in the prompt box," prompting and coordinating the human writers to articulate the theo-drama.[107]

Though Vanhoozer cleverly renders inspiration, he stretches the script model too far here. Customarily, a script finds completion long before the actors take the stage, and the stage manager sits in the prompt box to prompt the actors when they forget their already-written lines. To picture the Spirit in the prompt box, then, seems to present the wrong portrayal of inspiration as rigid repetition rather than inspired dual authorship. The voices of the human actors become parroted echoes of the Spirit's voice rather than authentic statements from the actors themselves. So the theatrical sense of "prompting" seems a far cry from inspiration as it pertains to Scripture.

The same problem haunts the musical score. One can envision two musicians cooperating to write a score, but such dual authorship remains inadequate to depict dual authorship of Scripture, which involves a divine author entering into the life and creative process of the human author in a way that maintains the integrity of both authors yet without violating the human author's personality or writing style. This situation proves difficult for any model to depict.

To their credit, the score and script models do uphold humanity's special place as God's image, which in turn might bolster the doctrine of inspiration. Only human beings create music and theater, employing complex

---

105. Vanhoozer, *Drama of Doctrine*, 227, 230, emphasis his.
106. Vanhoozer, *Drama of Doctrine*, 230.
107. Vanhoozer, *Drama of Doctrine*, 228.

language systems to do so. Music and theater, therefore, serve to remind humanity of its special link to God through language, a link emphasized in the doctrine of the inspiration of Scripture.

Light comes closest to depicting inspiration for two reasons: (1) it reflects God's own nature; and (2) it enables sight in the first place, thus depicting how humanity participates in God's nature of light, as described by the apostle John (cf. 1 John 1:5). This model thus depicts how God's light enters a human being, thus illuminating and enabling individuals to receive that light and transmit it in a way that maintains the integrity of both the divine and human author. So light communicates that the Holy Spirit first enters into and enables a person to produce Scripture in a way that prioritizes God's initiative and empowers that person's contribution.

Authority

The authority of Scripture refers to its supreme sovereignty and command over all creation and especially the church. Scripture derives its authority from God, the highest authority, who speaks through Scripture.[108] In Herman Bavinck's words, "authority is the power of a person who has something to say, the right to have a voice in some matter. Now one can speak of authority only between nonequals: it always expresses a relation between a superior to his inferior."[109] The models of a musical score and theatrical script do well in capturing this authority and sense of command for the church. A musical score requires adherence to its notes and structures to remain faithful in its performance, and the same goes for the written directions and dialogue in a script.[110] So both a score and script wield an unmistakable authority over the performers, demanding that performers obey the instructions on the page to enact the concert or play. These models thus convey the authority of Scripture to command the church's practice, and they make clear that the church stands under the authority of the score or script rather than equal as a second locus of authority. At the same time, a score or script does not call for slavish obedience but allows for creativity, improvisation, and diversity with each performance.

A possible problem with these models, however, regards the scope of their authority. Though a score and script make good sense of how Scripture

---

108. See Ward, *Words of Life*, 128; and Bavinck, *Reformed Dogmatics*, I.449–50.
109. Bavinck, *Reformed Dogmatics*, 1.463.
110. See Vanhoozer, *Drama of Doctrine*, 30.

exercises authority over the church as the performers on the stage, what about the audience or those outside of the orchestra or troupe of actors? A score or script thus posits an unhelpful dichotomy between participators and spectators rather than including all in joint participation. People who view themselves as outside the circle of musicians or actors may assume wrongly that the authority of Scripture does not apply to them, or people within the circle may assume wrongly that the authority of Scripture applies only to them but not to those outside. So these performative models may limit the scope of the authority of Scripture inadvertently, as if that authority pertains only to the church community, whereas Scripture obligates all to respond to and participate in its universally authoritative words.[111] It does not allow any person merely to sit in the spectator's position outside of the direct action. Of course, a proponent of these models might say that they do not imply such a dichotomy and that the score and script exercise authority over everyone in the concert hall or theater, but the question remains as to whether the context of a concert hall or theater make the best sense of the universality of the authority of Scripture.[112]

The authority of Scripture also proves problematic for the model of light. Feinberg titles his chapter on the authority of Scripture "Commanding Light," but nothing about light in and of itself necessitates command. Feinberg does not address how light entails such command, though the scriptural connection between God as light and Scripture as the light of God's Word perhaps implies an ability to command and enforce obedience.

Light more clearly conveys than a score or script the universality of the authority of Scripture. Light holds almost universal significance, as most living beings rely on light to exist. Light also carries a sense of priority

111. Lindbeck and Cantwell Smith both make this mistake regarding the authority of Scripture by limiting the regulative scope of its authority only to the church community. Cf. Lindbeck, *The Nature of Doctrine*, 18–27; and Cantwell Smith, 237.

112. Regarding the theatrical model, D. A. Carson warns that one loses a comprehensive grasp of the authority of Scripture when that "authority is tied exclusively to the notion of kingdom, understood to be advancing through the four acts of Scripture, and still advancing today in the fifth act. We have already seen how the actors in the fourth act, Jesus and the apostolic church, habitually speak of antecedent Scripture in more comprehensive terms . . . of truth, God speaking, the fact that Scripture cannot be broken, and the like—the kind of ways that Jesus himself spoke of Scripture. Shouldn't those who live in the fifth act adopt the same stance toward Scripture as that held by Jesus himself, the star of the fourth act?" Carson, *Collected Writings on Scripture*, 301. In other words, one must be careful not to allow a theatrical model of the scriptural narrative—even one as prominent as "kingdom"—to limit one's view the universal and truth-telling authority of Scripture.

since it enables one to see in the first place, which undergirds two implications for the function of Scripture that (1) all doctrinal formulations should fit with scriptural teaching, and (2) Scripture takes precedence over church tradition. Without the light of Scripture, all doctrinal formulations would operate blindly, with no sure guidance or confidence of progress. Tradition, lacking the light of Scripture, would reflect only humanity's thoughts rather than God's. The priority of light thus illuminates these points, though Feinberg does not explicitly say as much.

In summary, the score and script models do well at conveying the authority of Scripture in terms of direction and command, but they fail to show the universal scope of that authority. Light, on the other hand, has a less direct connection with authority, but it captures well the universal scope and priority of Scripture since, as God's Word, Scripture "stands on a level high above all human authority in state and society, science and art. Before it, all else must yield."[113]

Necessity

The necessity of Scripture speaks to its indispensability for true and saving knowledge of God "because without such a Word our knowledge of God would be insufficiently grounded, unreliable and even ... too subjective."[114] Scripture is essential for eternal life rooted in the truth found only in fellowship with Jesus Christ.[115] So Scripture never becomes superfluous, and Scripture sustains the church.

While scores and scripts need people to perform them, people do not necessarily need scores or scripts to perform. A musician or actor may learn the score of script sufficiently and leave it behind after several performances since the performers are the actual source of the music or theater. Similarly, theologians could leave Scripture behind after using it to form their comprehensive theological system, or the Catholic Church could claim that the Bible "strictly speaking is not necessary; Scripture does need the church for its authority and interpretation. . . . The 'church' survives the vanishing of Scripture because it produced Scripture."[116] The models of

---

113. Bavinck, *Reformed Dogmatics*, 1.465.
114. Ward, *Words of Life*, 99.
115. See Bavinck, *Reformed Dogmatics*, 1.450.
116. Bavinck, *Reformed Dogmatics*, 1.450.

score and script leave open these possibilities and perhaps even sanction them inadvertently.

The model of light, however, tends to avoid these liabilities. Light remains necessary for the possibility of sight, and it enables most living beings to stay alive. Light thus amounts to a constant and urgent need that one cannot leave behind without devastating consequences, like blindness or even death. Given its natural necessity, then, light fittingly models the desperate and perpetual need for Scripture. Scripture enables and sustains people's lives with the truth of God's Word; it also continually enables people to walk in God's truth, upheld by the crucial empowerment it provides. So people constantly need the light of Scripture, and light shows the necessity and priority of Scripture more seriously than a score or script.

The issue of seriousness presents another liability for the score and script models. While light shows that lives are at stake, scores and scripts do not naturally carry the same weight. Living without music or theater can lead to an impoverished quality of life, but living without light constitutes a much greater disability. So a lack of light brings a sense of terror and desperation missing from the score and script models, and this terror testifies to the necessity of light. Using light to model Scripture, therefore, underscores the abject necessity of Scripture, such that lack of it proves terrifying and life threatening. Such life-threatening terror does not factor into the context of a script or score since they pertain more to an entertaining event than the reality of daily mortality. The model of light thus makes clear that Scripture is no mere game but an issue of life or death, whereas a score or script may tend to lighten—or even leave out—the gravity of Scripture, including the threat of darkness and death if one lacks or disobeys it.

Even if one does have Scripture, it can prove dangerous if one does not rightly handle or obey it (cf. 2 Tim 2:15; Jas 1:22). Light captures this sense of danger since concentrated light turns into a laser that can literally cut through "both joints and marrow" (Heb 4:12). So light can capture the real terror of God's judgment when one lacks or disobeys Scripture, while this sense of real terror and mortal danger seems wholly absent in a script or score. With music and theater, the stakes are just not that high; while models drawn from music and theater stress the beauty and enjoyment of Scripture, they do so at the expense of accounting for the necessity of Scripture.[117]

---

117. Avis argues that revelation (and thus Scripture) calls for more than cognitive but aesthetic response "by indwelling its beauty—just as we would respond to a work

Sufficiency

The sufficiency, or perfection, of Scripture speaks of its complete and sole adequacy to impart the knowledge of God, accomplish his purposes, and save his covenant people. Scripture is thus in no "sense inadequate and therefore needing to be augmented by ecclesiastical tradition."[118] Rather, "*Scripture is sufficient as the means by which God continues to present himself to us such that we can know him, repeating through Scripture the covenant promise he has brought to fulfillment in Jesus Christ.*"[119] Scripture tells people everything they need to know about God and his salvation.

The score and script models can capture well that Scripture includes all the directions needed for a sufficient and faithful performance. A good score would contain all the markings and notes that musicians would need to know for the concert, and a good script would include all the spoken lines and instructions for cast and crew to enact a complete play.

Light also captures the sufficiency of Scripture. As a gift that helps people see in the first place, light highlights the sufficient enablement provided by God through Scripture. As sufficient light, Scripture empowers those who would receive its words with "everything a person needs to know" about God and his salvation.[120]

Clarity

The clarity, or perspicuity, of Scripture means that in Scripture God clearly communicates his nature, ways, purposes, and salvation to all who hear its words in good faith.[121] Mark D. Thompson defines the clarity of Scripture as "*that quality of the biblical text that, as God's communicative act, ensures

---

of art or beauty: reading poetry aloud, listening to music, enjoying a painting, relaxing in a garden, relishing a good meal, taking delight in the face of a beloved. The aesthetic response is not our whole response, but it is an important—and neglected—part of it." Avis, *God and the Creative Imagination*, 59. I agree with his sentiment but wish to guard against the tendency of aesthetic models—such as a score and script—to overemphasize beauty to the point of losing mortal necessity.

118. Bavinck, *Reformed Dogmatics*, I.451.

119. Ward, *Words of Life*, 113. Ward identifies a distinction between the material sufficiency and formal sufficiency of Scripture. Material sufficiency means that Scripture "contains everything needed for Christian faith and life." Formal sufficiency entails "the ability of Scripture to be its own interpreter." Ward, *Words of Life*, 108–9.

120. Ward, *Words of Life*, 107.

121. Cf. Bavinck, *Reformed Dogmatics*, 450.

its meaning is accessible to all who come to it in faith."[122] Clarity emphasizes that Scripture speaks accessibly and understandably; its central message remains understandable and straightforward for anyone willing to hear and trust it.[123]

The model of light proves especially helpful here. Light naturally brings clarity. It literally makes things clear by allowing one to see. An unclear light seems oxymoronic, as one would use a lamp, headlight, or flashlight to clarify one's way through darkness. One might describe a clear thought as "a lightbulb turning on," one "brings to light" things that would otherwise prove obscure, and one "throws some light" on something to clarify it. So light readily depicts Scripture as clear and accessible rather than hidden. In fact, light portrays Scripture as something that not only makes sense but also enables other things to make sense, and thus "we speak of that through which we know things as 'light.'"[124] Only by light can one see all else.

The score and script models also speak to the clarity of Scripture, though not as well as light. The bars and notes of a score present the music's melodies and harmonies clearly enough for musicians to perform them, and a script delivers clear directions and dialogue to guide the action of the play. An unclear score or script would fail its function. Moreover, these models provide a clear conceptual link with Scripture since a score, script, and Scripture all consist of a system of symbols written with ink on parchment or paper. So a score or script entails the clarity of Scripture, though light does so uniquely by enabling one to see clearly in the first place.

Inerrancy

As an inerrant document, Scripture "does not assert any errors of fact: whether the Bible refers to events in the life of Christ, or to other details of history and geography, what it asserts is true. . . . Scripture does not err in everything it affirms."[125] Inerrancy speaks of the absolute truthfulness of

---

122. Thompson, *A Clear and Present Word: The Clarity of Scripture*, 169–70, emphasis his.

123. On the other hand, the clarity of Scripture does not mean that Scripture has no difficult passages to interpret, that its meaning requires no careful historical and literary study, or that Christian interpreters do not disagree on the meaning of Scripture. See Ward, *Words of Life*, 121–24.

124. Whidden, *Christ the Light*, 102.

125. Ward, *Words of Life*, 130, 133. Notably, Ward does not consider inerrancy its own category alongside the authority, necessity, sufficiency, and clarity of Scripture.

Scripture and its inability to lie based on the morally perfect nature of God as its author (cf. Num 23:19; Titus 1:2; Heb 6:18). In short, Scripture always tells the truth; its statements always correspond to reality.

Such congruence with reality poses another problem for the script and score models, which imply a dichotomy between reality and imagination. A theatrical play or musical performance tends to encourage people to "lose themselves" in the realm of imagination distinct from direct reality. Applied to Scripture, this subtle privileging of the imaginary may damage people's view of the link between Scripture and reality by relegating Scripture to the domain of make believe. By distancing Scripture from reality and rooting it in the world of pretend, these performance models may mask the grave and real-world seriousness of the teaching of Scripture. One can play lightheartedly in theater and music, but one cannot do the same with Scripture since one's response to Scripture proves literally a matter of life or death that will "alter one's eternal destiny."[126] Just as Scripture does not take this eternal matter lightly, models describing Scripture should not either; they must fit reality, as Scripture does. Though it does include aesthetic and beautiful components, Scripture is not the arena for mere aesthetics, luxuries, or flights of fancy; it is the most serious of life essentials. While music and theater remain optional engagements that people can—though few would—live without, Scripture is no luxury but a bare necessity, a non-negotiable, real-world need.

So the danger with models like a script or score lies in that they may mislead people into thinking that the biblical world is distinct from the real one, such as when Vanhoozer claims, "By entering the worlds that the canonical authors create for us, therefore, we develop the ability to interpret our own world and, more important, the ability to see, say, judge, and do what is Christo-dramatically fitting in our own situations."[127] This separation between the "worlds that the canonical authors create for us" and "our own world" comes with the territory of theater; but, as with theater, it too

---

Instead, he considers inerrancy a subset of authority. See Ward, *Words of Life*, 130–40. I disagree with Ward on this point because a document can hold authority over a community without always telling the truth, such as the Book of Mormon or the Bhagavad Gita. In my view, inerrancy belongs in its own category since it reinforces all the other attributes of Scripture while necessarily affirming the utter truthfulness of Scripture and its correspondence to reality.

126. Feinberg, *Light in a Dark Place*, 662.
127. Vanhoozer, *Drama of Doctrine*, 331, emphasis his.

easily entails a bifurcation between Scripture and reality, putting a damaging distance between Scripture and its reality-describing inerrancy.

In Vanhoozer's defense, he does not mean to forge this distance; he states explicitly that doctrines based on Scripture "*are intellectual habits that draw upon the synthetic power of the imagination to enable us to see this world in otherworldly—which is to say, eschatological—terms.*"[128] By "otherworldly," then, Vanhoozer does not mean an imaginary world but rather a real, eschatological one. The pretend, "otherworldly" sense of theater, however, might cause confusion and misunderstanding, misleading his hearers to think that the "theater of the strange new world of the gospel" simply represents an imaginary Christian world rather than the this-worldly reality, which is anything but pretend.[129] So models like a score or script, which lead one to think of retreating from the real world into that of fantasy, do harm to conveying the truth-telling, reality-denoting inerrancy of Scripture.

The model of light, on the other hand, readily expresses the correspondence of Scripture to reality. Light can play a role in a theater or concert hall, but its range stretches far beyond these contexts. Light plays a crucial role in all of life in its daily reality. Light is serious, and blindness is tragic. The crucial importance of light reflects historically in philosophy and science. Plato links light with truth,[130] and modern physics makes much of light's properties and its relation to physical reality.[131] To this day, to "come to the light" means to admit the truth and to "bring to the light" denotes the public discovery of truth or reality. In modeling Scripture, then, light both philosophically and naturally helps to communicate the reality-describing truthfulness and inerrancy of Scripture.

In summary, the best model for Scripture fittingly communicates its inspiration, authority, necessity, sufficiency, clarity, and inerrancy. The score and script models depict the inspiration of Scripture rather well and its authority even better than light, but light better fits all the other attributes, especially the necessity of Scripture.

---

128. Vanhoozer, *Drama of Doctrine*, 377.
129. Vanhoozer, *Drama of Doctrine*, 457.
130. See Plato, *Republic*, 508b–520a.
131. See Waldman, *Introduction to Light*.

Fittingness to Current Culture

A good model discloses its subject clearly and coherently to the current culture, raising as few problems as possible. Both Thiselton's score and Vanhoozer's script appropriately describe the conduct, creativity, and community necessary to respond appropriately to the Bible in the current context. In addressing conduct, both a musical score and a theatrical script call for performance. After all, a "drama exists only when it is played. Music is experienced not simply in reading the composer's score privately, but in the actual event of the concert."[132] In the same way, the words of Scripture demand the "performance" of obedient conduct and faith, not just mental assent, just as in "a work of art its actual being cannot be detached from its representation which makes interpretation."[133] A score and script also capture the need for creative interpretation since interpreting the signs on the page "is not a mechanical reproduction of the past in the present, but a creative event in its own right."[134] With regard to community, a score and script reflect "the self-preserving qualities of Christian corporate memory" required to interpret the Bible today.[135] Interpretation is a corporate event drawing from corporate traditions.

However, a danger that lurks behind using the models of score and script concerns their cultural scope.[136] Since metaphors can shape culture and influence how people think and behave, one can raise questions as to how these models influence the way the current culture thinks about Scripture, and what kind of culture these models promote. A possible problem arises from the fact that both models come from the context of the arts and entertainment. Of course, there is nothing wrong with the arts or entertainment, but given the current cultural context—in which schools tend to

---

132. Thiselton, *The Two Horizons*, 298.
133. Vanhoozer, *Drama of Doctrine*, 298–99.
134. Vanhoozer, *Drama of Doctrine*, 299; cf. Peterson, *Eat This Book*, 76–77.
135. Putman, *In Defense of Doctrine*, 245.
136. By "cultural scope," I mean the kinds of culture being promoted by these models. Brümmer describes well the power of a model to shape believers' actions and attitudes: "Religious models determine the actions and attitudes to which believers commit themselves, in two main ways. First, in coming to understand themselves and their own lives in terms of the conceptual models derived from their religious tradition, believers discover the role they have to play in their lives and actions. . . . Secondly, by interpreting their experience of the world in terms of such models, believers come to see which actions and attitudes are called for in relation to the world and in the various situations in which they have to act." Brümmer, *Model of Love*, 16.

devalue the arts and scale back arts programs—one wonders whether such models might influence those in this culture to devalue and scale back use of the Bible.[137]

One might question also whether the theatrical (and in today's culture, cinematic) model of "Scripture is a script" places the Bible too much in the context of entertainment, which in the current culture may influence people to consider approaching the Bible as an escape from reality rather than engagement with reality.[138] David Buschart and Kent Eilers have mentioned how church buildings are being modeled after theaters or cinemas, a phenomenon that may reflect how entertainment contexts are influencing even the physical space of church culture:

> In both design and aesthetic, the worship center is closer to a performance hall or auditorium than it is to a "traditional" church building. With theater-style seats and an absence of explicitly Christian symbolism, it is a multipurpose space that, in addition to weekly worship services, very comfortably hosts concerts, conferences and other local-community events.[139]

So a model of Scripture as "script" may mislead people in contemporary culture to think of church as merely a theater that lacks "explicitly Christian symbolism" and implicitly promotes "very comfortably" cushioned lives.

The theatrical model also might have the troubling effect of limiting the scope of Scripture to only the highly educated. Aristotle says that a good metaphor must be clear and *immediately* accessible to its audience, but the theatrical model requires its audience first to understand the context of theater and its technical terms, such as "auctor," "mise en scène," "Performance I and II," "raconteur," "provocateur," "dramaturge," and "*sub specie theo-dramatis.*"[140]

---

137. The arts should not be devalued in the educational system, but such is the case, and I have concern that the current culture's dismissive attitude toward art might engender such dismissiveness toward Scripture.

138. As a personal example, my friends and I most often go to the theater or cinema to "escape real life," not to wrestle with it. This is not to say that movies and plays do not engage with real issues, but their context as entertainment does suggest to me a mental distance from the direct engagement of real life. As a preacher, I would not want my model for Scripture to create such "mental distance" within the minds of my audience. Though often entertaining, the Bible is not mere entertainment; it is as directly real as life and death, as food and starvation.

139. Buschart and Eilers, *Theology as Retrieval*, 142.

140. Vanhoozer, *Drama of Doctrine*, 177, 173, 176, 237, 239, 334. With regard to

THE APPETIZERS

These terms create a steeper learning curve for the audience rather than immediate clarity, and they require that an audience be highly educated in theatrical terminology to grasp the metaphor (and thus the Bible). Such selective terminology tends to limit the scope of a play to only the small circle of actors, artists, and those who like the genre, thus limiting applicability to all. In this way, theater can become elitist, favoring only "cultured" people who can grasp the complexity of the art form, while people outside the inner circle might ignore or disregard the performance as irrelevant or unnecessary to them. The person on the street will not readily grasp the nuance and terminology required to understand and apply the theater and music models. Such terms might thus discourage the lesser educated from approaching the Bible because of the faulty assumption that the Bible is too complicated or highbrow, which would be a lamentable repercussion. In a similar vein, people who see Scripture as a score or script may tend to think of Scripture as something only of interest to a privileged few rather than of crucial import to all people.

In addition to the dichotomy between the more and lesser educated, the current context of music and theater may imply another unhelpful dichotomy between rehearsal and performance.[141] One does not perform a score or script constantly but only during the event of the performance. These models may lead people away from the daily rhythms of consistent discipline in spiritual growth by relegating the "performance" of Scripture

---

Performance I and II, Vanhoozer spends pages and pages trying to clarify what he means by right performance so as not to conflate Performance I and Performance II. He lays out Lindbeck's view of Scripture under Performance II interpretation (wherein the actors disregard the author's intentions and replace them with only the actors' own intentions) to argue against it in favor of Performance I interpretation (wherein the actors uphold the author's or playwright's intentions). See Vanhoozer, 180. Putman agrees with this criticism of Performance II: "This approach veers toward antirealism. God-talk does not describe the reality of God as much as it describes communal beliefs about God." Putman, *In Defense of Doctrine*, 249. Though this distinction remains important to maintain the divine authority of Scripture, the reason Vanhoozer must address this issue in the first place is because his model entails it.

141. Ironically, Vanhoozer sees his script model as subverting rather than creating longstanding dichotomies: "The working assumption . . . is that the *analogia dramatis* remains theologically fruitful: both adequate to the subject matter of Christian theology and conducive to resolving certain long-standing dichotomies (e.g., word versus act, theory versus life) that have led the church to undervalue, or even to neglect its rich doctrinal heritage. The theatrical metaphor illumines both what happens in the church and the relationship between church and world." Vanhoozer, *Drama of Doctrine*, 402. In my view, the model creates as many dichotomies as it may abolish.

to isolated events like the Sunday church service or the Wednesday prayer meeting. As with a musical performance or theatrical play, people might exit the church building and leave Scripture behind rather than carrying it with them throughout their daily lives.

The stress on performance may continue also to reinforce the current culture's idolization of celebrity pastors. Theater and music tend to promote a celebrity culture that idolizes musicians or actors who perform the score or script exceptionally well. In a similar way, these models may feed into the already problematic American tendency to elevate celebrity pastors with almost cult followers, resulting in the glory going not to God but to human beings. For these famous pastors, excellence in performance and lack of rest can lead to burnout, just as with famous musicians and actors. So these performative models of score and script might feed more into the harmful effects often associated with such pressurized, performance-based careers. Moreover, congregants might make the faulty assumption that the pastor on stage constitutes the only real actor, leading to the repercussion that the congregation sits outside the performance, exempt from the action and instead sitting in judgment over it.

This model also may perpetuate the current problem of Christians merely acting a role in church or putting on a face that they really are not in their homes and "real life." Once again, models of score and script are not unhelpful, but one should take to heart Putman's warning always to "approach theological metaphor making cautiously,"[142] evaluating models carefully to ensure that they promote the right cultural customs (those taught in Scripture) and submit to the right source (Scripture as God's written Word).

Light avoids the cultural misapplications above but also comes with its own liabilities. To its credit, light enjoys a pan-cultural scope. In every culture, "light warms and it also uncovers things hidden in our way. If we attend to it, light can keep us from stumbling and falling over obstacles in our path. On the other hand, darkness is a problem."[143] People in modern society still associate light with sight, productivity, progress, and moral clarity while darkness remains descriptive of blindness, blockage, stagnation, and moral decay. In Feinberg's words, "Darkness challenges every aspect of our existence,"[144] no matter the culture. So light communicates to any

---

142. Putman, *In Defense of Doctrine*, 306.
143. Feinberg, *Light in a Dark Place*, 31.
144. Feinberg, *Light in a Dark Place*, 23.

culture that Scripture guides away from corruption toward righteousness and spiritual progress.

A liability for light, however, may pertain to its history in Western philosophy. For Western societies that depict knowledge as light, "vision is a suitable sense to employ in metaphors for the disembodied wisdom of true philosophy."[145] Light may promote the philosophical bifurcation between the mind and body, privileging a disembodied view of knowledge as a merely intellectual or cognitive enterprise rather than one that involves corporeal participation. Seen from this angle, light would encourage seeing Scripture as merely an academic enterprise rather than one that holistically involves one's whole, embodied self.[146]

As the premier proponent of disembodied knowledge, Plato promotes vision as "the most sunlike of all the instruments of sense."[147] Thus "knowing" becomes synonymous with "seeing":

> Western philosophy focuses its epistemological interests by an appeal to two sorts of "seeing"—one which entertains what appears to the senses, primarily the sense of sight; the other which "envisions" a reality lying behind appearances. Until recently, the assumption that knowing is a kind of "seeing" has guided epistemological reflections in the West. And from this understanding our principal meaning of truth has been derived.[148]

In Plato's view, "seeing the light" means to grasp "a reality behind appearances" as the "principal meaning of truth." On the one hand, applying this view to Scripture rightly affirms that Scripture reveals the deeper meaning of reality. On the other hand, this view may relegate one's understanding of truth only to an abstract, intellectual realm divorced from earthly, embodied existence, and it also may reinforce a false sense that truth is

---

145. Korsmeyer, *Making Sense of Taste*, 18. Plato famously uses visual metaphors in the *Republic* to connect wisdom and knowledge, reality and appearance, including "a cave, a fire, the sun, and a divided line. In Plato's epistemology, *seeing clearly* is so powerful a metaphor for knowing that it almost ceases to be metaphorical.... Centuries before the rise of modern philosophy, vision already stood in for knowledge." Boisvert and Heldke, *Philosophers at Table*, 113; cf. Cohen, *I Think*, 285.

146. Plato argues—and later Kant—that "only our senses of sight and hearing—our 'intellectual' senses—afford us profound aesthetic pleasures. The bodily senses of taste, smell, and touch lack a spiritual focus that renders them incapable of providing experiences of the beautiful." Sweeney, "Hunger Is the Best Sauce," 52; cf. Kant, *The Critique of Judgment*; and Guyer, *Kant and the Claims of Taste*, 148–83.

147. Plato, *Republic*, 508b; cf. Korsmeyer, *Making Sense of Taste*, 16.

148. Hall, "The Way and the Truth," 214.

not accessible to all but only to the initiated and highly educated elite. So while light does very well at expressing contrast with darkness—and thus the contrast of truth with falsehood—one must not allow such a contrast to separate head and heart in engaging Scripture, nor allow it to make the less educated feel that only the smart, educated people can understand the truth of Scripture.

Light also falls short in accounting for diversity and the morally gray areas of life. Ethically speaking, not everything in the culture is black and white, dark and light. Many gray areas require diverse perspectives and careful nuance to parse through such issues wisely. The stark contrast of light and darkness may not inherently capture the need for such diversity and nuance, which in the current "cancel culture" may mislead some proponents of the "light" of Scripture to denounce others immediately as "darkness" without carefully listening to their arguments. Light also may not capture well the process by which understanding happens, as usually understanding comes through discourse over a long period of time rather than an immediate "light turning on." In this way, light may lead toward a wrong view of Scripture as harsh, black-and-white, exclusionary, and abstract as opposed to properly nuanced, universally accessible, and eminently practical. As light tends to divide the world into brightness and darkness, the model of light may encourage people to divide one another tribally into just "the good guys" and "the bad guys." In contrast to the score and script, then, light may not capture as well the communal aspect of Scripture as a document that brings together a diverse, corporate body, sometimes uniting even former enemies.

Light is also not entirely universal, as the blind cannot see light yet find other ways to navigate life. As important as light is, it may not communicate strongly enough that Scripture is a universal matter of life and death. So while light does convey gravity and seriousness, it may not capture sufficiently the mortal danger people face if they lack or ignore the teaching of Scripture.

Evaluating Fruitfulness

A good model proves fruitful conceptually and practically. Regarding Scripture, conceptual fruitfulness regards a model's ability to elaborate the nature of Scripture in such a way as to inform other doctrines in systematic theology. Practical fruitfulness concerns how a model informs church practices based on the nature of Scripture depicted by the model.

Conceptual Fruitfulness

Since limited space prevents elaboration on all categories of systematic theology, three categories will suffice: (1) theological anthropology, (2) soteriology, and (3) ecclesiology. In terms of theological anthropology, the script and score models help preserve the specialness of humanity made in God's image since only humans create music and theater, including their complex language systems. Music and theater, then, constitute uniquely human practices and cultural projects, which can illustrate how Scripture results from dual authorship, the collaboration of God and humanity to produce Scripture as a complex, beautiful, and unique form of special revelation. At the same time, one must resist the temptation to misconstrue such dual authorship and thus blur the Creator-creature distinction (God is a much different kind of director than a human conductor or playwright); but these models beautifully emphasize mutual interaction and participation, whereas light seems more associated with objectivity and the natural world, independent of humanity.

Given its independence from human artifice, light depicts mystery well, as physicists still struggle to define what it is. Light may capture the complexity and mystery of Scripture, especially its difficulties in interpretation that require careful study and meditation. Whereas a script or score tends to imply a possible mastery of their contents, light implies being mastered or enabled by another to "live and move and have our being" (Acts 17:28). In other words, light depicts humanity as entirely dependent on God's enablement to survive and thrive.

Such divine enablement, taken seriously, guards against misconceiving human persons as autonomous or self-sufficient. In Norman Wirzba's words, "When we consider humans as touching and tasting beings, we discover that we have never been alone, and could not ever be singular."[149] Humans cannot be separate from or independent of God and should not be conceived of as such; rather, "dependence and the insufficiency of man's mortal life are facts which belong to God's plan of creation and must be accepted with reverence and humility."[150] In other words, food should lead

---

149. Wirzba, *Food and Faith*, xvi.

150. Niebuhr, *The Nature and Destiny of Man*, 167; cf. Farris, *Introduction to Theological Anthropology*, 11.

to a theological anthropology rooted in reverence and humility before God, one in which human persons "finds [their] true identity only in relation to God."[151] Such a relation proclaims God as "beneficent Provider" and humanity as humble beneficiary.

Soteriologically, the score and script models posit the dance and drama of redemptive history, thus depicting Scripture as God's gripping story of a rescue mission. Building the dramatic action through the four theatrical acts of creation, the fall into sin, redemption at the cross, and consummation with a new heaven and earth, a score and script together portray history as a cinematic masterpiece of narrative theo-drama wherein God acts as the main character to deliver his otherwise doomed people. The progression from darkness to light also includes the model of light and denotes the hope that God brings in saving humanity from the darkness of sin and "the world forces of this darkness" (Eph 6:12). Light thus depicts the empowerment and hope that overcome sin and the forces of darkness, leading to heaven as the place of perpetual light in God's presence (Rev 21:23).

Light also does well to depict why people need salvation: the darkness of sin. Whereas a score and script do not make clear the real danger that threatens people, the contrast of light with darkness illustrates the terrible moral and spiritual darkness in which one dwells if one does not have the light of God's Word. Light shows how Scripture, in Feinberg's words, is "something all can stake their very life on!"[152] Such dire consequences do not immediately apply to theater and music, though theater may depict characters facing difficult problems within the plot. On the other hand, the score model taken by itself falls the shortest in terms of soteriological fruitfulness because few people—perhaps musicians excepted—would stake their lives on music or connect music with the salvation of their lives.

Regarding ecclesiology, the score and script emphasize the need for faithful interpretation of Scripture, which implies the helpfulness of church tradition to understand Scripture correctly. Though always secondary to Scripture, church tradition aids Christians as a supplementary resource in seeing how past Christians have interpreted and enacted the authoritative teaching of Scripture, just as previous groups of musicians or acting troupes provide insightful precedents for future interpretations of a score or script. So these models affirm the human agency and ecclesial involvement pertaining to Scripture and theology. Music in particular stresses community

---

151. Green, *Body, Soul, and Human Life*, 73.
152. Feinberg, *Light in a Dark Place*, 25.

in its ability to bind people together, as with national anthems, and music even invites new people to join in through the enjoyment of pop songs. So the score model connects well both with binding together and energizing the church community and inviting others evangelistically to hear God's voice in Scripture. Music thus includes a strong component of universal accessibility and inclusion that should ring true of Scripture, but a musical *score*, on the other hand, may imply a steeper learning curve rather than ready accessibility.

Vanhoozer's script model in particular carries profound implications for the nature of the church. Given its script, the church becomes the acting company of the gospel charged with exhibiting and performing the words of the script in the power of the Spirit.[153] The church is "holy and vital theater" performed with "passion" for God, "rehearsing the kingdom" in a way no other institution can. In this sense, the church is the "body" of the text.[154] Vanhoozer thus calls the church's vocation a "*command* performance" and a "*parable of the kingdom*, a moving picture of 'the extraordinary in the ordinary,' an instantiation of an economy of love that surpasses the mundane economies of give and take," and pastors are "local directors," helping their local churches learn and perform God's Word.[155] Moreover, evangelism takes the form of "interactive theater" that invites an audience into the action.[156]

Vanhoozer's script model, however, proves problematic in its vision of the church in an "empty space."[157] In theater, an "empty space" refers to the empty stage on which "*that which is mediated is left free to be and act*,"[158] and Vanhoozer suggests that Christ's empty tomb serves as spiritual "empty space" to inform how the church acts as Christ's body. The church fills this "empty space" created by Christ's resurrection "*with redemptive speech and redemptive action.*"[159] Though an interesting idea, such "empty space" could give the wrong impression of the conflict that the church still

---

153. See Vanhoozer, *Drama of Doctrine*, 401.

154. Vanhoozer, *Drama of Doctrine*, 441–43, 418.

155. Vanhoozer, *Drama of Doctrine*, 443, 456, emphasis his.

156. Vanhoozer, *Drama of Doctrine*, 416–17.

157. Vanhoozer, *Drama of Doctrine*, 401–3. The idea of theater as "empty space" first comes from Peter Brook, *The Empty Space*.

158. Vanhoozer, *Drama of Doctrine*, 402, emphasis his.

159. Vanhoozer, *Drama of Doctrine*, 403, emphasis his. For more on church and "empty space," see Craigo-Snell, *The Empty Church*.

faces today. As Feinberg points out, the church does not exist in a merely "empty space" rife with creative possibility; rather, the church lives within a grave conflict wherein spiritual darkness "challenges every aspect of our existence."[160] The church thus exists as "light in a dark place," not "actors in an empty space." Vanhoozer does hint at this conflict with darkness in calling the church's actions "redemptive," but he leaves unclear how "empty space" captures the real danger in which the church acts within a dangerous, sinful system threatened with darkness unless the light of Scripture pierces through it. The empty space metaphor thus ignores the atmosphere of danger, negativity, sin, and mortality that are all too real and threaten this present world; the church does not merely fill "empty space" but meets a troubled, dying, conflicted, and starving place with the needed remedy of God's saving Word.

"Light in a dark place" better captures this grave context. Jesus describes his church as the light of the world and city on a hill, shining as a light to the nations (Matt 5:14–16). The church thus embodies and reflects God's light to the rest of the world, displaying God's gospel and drawing others into his kingdom. At the same time, light exposes darkness rather than hides it; light depicts the church as an entity that exposes sin and turns itself and others to face the light of God's righteousness. Moreover, the light model depicts how the church serves as light to the world: Scripture illumines the church, who then reflects that light to others (cf. Matt 5:14).

Practical Fruitfulness

Practical fruitfulness can prove tricky because Scripture can be used for "fruitful" practices other than those taught in Scripture, such as demanding from God health, wealth, and prosperity.[161] Yet Scripture prescribes the fruitful practices of faith, hope, and love (1 Cor 13:13). Truly fruitful models should foster these three practices.

Faith

Faith, which corresponds to the verb "believe," means "trust in God through Christ" that "involves right belief about God . . . rests on divine testimony

---

160. Feinberg, *Light in a Dark Place*, 23.

161. For examples of prosperity preaching from the letters of Paul, see Braxton, "Preaching, Politics, and Paul," 563, 569–73.

... [and] is a supernatural divine gift."[162] The script and score models do well in depicting faith as action, especially interactive and improvised action. For example, Scripture, as a musical score, gives "attention to the role played by *expectation, construction, projection, and surprise in processes of engagement between readers and texts,*" which carries profound implications for pastoral theology and how the church community lives out its faith. First, as aforesaid, Scripture requires concrete action: "the musical score *must be played,* whether by a soloist, or by a chorus, or orchestra as a temporal process which is of an *eventful nature.*"[163] Second, Scripture calls for creative improvisation that yet remains faithful to the score, which guards against *"wooden, mechanical, or repetitive routine. Readers are invited to perform active and creative roles in reading-processes."*[164] Third, such improvised performances of the text call into question the current presuppositions and interpretations held by the community. So seeing Scripture as a musical score (or theatrical script, for that matter) allows room to challenge those conventional interpretations rooted merely in routine and tradition.[165] So these performative models like score and script provide space for needed critique of communal norms that may not actually stem from the Bible. Fourth, music and theater should aim at moving an audience in a noncoercive way, which carries implications for preaching. Preaching involves "striking up the music" or "inviting into the action," moving people to "catch the vision" of Scripture without forcing a certain way of thinking upon them.[166] Preaching seeks to attract rather than pressure people to respond faithfully to God.

The notion of improvisation, however, also comes with significant problems. For many, improvisation means something *"unscripted . . .* to do something extempore, without preparation, or 'off the cuff,' which seems a far cry from the faithful obedience Scripture requires."[167] So improvisation

---

162. Packer, "Faith," 208–10.
163. Thiselton, *New Horizons in Hermeneutics,* 587, emphasis his.
164. Thiselton, *New Horizons in Hermeneutics,* 587, emphasis his.
165. Thiselton, *New Horizons in Hermeneutics,* 587.
166. Thiselton, *New Horizons in Hermeneutics,* 212.
167. Vanhoozer, *Drama of Doctrine,* 336. Vanhoozer recognizes this view of improvisation and makes an effort to address it as a "misleading picture." Vanhoozer, 336. Yet improvisation remains most often "off the cuff" and unscripted. Seen in this way, improvisation jeopardizes obedience to the authority of Scripture.

can mislead one to think that one's spiritual life does not need a script like Scripture at all but only spontaneous and subjective "ad-libbing."[168]

Improvisation also lacks objectivity and universality. Forms of art, including theater and music, stress subjectivity. So while almost boundless in its possibilities, art often lacks a connection to objective truth, which becomes a liability when subjective artistic practices, like improvisation regarding a score and script, become associated with the objective truth of Scripture. For this very reason, Porter criticizes Vanhoozer's theatrical model, alleging that it would be "difficult to know how it is that [Vanhoozer] would adjudicate a dispute over a crucial or contentious issue using his method."[169] Porter finds troubling that the model lacks sufficient objective boundaries or reference points to judge the truth or falsity of certain improvisations, or whether certain improvisations are right or wrong. In fact, Vanhoozer remains unclear as to how exactly one should "improvise" on the text, raising the question of how exactly the script applies to practicing Scripture; Scripture itself does not take the form of a script, and many of its passages do not instruct in what to do but rather provide examples of what not to do. So while improvisation sounds creative and exciting, it seems quite different from biblical obedience.

Furthermore, improvisation is not universal for at least two reasons. First, the kind of skilled improvisation described by Thiselton and Vanhoozer can be performed only by seasoned experts. Such improvisation tends to privilege highly educated scholars while excluding most people from participating, which may make Scripture appear inaccessible to the masses. Of course, engaging Scripture does require some level of education and training, and Scripture does require a good amount of "improvising" to

168. To his credit, Vanhoozer addresses both ad-libbing and preplanning at length, identifying them as pitfalls one should avoid in improvisation. Ad-libbing means breaking away from others to go one's own way and "is the theatrical equivalent of heresy" since true improvisers "work together; they are 'one body' who all contribute to the outcome of the play." Vanhoozer, *Drama of Doctrine*, 338. Preplanning, on the other hand, is tantamount to eisegesis, wherein would-be improvisers "seek to wrest control of the game by 'scriptwriting' the play, manipulating the situation and their fellow actors according to a preplanned mental map. The history of Christian mission, and theology, has its fair share of scriptwriters who have sought to control the action in new situations. Other actors follow conventional scripts without even being aware of it." Vanhoozer, 337. In other words, preplanning violates the integrity of the script by trying to impose an external script derived from one's own preferences or sociocultural proclivities. While Vanhoozer provides here a creative rendering of both problems, the problems arise in the first place because of Vanhoozer's commitment to the problematic notion of improvisation.

169. Porter, "Hermeneutics, Biblical Interpretation, and Theology," 118.

apply its teachings in the modern day, so long as such improvisation stays within justifiable limits of the text. Second, improvisation works in only some musical genres, like jazz, whereas genres like classical for an orchestra would fall apart if improvisation were to be allowed. Orchestras must stay as close to the written score as possible, and one could argue that that is exactly how God wants his orchestra to play (cf. Lev 10). While improvisation promotes personal expression and imagination, such practices may contradict God's stated intention that his people not turn "to the right or to the left" but instead "be careful to do just as the LORD your God has commanded you" (Deut 5:32). Improvisation, then, may promote faith and dependence not on Scripture but on oneself and one's own creative abilities or those of other human beings.

The script and score thus may lead inadvertently to merit-based rather than grace-based systems of behavior. As systems that put front-and-center the creative abilities of trained professionals, theater and music are inherently merit-based and stress the excellence of one's performance. Excellence in performance is not in itself bad or evil, but it may tend toward action before reception or output before enablement, leading to ministry burnout or overdependence upon human ministers instead of the thankfulness and peace that accompany dependence on God's unmerited grace shown through Scripture. The model of light, however, escapes the implication of merit since one cannot "earn" light but only receive its enablement.

Light thus ties one's dependence directly to Scripture. As light, Scripture enables people to see in the first place, which illustrates that salvation, according to Scripture, requires faith and dependence on the Word of God to supply that saving light. Without light, one dwells in blindness and darkness; without God's Word, one dwells hopelessly in sin. Light thus emphasizes the necessity of faith in God's provision and enablement to dispel one's darkness and "walk in the light" (1 John 1:7) supplied by God's Word. The priority of light thus ensures that if one walks with God at all, God gets the glory for providing that light by which to walk. In this way, light also envisions faith not as a punctiliar event but as a lifelong need for enablement; for if that light were to cease or fail in some way, one would fall back into blindness and darkness. Thus light both emphasizes the sufficiency of Scripture and fosters humility, humility that comes from realizing the unceasing need to depend on Scripture to provide the light to see and walk in an otherwise dark world. So the light model helps people see why they must return to Scripture continually. Presumably one can learn the lines or notes of the script and score and not need to return to the document, but light requires that one always return to the written Word to provide the light to see. Of course, the script and score models also encourage habitual return to the written word and even memorization of its contents, but the sense of continual dependence seems to disappear once the actors or musicians become familiar with the performance. At that point, the script or score may no longer be necessary.

The script and score do better than light, however, in conveying the embodiment of faith. Biblical faith must not remain merely intellectual or cognitive but embodied and lived. The models of script and score helpfully promote "attention to embodied knowledge" and committed action, which always accompany true faith since "faith without works is dead" (Jas 2:26; cf. 1:22–26; 2:17–25).[170] Based on his script model, Vanhoozer promotes two theatrical techniques to foster a faithful, embodied response to Scripture: reincorporation and overaccepting. Reincorporation involves recapitulating events of Scripture such that the church becomes richly aware of and responsive to "everything that has been going on up until the present moment."[171] This recapitulation precludes simply memorizing verses by rote or repeating the same lines; rather, the church approaches the script of Scripture knowing that in it, God offers his divine action in history that structures the church's response and subsequent action.[172] Such divine action then calls each person to overaccept God's offer, incorporating God's offers into one's current life story and ultimately into "the overall coherence of the developing theo-drama."[173] The church thus engages in "fitting participation" as it becomes the "body" of the text by doing (not just mentally accepting) the truth of Scripture.[174] A musical score also heads in this direction of embodied action in that music tends to compel movement in dance. The problem with light

---

170. Craigo-Snell, *The Empty Church*, 145.

171. Vanhoozer, *Drama of Doctrine*, 340.

172. See Vanhoozer, *Drama of Doctrine*, 338–39.

173. Vanhoozer, *Drama of Doctrine*, 340. In Vanhoozer's view, the entire theo-drama of the gospel involves God's overacceptance of humanity, not just humanity's overacceptance of God's Word. God is thus the ultimate improviser and central actor who initiates and reincorporates all of history as the theater of his gospel. God offers himself as humanity's covenantal partner, overaccepts all of humanity's attempts at blocking his covenant, and even incorporates humanity's rebellion into his story, ultimately improvising by becoming incarnate to reincorporate all of history into his redemptive play. See Vanhoozer, *Drama of Doctrine*, 340–41.

174. Vanhoozer, *Drama of Doctrine*, 411, 418–21.

in terms of embodiment has to do with its history in Western philosophy, wherein light becomes associated more with the cognitive, abstract, and detached rather than the embodied, physical, and sensory.[175] As a metaphor for knowledge, then, light tends to remain merely intellectual.

A strength of the score model remains its emphasis on hearing, which Scripture describes as the source of faith: "Faith comes from hearing, and hearing by the word of Christ" (Rom 10:17). Jesus calls hearing his word the "one thing [that] is necessary" (Luke 10:42). Music describes how Scripture "gets into" the head of people who repeatedly listen to it such that it "sets the tone" or "conveys an atmosphere" for the entire community.[176] So music communicates how Scripture "gets into" the minds of listeners and "sets the mood" or "provides the atmosphere" for church gatherings. Scripture should saturate the church community, providing an atmosphere of comfort and healing much like David's music did for Saul (cf. 1 Sam 16:23).

Hope

Hope means an "expectation of good" based on trust in God that actively anticipates his blessing; it "relates to salvation and is an essential grace like faith and love . . . but where faith refers to past and present, hope includes the future . . . [and] its object is the ultimate blessedness of God's kingdom."[177] According to McFague, theater does well to provide a "shock of recognition": "'Yes,' we say, 'life is like that'—not life as conventionally lived or usually understood, but at its deepest level, or as it could be, ought to be, might have been. The basic structure of experience is illuminated."[178] Theater can envision a better world, a world that should be, and the model of a theatrical script can depict the hope-giving power of Scripture as it illuminates human experience with divine truth and moves people with God's vision of a better world. A musical score, performed well, moves people with the beauty of God's creation.

The requirement of excellence in these "performance models," however, may hamper their ability to provide hope. Scripts and scores tend to

---

175. See Boisvert and Heldke, *Philosophers at Table*, 113; cf. Cohen, *I Think, Therefore I Eat*, 285.

176. The phrase "conveys an atmosphere" comes from Boersma, *Violence, Hospitality, and the Cross*, 102.

177. Tongue, "Hope," 271.

178. McFague, *Metaphorical Theology*, 141–42.

emphasize directions, instructions, or lines to speak, but much of Scripture does not consist of such directions; rather, much of Scripture consists of a narrative often containing characters that should *not* be imitated. So the actual composition of Scripture seems to militate against using it as a script. While Scripture does contain a divine drama that covers all human history, it very rarely offers literal lines to speak, as an actor might expect. Instead, readers must parse through normative versus phenomenal passages,[179] carefully discerning what parts should or should not be performed. The script model thus may mischaracterize the many descriptive rather than prescriptive parts of the Bible; and though Vanhoozer admirably tries to link reading Scripture with obeying it, the push for performance implicit in the script model might not prove all that helpful since much of Scripture *should not* be performed. Rather, Scripture mainly has to do with what God performs for us. In Vanhoozer's defense, he calls his model "theo-dramatic" to emphasize that God plays the main acting role, but a script nonetheless encourages readers of Scripture perhaps to overemphasize their role in the performance.

The implicit dichotomy between imagination and reality in the script model hampers its ability to provide real hope. While McFague rightly points out that theater can depict life "as it could be, ought to be, [or] might have been,"[180] these categories fall short of being life as it actually is. In other words, theater can reflect the realities of life but remains distinct from them since theater remains only an imaginary representation. However, Scripture offers real hope, not imaginary hope. People may feel better if they imagine a better world, but Scripture presents the actual reality of a better world based on the real actions of a real God who has done "far more abundantly beyond all that we ask or think" (Eph 3:20). For hope to be real hope, it cannot remain imaginary, and the theatrical context of imagination thus restricts the script from providing hope that not only feels real but is real. It bears repeating that there should be no difference between the biblical world and the real one; otherwise, the hope of the biblical world may not be real and thus fail to be hope at all.

Light, on the other hand, stays firmly connected to reality and does not entail dependence on human performance. Rather, light communicates real-world hope despite human inability since light enables the ability to

---

179. Feinberg points out this distinction between normative and phenomenal passages of Scripture in his discussion on theological method. Feinberg, *Light in a Dark Place*, 112–16.

180. McFague, *Metaphorical Theology*, 141.

see—and thus to act—in the first place. As light, then, Scripture puts first things first: reception before action, and enablement before performance. In other words, light avoids any immediate demand for human performance and stresses the more basic posture of reception and enablement, thus placing the reliance in the right place: Scripture does not rely on the church's agency, but the church relies on the agency of Scripture. The church thus grounds its hope not in human performance at all but firmly and wholly in God's performance through Scripture. Put another way, Scripture provides the church's hope for survival; the church does not provide the hope for the survival of Scripture. Therefore, the church must deeply internalize the hope within Scripture before rushing to performance.

The internalization of this hope occurs in everyday, habitual practices more than in spectacular, sensational events. In the current culture addicted to entertainment, scripts and scores tend to emphasize spectacle and feature exciting and extraordinary events rather than the ordinary parts of life. According to Vanhoozer, in some forms of theater the "most important qualification . . . is the ability to fascinate the guests."[181] Applied to Scripture, this tendency in theater may tend toward seeking only dramatic, spectacular, and extraordinary experiences through Scripture while downplaying the effectiveness of Scripture during the mundane, dull, and painful realities of earthly life. So a more "basic" model, like light, better communicates seeking God's hope in Scripture through the daily grind. Rather than staging one spectacular event after another, churches should encourage people to find hope through Scripture in the everyday mundanity of life, seeking God's sustenance even in quiet and humdrum moments.

Scripture not only provides hope for every moment but also for every person. A model for Scripture, then, should foster social inclusiveness and universal invitation rather than elitism or parochialism. Here again, light proves more helpful than a script or score. Plays and concerts usually operate within the context of friends, or at least those initiated or "cultured" enough to appreciate the art form. A script or score, therefore, may encourage people to limit the relevance of Scripture to only the church community or Christian culture. Light, however, holds immediate relevance for almost everyone, thus encouraging sharing Scripture to everyone so that all may see by the hope it provides. Even so, light has a limitation in that light also falls short of being entirely universal; the blind who cannot see light may feel excluded by the model.

181. Vanhoozer, *Drama of Doctrine*, 417.

Love

Scripture defines love

> in the only way that it can or ought to be defined; namely, by listing its attributes: "Love is patient and kind; love is not jealous or boastful; it is not arrogant or rude. Love does not insist on its own way; it is not irritable or resentful; it does not rejoice at wrong, but rejoices in the right. Love bears all things, believes all things, hopes, all things, endures all things" (1 Cor 13:4–7). Love is fellowship between persons; it is an act of self-surrender. . . . Love may or may not be accompanied by personal affection. We can be kind and thoughtful to a person, even though we may dislike him. Love is the key to happiness as well as virtue, for without love there is no life.[182]

So love seeks the blessing of and communion with the beloved, and each of these models promotes God's love in Scripture. Thiselton's score model taps into the ability of music to create new loves and alliances. For example, Thiselton points out that youths might be drawn together through an interest in rock music, or that two youths with different musical tastes might fall in love and thus have their tastes mutually expanded and transformed by each other's, leading to a situation where interests "*which have hitherto gathered round the self as a system of self-centred relevance begin to be re-grouped and re-ranked round the self of another, or even the Other*"; in other words, love of another can cause musical tastes to change and even dislodge one's selfishness in favor of another. In the same way, God's love conveyed through Scripture expands and transforms people and reorients them around God's purposes, and the "biblical narrative texts [play] a decisive part in allowing and enabling readers *to identify* God's personhood and purposes through Christ."[183] As God's musical score, Scripture moves hearers in a noncoercive way, inviting them to receive and share God's love.

Similarly, Vanhoozer seeks to employ his theatrical model to draw outsiders into God's love. Vanhoozer uses the concept of "interactive theater," which he admits has "typically no script" but aims at drawing "the 'guests' into the play."[184] In interactive theater, actors include and interact with the audience "in such a way that [the audience] will want to join in."[185]

---

182. Carnell, "Love," 332–33.
183. Thiselton, *New Horizons in Hermeneutics*, 609, emphasis his.
184. Vanhoozer, *Drama of Doctrine*, 416.
185. Vanhoozer, *Drama of Doctrine*, 417.

This type of theater thus makes up a ready illustration for evangelism, the interactive outreach of God's love to include others through the gospel. While this application of theater certainly stretches the script model, Vanhoozer highlights the tendency in theater to transport an audience into the action, which he likens to being drawn into the community of God's love.[186]

Light may seem distant from love, but it captures the ethical component of love, moving a person out of moral darkness into the light of God's righteousness.[187] Light "breaks through" darkness, which underscores God's victory over spiritual and moral forces of darkness. Practically speaking, then, the model of light encourages people to share in God's love by receiving the light of his truth in Scripture, using Scripture to expose corruption, sharing Scripture to help others see God's righteousness and wisdom in all of life, and drawing together a loving community around Scripture to be God's light to the world (cf. Matt 5:14–16). This loving community should include people of all types, cultures, and ages, especially children, teaching them to grow in hearing Scripture and applying its light to every facet of life as a means of experiencing God's love for oneself and others. Given the association of light with abstract truth in Western philosophy, however, one must ensure that love does not remain merely the sharing of cognitive and intellectual information but also include tangible, embodied action.

Furthermore, light touches upon the necessity of prayer to appropriate God's light since understanding Scripture requires *illumination* by the Holy Spirit. Though illumination stretches into pneumatology, it certainly concerns the nature of Scripture by underscoring the continual need for prayer to abide in the Spirit's love and rely on his help to understand Scripture.

In summary, the models of score, script, and light fruitfully inform the church's practices of faith, hope, and love. While the score and script models do better at encouraging embodiment of these practices, light more firmly captures the universal hope grounded in the sufficiency of Scripture to sustain all who receive its light. The larger scope of light also encourages living in continual and humble dependence on God's enablement, not

---

186. For more on the church as an embodied, collaborative community of God's love, see Johnson and Savidge, *Performing the Sacred*, 129–36.

187. Theater also can capture this ethical component since its plot often portrays good overcoming evil, though this outcome does not always happen. Music, however, seems weakest regarding ethics since an ethical component is not inherent in the notes of a score. One could say that ethics in music has to do with that music's use, such as in music therapy (a good use) or political manipulation (an evil use). Still, a score by itself seems ethically ambiguous.

seeking the next spiritual high or spectacular experience but abiding in Scripture through the mundanity of day-to-day life.

While these models prove faithful to Scripture and tradition, fitting to the subject and current culture, and fruitful conceptually and practically, the above discussion also shows that each comes with significant weaknesses that may hamper the church's understanding of and response to Scripture. In terms of faithfulness, the script and score rely overmuch on extrabiblical sources like Gadamer's or Austin's books, and the score falls especially short in finding precedents in the theological tradition. As for fittingness, the script and score inadequately render the necessity, sufficiency, inspiration, and inerrancy of Scripture, while light remains insufficient to capture the authority of Scripture. Light also carries philosophical liabilities within the current culture that may limit light to the realm of intellectual, abstract cognition instead of embodied, concrete action. Cultural liabilities also haunt the script and score, as both can bolster unhelpful dichotomies between the educated and uneducated, between rehearsal and performance, and between reality and make believe, which restrict the accessibility of these models. In addition, all three models fall short of being entirely universal, as even light may exclude the blind, fall short in reckoning with the morally gray areas of life, and fail to capture the long process involved in understanding rather than the immediacy of a "lightbulb turning on." Regarding fruitfulness, the script and score tend to overstress human performance since they require humans to "complete" the script or score by performing it. As models based in entertainment, they also fail to account adequately for the very serious and real dangers involved in following Scripture, which occur not in an "empty space" but in a fallen world.

Of course, no one model captures all that can be said but should allow room for insights from other models.[188] No single model of Scripture will suffice to encompass the Bible's complexity and significance, but the above inadequacies in the present models raise the question of whether another model might avoid these deficiencies and convey a more comprehensive understanding of the nature of Scripture. That model, I argue, is Scripture as food.

---

188. See McFague, *Metaphorical Theology*, 137.

3

The Main Course

Scripture Is Food

To develop the model "Scripture is food," I first query the biblical data to trace the consistent connection between Scripture and food, supporting these data with voices from historical theology both to show the consistency of the food model with church tradition and to glean insights into how food informs the nature of Scripture. I then evaluate the food model over against the three models of score, script, and light to demonstrate how the food model proves exceptionally and comprehensively faithful, fitting, and fruitful by not only maintaining the strengths of the previous models but also making up for their weaknesses.

The Food Model in Scripture

Scripture offers several models for itself in its pages, and food figures as one of the most prominent.[1] Jesus says in Matt 4:4: "Man shall not live on bread

---

1. Besides food, other models include a lamp (Ps 119:105), fire (Jer 23:29a), hammer (Jer 23:29b), sword (Heb 4:12–13), mirror (Jas 1:23), and seed (1 Pet 1:23). See Standridge, "Seven Metaphors for God's Word," https://thecripplegate.com/seven-metaphors-for-gods-word. McFague insists that many metaphors and models prove necessary "to avoid idolatry and to attempt to express the richness and variety of the divine-human relationship." McFague, *Metaphorical Theology*, 20; cf. Brümmer, *Model of Love*, 19–20.

alone, but on every word that proceeds out of the mouth of God."[2] Here, Jesus quotes Deut 8:3, echoing the consistent witness of the OT and NT that "eating" God's Word is not trivial but a matter of life and death. By coupling Jesus's statement in Matt 4:4 with 2 Tim 3:16 ("All Scripture is God-breathed and profitable . . ."), Scripture becomes a part of that "word that proceeds out of the mouth of God," which makes the "eating" of Scripture essential for human life. The intake of Scripture thus becomes inextricably linked to "the first and most urgent activity of all animal and human life: We are only because we eat."[3] Just as human beings survive by eating, they also survive by receiving God's words in Scripture.[4]

This model first arises in the OT, wherein God explicitly connects his saving word to food. In Exod 13:9, God designates the Passover's unleavened bread as a reminder "that the law of the LORD may be in your mouth; for with a powerful hand the LORD brought you out of Egypt." God thus uses this food to symbolize his "law," or word, which his people should have in their mouths constantly. God does the same with manna, a food that symbolizes God's provision for his people's hunger and makes them "understand that man does not live by bread alone, but man lives by everything that proceeds out of the mouth of the LORD" (Deut 8:3), emphasizing again that "the food God provides is his word; the food embodies his wisdom."[5]

The model also figures prominently in the prophets and psalms. When God's people face impending judgment, God gives Jeremiah his words to eat: "Your words were found and I ate them, and Your words became for me a joy and the delight of my heart" (Jer 15:16).[6] While God's people languish

---

2. I assume that the *Bible*, *Scripture*, and the written *Word of God* are all identical and interchangeable terms in my evangelical theological perspective. Proving that these terms are identical falls outside the purview of this book, and many fine systematic theologies deal directly with this issue. Cf. Grudem, *Systematic Theology*, 31–168; and Erickson, *Christian Theology*, 143–232.

3. Kass, *The Hungry Soul*, 2. Bartholomew and O'Dowd call eating "perhaps the most powerful act we do as physical creatures." Bartholomew and O'Dowd, *Old Testament Wisdom Literature*, 114.

4. Lakoff and Johnson point out that modern culture often uses metaphors that have a book as the tenor and food as the vehicle. For example, "That's *food for thought*. He's a *voracious* reader . . . He *devoured* the book . . . This is the *meaty* part of the paper." Lakoff and Johnson, *Metaphors We Live By*, 47.

5. Feeley-Harnik, *The Lord's Table*, 82; cf. Exod 16:32–35.

6. Craigie, Kelley, and Drinkard Jr. comment that this metaphor describes how Jeremiah "had joyfully made the Lord's words a part of his life (cf. 1:9)." Craigie, Kelley, and Drinkard Jr., *Jeremiah 1–25*, 210.

in exile, God commands Ezekiel to open his mouth and eat the scroll of God's Word (Ezek 2:8—3:3).[7] Both prophets ingest God's Word as sweet food during bitter days of struggle, food that they would assimilate and then serve to God's people to sustain their very lives.[8] The Psalms again refer to God's Word as sweet food: "How sweet are Your words to my taste! Yes, sweeter than honey to my mouth!" (Ps 119:103; cf. 19:10). This satisfying, life-sustaining ingestion of God's Word leads to life, as Isaiah proclaims:

> Everyone who thirsts come to the waters and you who have no money come, buy and eat.
> Come, buy wine and milk without money and without cost.
> Why do you spend money for that which is not bread,
> Your wages for what does not satisfy?
> Listen carefully to Me, and eat what is good, and delight yourself in abundance.
> Incline your ear to Me. Listen that you may live;
> And I will make an everlasting covenant with you,
> According to the faithful mercies shown to David. (Isa 55:1–3)

So "eating" God's word leads not only to survival but to satisfaction, abundance, and delight (cf. Ps 34:8).[9] Drawing on the metaphor of food, this passage makes clear that "the essential ingredients for a person's life... are listening to God and coming to him.... It is speaking about the fullest reality of human life. If we do not listen to God, we cannot be fully human."[10] This full humanity, according to verse 3, requires partaking of God's feast and thus entering into covenant with him.[11] One eats by "listening carefully

---

7. Allen connects eating God's word to submission to God's will: "He has opened his life to the divine will and undertaken to submit his own will to his Lord's.... He has committed himself to the prophetic ministry that will invoke hostility and rejection, but the privilege far outweighs such hardness." Allen, *Ezekiel 1–19*, 41.

8. Seitz sees Ezekiel's swallowing of the scroll as "a metaphor perhaps for more direct involvement in the compositional achievement of prophetic witness." Seitz, *Colossians*, 46. Allen draws from this verse that God's Word must "be swallowed down and digested." Allen, *Ezekiel 1–19*, 41.

9. According to Motyer, the language of Isa 55:3 suggests that the "Lord is himself the feast." Motyer, *The Prophecy of Isaiah*, 453. For more on the rich meaning of food in Isaiah, see Abernethy, *Eating in Isaiah*.

10. Oswalt, *The Book of Isaiah: Chapters 44–66*, 437.

11. Eating God's Word establishes "a binding agreement, a covenant, among the eaters to abide by his word." Feeley-Harnik, *The Lord's Table*, 82.

(the verb is emphasized by the infinitive absolute immediately following) to the words that God speaks to the prophet."[12]

Conversely, not eating leads to death. God bitterly judges his people not with "a famine for bread or a thirst for water, but rather for hearing the words of the LORD. People will stagger from sea to sea and from the north even to the east. They will go to and fro to seek the word of the LORD. But they will not find it" (Amos 8:11b–12; Isa 5:13).[13] So God's Word carries life-or-death consequences. Without it, people die. With it, they live.[14] As Gillian Feeley-Harnik says, "God's word, as represented in scripture, was not a dead formula. The word was realized in creative, life-giving, death-dealing speech, which transformed wisdom into practice, as food is transformed into flesh."[15] As both life-giving and death-dealing, the food of Scripture seamlessly illustrates God's kindness and severity; kindness and blessing to those who eat his word, but severity and judgment to those who refuse to receive it and thus starve to death. Those who eat, however, find new energy as divine wisdom metabolizes into daily practice, bringing "healing to [their] body and refreshment to [their] bones" (Prov 3:8).

Proverbs thus speaks of God's "wisdom" as something to eat. In Prov 9:5–6, God's wisdom calls to the foolish, "Come, eat of my food, and drink of the wine I have mixed. Forsake your folly and live, and proceed in the

---

12. Oswalt, *The Book of Isaiah*, 436. According to Abernethy, looming in the background of the imperatives in Isa 55 "is God's case against those who persist in not listening (42:18–25; 48:1–8), God's hope for a people who will listen (48:14; 50:8), and God's servant who is a model listener (50:4). It is likely that 55:2b–3a presents a culminating offer for the reader to respond to Isa 40–55 by finally taking on board what YHWH has been saying all along: turn and listen to me." Abernethy, *Eating in Isaiah*, 137.

13. Stuart describes the gravity of this judgment: "The human need for God's word is well established in the Pentateuch (e.g. Deut 8:3). Absence of that word is one of the agonies of the exile (Deut 4:28; 32:21; Hos 3:4)." Stuart, *Hosea-Jonah*, 386.

14. MacDonald recognizes food as a concern throughout the OT: "It is little wonder then that the perennial concern for food makes an impression on the texts that have survived from ancient Israel. Even for the scribal authors who composed the Old Testament, belonging as they did to the social elite, a regular supply of food probably could not be taken for granted." MacDonald, *Not Bread Alone*, 1. MacDonald points out that food shortages in the OT prove common, reinforcing the OT authors' insistence that the Creator provides food. See MacDonald, 1; and Ps 136:25.

15. Feeley-Harnik, *The Lord's Table*, 107. Feeley-Harnik's study uncovers that food "was identified with God's word as the foundation of the covenant relationship in scripture and in sectarianism. During the inter-Testamental period, as God's word became increasingly identified with the law, food came to represent the whole law." Feeley-Harnik, *The Lord's Table*, 165.

way of understanding." Proverbs 13:14 compares God's wise teaching to "a fountain of life, to turn aside from the snares of death," and Prov 24:13–14 likens his wisdom to honey.[16]

This same connection between food and Scripture carries over into the NT. John eats the book of God's words, which taste sweet but then give him "a severe case of indigestion" (Rev 10:9–10).[17] In 1 Tim 4:6, Paul exhorts Timothy to be "constantly nourished on the words of the faith and of the sound doctrine which you have been following." All these references portray food as a strong model for Scripture.

These references echo the teaching of Jesus himself, who not only compares God's Word to bread in Matt 4:4 but also makes the implicit connection in John 4:34 when he says, "My food is to do the will of him who sent me and to accomplish his work." If one sees doing God's will as synonymous with obeying God's Word, as John does (cf. John 5:30, 36), Jesus's meaning here includes that he derives his vital sustenance from receiving and obeying God's words.[18] Jesus repeatedly claims only to say and do what his father has taught him (John 5:19, 30; 6:38; 8:28; 12:49, 50; 14:10). For him, fulfilling God's Word and completing his work means "to go to his death. It is fitting, therefore, that Jesus takes a drink when his work is complete, at the moment of his death. This action, however, makes it possible for others to eat and drink that which Jesus offers, namely, eternal life."[19] Jesus thus "offers himself as food, giving life to others through his death,"[20] highlighted also by his birth in a feeding trough (Luke 2:7, 12, 16) and his self-identity as bread of life, the food to whom Scripture ultimately points (John 6:33, 35, 41, 48, 50, 51; cf. 5:39–40; Luke 24:27).[21]

---

16. Cf. Feeley-Harnik, *The Lord's Table*, 83; Prov 10:11; 14:27; 16:22.

17. Peterson, *Eat This Book*, 64.

18. Radner observes that in Christ's incarnation, God eats: "The fact that God incarnate placed in his mouth, chewed, tasted, savored, swallowed, delighted in, and was nourished by the very creatures he had, in his wisdom, made from nothing stands, in relation to human understanding, in the same incomprehensible place as does the creation itself. It is also, just there, one of the overwhelming mysteries of our existence." Radner, *A Time to Keep*, 217.

19. Webster, *Ingesting Jesus*, 131.

20. Webster, *Ingesting Jesus*, 149.

21. Jeremias argues that Jesus's use of the metaphor "bread of life" speaks to the covenantal, sacrificial, and hospitable aspects of God's word. The breaking of bread often "binds the table companions into a table fellowship," with firm obligations and covenantal overtones of membership and blessing. Jeremias, *The Eucharistic Words of Jesus*, 232. Through Jesus's references to bread and water, "divine gifts are imparted in

Jesus also treats Scripture as his life-sustaining food throughout his earthly ministry. During his temptation, Scripture sustains him against each of Satan's attacks (cf. Matt 4:4, 7, 10). While carrying his cross, he quotes Hos 10:8, and during his crucifixion, he cites Ps 22:1 and 31:5. In Tim and Kathy Keller's words, "Jesus was so saturated in the Word of God that it spontaneously came to his mind, enabling him to interpret and face every challenge. . . . God's Word was what sustained God's incarnate Word when he lived and when he died."[22] That Jesus treats God's Word as his food and refers to himself as living bread deepens the connection between Jesus and Scripture as God's Word and between God's Word and food as life-giving necessities.[23] No wonder the bread of life discourse ends with Peter's confession: "Lord, to whom shall we go? You have words of eternal life" (John 6:68).

Ingesting Jesus's words, then, leads to life and averts death. Jesus says in John 8:51, "Truly, truly, I say to you, if anyone keeps My word he will never see death," to which the Jews retort with an eating metaphor: "You say, 'If anyone keeps My word, he will never taste of death'" (John 8:52). So the "way to avoid 'tasting death' . . . is to keep Jesus' word (his commandments) out of love for Jesus (14:15–23; 15:10)."[24] Hearing and obeying Jesus's words proves synonymous with eating Jesus as God's incarnate Word since "the one who keeps Jesus' word tastes life, not death."[25] His words

---

eating and drinking." Jeremias, 234. Bread also speaks to the accessibility of God's Word offered freely to all, suggested by the promise in Isa. 55 of free food as well as Jesus's tendency to eat "with tax collectors and sinners" (Matt 9:11; Mark 2:16; Luke 5:30). Cf. Jeremias, 234–35.

22. Keller and Keller, *The Songs of Jesus*, 37.

23. Webster emphasizes that Jesus not only provides and is the food of salvation but that he "also provides the word(s)/light and is the word/light that gives salvation. Similarly, as those who eat Jesus feed others, those who believe because of what they have seen or heard are to testify so that others will believe (1:41, 45; 4:39–42; 12:22; 19:35; 20:2, 18, 24, 30; 21:24–25)." Webster, *Ingesting Jesus*, 151. Thus "eating" Jesus means "to internalize his words or his spirit" by believing and sharing his words, now written as Scripture. See Webster, *Ingesting Jesus*, 151.

24. Webster, *Ingesting Jesus*, 90.

25. Webster, *Ingesting Jesus*, 90. The close connection between receiving a person and receiving that person's words has support in Scripture. The prophet Samuel receives God's person by receiving his words (cf. 1 Sam 3:7, 21). Jesus rebukes the Pharisees for ignoring God's Word, thus having hearts far from God (cf. Matt 15:5–8). He also connects abiding in him with his words abiding in us (cf. John 15:7) and receiving his disciples with receiving their words: "Whoever does not receive you, nor heed your words, as you go out of that house or that city, shake the dust off your feet" (Matt 10:14; cf. Mark 6:11).

comprise the food that provide eternal life to people who "eat" them by believing and obeying them, while people who do not eat will die.

In John 21, Jesus reinstates Peter after his threefold denial and, after eating breakfast with him, charges him three times to feed his sheep (John 21:15–17). Christ thus appoints Peter to "govern the Church by the ministry of the word under Christ, who is their Head."[26] Feeding Jesus's sheep, then, involves nourishing his church with his authoritative "words of eternal life" (John 6:68), now written as Scripture. Such feeding involves sharing his words and obeying them, thus "doing the works that Jesus has done (see 14:12; 13:14). The extreme act of love, according to the Gospel, is to give up one's life willingly for another (15:13), as Jesus does (10:17–18)."[27] Jesus thus calls Peter and all his disciples not only to speak his words but to practice them with a Christlike "willingness to love and to serve to the point of death."[28] To feed others God's Word requires costly personal sacrifice, as it does for Jesus himself.

A further reference to God's Word as food comes in Luke 10:38–42. Mary and Martha invite Jesus over for a meal, and while Martha is busy preparing,[29] she gets upset at finding Mary merely "seated at the Lord's feet, listening to his word" (Luke 10:39). As Martha complains to Jesus, he curiously replies that "only one thing is necessary, for Mary has chosen the good part (*tein agathein merida*), which shall not be taken away from her." What is this "good part," or portion? John Nolland points out that the Septuagint uses *meris* (part) "for portions in a meal (Gen 43:34; 1 Sam 1:4–5; 9:23; Neh 8:10, 12; Esth 9:19, 22)."[30] So Mary's choice to listen to Jesus's word "may be viewed metaphorically as the choice of the best meal (cf. 4:4), or it could be that *necessity* is seen from a double aspect; for a meal a few things will

---

26. Calvin, *Commentary on the Holy Gospel*, 18:290. Calvin denies that this passage legitimizes the pope and views Christ's command as applying to all Christians: "Nothing was given to Peter by these words, that is not also given to all the ministers of the Gospel." Calvin, *Commentary on the Holy Gospel*, 290.

27. Webster, *Ingesting Jesus*, 142.

28. Webster, *Ingesting Jesus*, 143.

29. Nolland points out that this "preparing," or "service" (*diakonia*), refers "to domestic affairs (with a particular focus on what pertains to meals) in the interest of her honored guest. . . . Jesus is a meal guest," which happens often in Luke. Nolland, *Luke 9:21—18:34*, 604; cf. Luke 5:27–32; 7:36–50; 14:1–14; 24:13–35.

30. Nolland, *Luke 9:21—18:34*, 604; cf. Garland, *Luke*, 454.

do; for one's salvation receiving the word of God is the necessary thing."[31] Either way, the passage suggests food as a model for God's Word.[32]

Another implicit comparison appears in Acts 6, which concerns feeding widows in the church. When approached with the problem that some widows were being overlooked in the food distribution, the twelve apostles respond in a way that shows they have not forgotten Jesus's teaching about the one necessary thing: "It is not desirable for us to neglect the word of God in order to serve tables. Therefore, brethren, select from among you seven men of good reputation, full of the Spirit and of wisdom, whom we may put in charge of this task. But we will devote ourselves to prayer and to the ministry of the word" (Acts 6:2b–4). Feeding widows is certainly important, but not as important as feeding God's Word to everyone.

Both 1 Cor 3:1–3 and Heb 5:12–14 refer to God's Word as milk and solid food, and letters rebuke certain Christians for staying infants in their digestion of the word instead of growing in God's righteousness to eat more solid food.[33] David E. Garland argues that this contrast between milk and meat does not divide Christians into "lower-level beginners who need to be fed a diet of theological pabulum and an upper-level elite who can receive advanced, esoteric doctrine.... Nor does he offer a two-stage wisdom, leading believers to the next stage of more arcane lessons when he thinks they can handle it."[34] Rather, Paul offers the same word of God's gospel to all, but the spiritually mature feed on and exercise it so intently that it matures them in godliness.[35] Others stubbornly insist on a diet of "synthetic substitutes" and thus remain "fleshly" (cf. 1 Cor 3:3), lacking in

---

31. Nolland, *Luke 9:21—18:34*, 604–5.

32. Luke's gospel makes much of food. In Karris's words, "In Luke's Gospel Jesus is either going to a meal, at a meal, or coming from a meal. References to food abound on almost every single page of Luke's Gospel." Karris, *Eating Your Way through Luke's Gospel*, 14.

33. According to Calvin, milk "means an elementary doctrine suitable to the ignorant" while solid food involves a deeper grasp of God's word enabled by mature understanding so that "at first we must suck milk from Scripture, so that we may afterwards feed on its bread." Calvin, *Commentaries on the Epistle of Paul*, 128.

34. Garland, *1 Corinthians*, 108.

35. Gregory of Nyssa holds a similar view that Paul preaches the same message to all but tailors it to those of different spiritual maturity: "So teaches Paul the divine Apostle who spreads such a table as this for us—making his message strong meat for the more mature and greens for the weaker and milk for little children." Gregory of Nyssa, *The Life of Moses*, 88.

spiritual discernment.[36] For this reason, Heb 13:9 urges believers not to "be carried away by varied and strange teachings; for it is good for the heart to be strengthened by grace, not by foods through which those who were so occupied were not benefited." Here, God's grace—mediated through his Word—constitutes the food that truly strengthens and benefits a person. So abiding in God's Word forms and transforms a person just as food forms and transforms a person.[37]

The food model appears negatively in Matt 16:6, where Jesus warns his disciples to "beware of the leaven of the Pharisees and Sadducees." The disciples mistake this saying as a rebuke for not bringing bread, so Jesus reminds them that he has fed thousands miraculously and has no need for their provision, which prompts the disciples finally to understand that Jesus's warning pertains not to physical bread but to "the teaching of the Pharisees and Sadduccees" (cf. Matt 16:12). So just as one must live by eating the bread of God's Word, one also must avoid the poisonous teaching of God's enemies. Here, the food model works both ways, pointing toward the source of salvation and warning against sources of death.

The Bible is clear: Scripture is food. As God's written Word, Scripture is nothing less than life-giving, and lack of it means certain death. "Eating" Scripture sustains one's life on a fundamental level and brings unending delight as one partakes of God's salvation, enters his covenant community, and thus tastes that the Lord is good (cf. Ps 34:8).

I acknowledge that not all of the biblical quotations above refer directly to Scripture but also recount other words from God, such as prophetic oracles and other divine words. In developing this food model for Scripture, I am tracing what Scripture says about all of these words from God and applying it to Scripture itself as God's written Word, inferring that these specific descriptions of God's words as food can also apply to Scripture *as a whole*. I find legitimacy in making this hermeneutical move because Scripture itself does depict God's written words as food, and Scripture also is the now the source that records the other prophetic oracles and divine words such that people can be nourished by them.

---

36. See Garland, *1 Corinthians*, 108.

37. Gordon describes this process: "[The Scripture reader's] judgments and values will change. Any change in her understanding and judgments, though, is a change in *her*. Through attentive, intelligent, reasonable, responsible, and faithful engagement with Scripture, the reading subject will find herself changed to measure up to the technological, linguistic, and intelligible content of Scripture." Gordon, *Divine Scripture in Human Understanding*, 251–52, emphasis his.

The Food Model in Theology

The model "Scripture is food" enjoys firm support from not only Scripture but also the church's theological tradition. A brief survey of three ancient and three contemporary theologians testifies to the historical consistency and usefulness of the food model.

Three Ancient Theologians: Athanasius, Origen, and Gregory

The patristic fathers use the model "Scripture is food" to profound effect, as seen in the works of Athanasius, Origen, and Gregory the Great.

ATHANASIUS

In his seventh festal letter for Easter of 335, Athanasius calls Christians to "be nourished with living bread, by faith and love to God, knowing that without faith it is impossible to be partakers of such bread as this."[38] This "living bread" refers to Jesus, who "continually nourishe[s] His believing disciples with His words" that constitute "the food of the righteous" such that a righteous man lives on the power of these words and keeps "his soul always in health" by "being nurtured in faith and knowledge, and the observance of divine precepts."[39] So Athanasius quotes 1 Tim 4:6 and 2 Tim 1:13 to exhort Christians to "be nourished with the word of faith" and "the form of sound words," thus to "eat at this heavenly table" and "delight themselves not with that food which is cast out, but with that which produces life everlasting."[40] He follows Paul's pastoral letters in referring to Scripture as food.

Athanasius refers to Scripture as food even more explicitly in his letter to Dracontius, written in 354 or 355.[41] Athanasius urges Dracontius not to flee persecution but to fulfill his role as bishop of Hermupolis Parva since "the laity expect you to bring them food, namely instruction from the Scriptures. When then they expect, and suffer hunger, and you are feeding yourself only, and our Lord Jesus Christ comes and we stand before Him, what defense will you offer when He sees His own sheep hungering?"[42]

---

38. Athanasius, "Letter 7. Easter 335," 526.
39. Athanasius, "Letter 7," 526.
40. Athanasius, "Letter 7," 526.
41. Athanasius, "Letter 49: Letter to Dracontius," 558.
42. Athanasius, "Letter 49: Letter to Dracontius," 558.

Athanasius specifically highlights the prime responsibility of a pastor as feeding Christ's sheep the food of Scripture, and he warns of Christ's fearful judgment on the one who feeds himself but not the sheep, alluding to Ezek 34:2: "Son of man, prophesy against the shepherds of Israel. Prophesy and say to those shepherds, 'Thus says the Lord GOD, "Woe, shepherds of Israel who have been feeding themselves! Should not the shepherds feed the flock?"'" Athanasius thus speaks to the gravity and urgency of providing Scripture to satiate spiritual hunger.

Origen

In *The Philocalia*, Origen compares Scripture and food to provocative effect. In chapter 12, he proposes "that though at times our understanding is unfruitful, the faculties which assist the soul, and the understanding, and help us all, are nourished with rational nourishment drawn from the Holy Scriptures . . . and that being nourished they are better able to assist us."[43] According to Origen, then, Scripture provides the "rational nourishment" that enables the faculties of the soul to understand Scripture in the same way that food provides the strength for bodily faculties to operate. Origen thus encourages his "hearers not to faint as they read" Scripture even if they do not understand it at first, since Scripture will nourish "certain invisible departments of our being" to gain the faculties to understand over time.[44] In other words, one should continue to read Scripture even if one does not yet understand it because Scripture, over time, provides the ability to understand, just as food provides the ability to do what one cannot yet do until one eats.

Since the food of Scripture has this enabling power, Origen urges discouraged Christians in the following way: "Let us not then weary when we hear Scriptures which we do not understand; but let it be unto us according to our faith, by which we believe that all Scripture being inspired by God is profitable."[45] Origen likens this profitability to how certain foods improve eyesight, wherein "we do not, I suppose, while we are eating perceive that our eyesight is better, but after two or three days, when the food is assimilated which benefits the eye, we are convinced of the fact by experience; and the same remark applies to other foods which benefit other parts of

---

43. Origen, *The Philocalia*, 12.1.
44. Origen, *The Philocalia*, 12.1.
45. Origen, *The Philocalia*, 12.2.

the body."[46] Likewise, Christian should "have the like faith with regard to Divine Scripture; believe that thy soul is profited by the mere reading, even though thy understanding does not receive the fruit of profiting by these passages. Our inner nature is charmed; its better elements are nourished, the worse weakened and brought to nought."[47] So Scripture exerts a food-like agency, gradually nourishing and strengthening readers' ability to understand while weakening those faculties that oppose God's influence. Readers should therefore not despair when failing initially to understand but persist in "mere reading" with faith that, over time, even these difficult passages will profit them as they assimilate it as spiritual food.

Origen defends the colloquial writing style of Scripture against Greek philosophers who allege that such "poverty of style" lacks the greatness or intelligence fitting to convey the highest truths.[48] Origen responds with a brilliant food illustration: Cooks can prepare the same nutritious food either luxuriously to suit the tastes of the rich or plainly "to suit the tastes of the poor, of rustics, and the majority of men."[49] Food proves equally nourishing however one prepares it; thus, "the greatest public benefactors" are those cooks who cater to the masses and seek the health of the many. Such cooks provide a "greater service to the public than he who cares only for the health of the few."[50] In the same way, God means for his Scripture to feed not only "better-class patients" but instead reach the masses by adapting itself to their speech and "employing words familiar to them, [so that] it might encourage the unlearned multitude to hearken; for after the first introduction they can easily endeavour to get a hold on the deeper truths hidden in the Scriptures."[51] Origen thus ingeniously turns the Greek objection on its head by redefining the nature of greatness: Scripture proves greater than Greek wisdom because it condescends to make God's wisdom accessible to the greatest number of people, just as commonly cooked food feeds the greatest multitude. Origen also captures here the hospitable and inviting heart of God, who takes "thought not only for those who are reputed learned among the Greeks" but also for the starving, unlearned multitude.[52]

46. Origen, *The Philocalia*, 12.2.
47. Origen, *The Philocalia*, 12.2.
48. Origen, *The Philocalia*, 15.9.
49. Origen, *The Philocalia*, 15.9.
50. Origen, *The Philocalia*, 15.9.
51. Origen, *The Philocalia*, 15.10.
52. Origen, *The Philocalia*, 15.10.

Gregory the Great

In *Moralia in Job*, Gregory the Great comments on Job 1:4, wherein Job's sons "would go and hold a feast in the house of each one on his day, and they would send and invite their three sisters to eat and drink with them." In this feast, Gregory sees "the Apostles proclaim to hearers that are weak the joys of the refreshment above, and inasmuch as they see their souls to be starved of the food of truth, they feed them with the feast of God's Word."[53] In short, the food of the feast is Scripture.

Gregory also uses food to distinguish between the more obscure and plainer parts of Scripture: "Scripture is sometimes meat to us, and sometimes drink. It is meat in the harder parts, in that it is in a certain sense broken in pieces by being explained, and swallowed after chewing; and it is drink in the plainer parts, in that it is imbibed just as it is found."[54] The experience of eating meat illustrates his point: Meat cannot be swallowed right away but requires careful chewing to break it down into digestible pieces; likewise, "meatier" parts of Scripture require careful explanation to "break them down" into understandable truths: "the stronger declarations of holy Scripture might be crumbled for [weaker Christians] by explanation."[55] Drawing from Isa 55:1, Gregory affirms that Scripture is also drink, easily swallowed and understood by all people.[56]

Based on this depiction of Scripture as meat and drink, Gregory offers a fascinating interpretation of Isa 5:13: "Therefore my people go into exile for their lack of knowledge; and their honorable men are famished, and their multitude is parched with thirst." Gregory claims that Judah's leaders fail their people by treating Scripture only as drink and not as meat. By neglecting to digest the deeper meaning of Scripture and explain its more obscure parts for themselves, Judah's leaders thus let their "minds fall away from the inward sense, [and] the understanding of the little ones even in the outward meaning is dried up."[57] Since the leaders fail to digest Scripture as meat, the multitude under their care fail to drink Scripture as drink and become "parched with thirst." While one may not agree completely with Gregory's interpretation here, he makes a valid point that sheep follow their

---

53. Gregory the Great, *Moralia in Job*, 1.21.29.
54. Gregory the Great, *Moralia in Job*, 1.21.29.
55. Gregory the Great, *Moralia in Job*, 1.21.29.
56. Gregory the Great, *Moralia in Job*, 1.21.29.
57. Gregory the Great, *Moralia in Job*, 1.21.29.

shepherds: Church leaders can lead their sheep only as far as their own understanding of Scripture; and if they cease to digest Scripture themselves, their flocks will die of spiritual thirst.

In summary, this short survey of three church fathers shows that food serves as a faithful, accessible, and provocative model for Scripture. Athanasius connects the words of Scripture to Jesus as their source and "living bread," and he highlights the gravity and urgency of Scripture in his letter to the bishop Dracontius. Origen insightfully advises Christians to continue reading Scripture even when they do not yet understand it since Scripture, like food, provides the strength to grasp it over time. He also presents Scripture as God's accessible provision for all people regardless of education or social status. Gregory employs food with creative flexibility, using even the experience of eating to make theological distinctions that carry pastoral implications. For all three, Scripture, as food, provides "an accessible and ever-surprising resource" from which "to savor and take nourishment."[58]

Three Modern Theologians: Peterson, Wirzba, and Feinberg

The food model continues to generate creative and provocative insights in contemporary theology. Three prime examples include Eugene Peterson, Norman Wirzba, and John Feinberg.

Eugene Peterson

In *Eat This Book: A Conversation in the Art of Spiritual Reading*, Eugene Peterson uses food to promote reading Scripture "formatively, reading in order to live," rather than seeing Scripture merely as "an object to be honored," which leads to "a lifetime of reading marked by devout indifference."[59] Through the metaphor "eat this book," Peterson reflects on the meaning of receiving Scripture formatively.[60]

He draws most of his insights from Rev 10:9–11, where John eats the scroll given him by an angel. Identifying the scroll as "the Bible, or as much of the Bible as was written at that time,"[61] Peterson distinguishes between eating and mere reading: "[John] eats the book—not *just* reads it—he got

58. Reasoner, *Five Models of Scripture*, 6, 266.
59. Peterson, *Eat This Book*, xi–xii.
60. Peterson, *Eat This Book*, 38.
61. Peterson, *Eat This Book*, 20.

it into his nerve endings, his reflexes, his imagination. . . . Assimilated into his worship and prayer, his imagining and writing, the book he ate was metabolized into the book he wrote . . . the Revelation."[62] So he understands the angel to say, "Get this book into your gut; get the words of this book moving through your bloodstream, chew on these words and swallow them so they can be turned into muscle and gristle and bone."[63] Food thus expresses intimate embodiment of the words received, not just intellectual comprehension or rote transcription.[64]

Peterson contrasts such intimacy with the coercive externality of propaganda or mere information. Propaganda "works another person's will upon us, attempting to manipulate us to an action or a belief," turning people into soulless puppets.[65] Mere information also does violence by reducing words "to the condition of commodities that we can use however we will. Words are removed from their originating context in the moral universe and from personal relationships so that they can be used as tools or weapons," which in turn reduces the users of those words into mere commodities as well; in stark contrast, words "eaten" entail the freedom and dignity of personal communication "taken in, tasted, chewed, savored, swallowed, and digested."[66] Such words are "assimilated, taken into the soul—eaten, chewed, gnawed, received in unhurried delight."[67] Eating Scripture as food, then, maintains the dignity of being freely and fully human, made in God's image as personal and communicative beings.

Eating the book also gives John "a severe case of indigestion"; and while Scripture tastes good when put in his mouth, it makes him sick to his stomach.[68] Peterson draws from John's upset stomach that there "are

---

62. Peterson, *Eat This Book*, 9. Peterson justifies this distinction from the passage itself, pointing out that in the immediate context, John already "started to write down what he had just heard. A voice from heaven told him not to write what he had heard, but to take the book and eat it." Peterson, *Eat This Book*, 37; cf. Rev 10:1–4.

63. Peterson, *Eat This Book*, 37–38.

64. To stress this embodiment and materiality, Peterson even explicates how physical hearing works: "A word is not something spiritual as opposed to something material. Everything about a word is material: it begins as a puff of air, is put in motion by the contraction of our lungs, is pushed up the tunnel of the esophagus through the constrictions of larynx and pharynx, and is then worked on by that excellent trip, tongue, teeth, and lips, to make a word." Peterson, *Eat This Book*, 114.

65. Peterson, *Eat This Book*, 10.

66. Peterson, *Eat This Book*, 10.

67. Peterson, *Eat This Book*, 11.

68. Peterson, *Eat This Book*, 63–64.

hard things in this book, hard things to hear, hard things to obey. There are words in this book that are difficult to digest."[69] So while readers may find Scripture sweet at first, they soon discover that Scripture does not always conform to their liking: "we find that the book is not written to flatter us, but to involve us in a reality, God's reality, that doesn't cater to our fantasies of ourselves. There are hard things in this book, hard things to hear, hard things to obey,"[70] and it benefits people not only to taste its sweet and pleasant parts but also its bitter and difficult teachings. In eating Scripture, "we don't participate on our own terms"; rather, Scripture exerts the Holy Spirit's agency and "generative power" outside human control to "call forth, stimulate, rebuke, prune us. We don't end up the same."[71] Just as food mysteriously acts to transform the body, Scripture acts with the Spirit's mysterious agency to transform its readers.[72]

Treating Scripture as food also helps Peterson conceive of Scripture as more than "one-dimensional, systematized, or theologized" but as "intimately and organically linked to lived reality."[73] Rather than presenting an abstract system of theology, Scripture "makes us participants in the world of God's being and action."[74] So eating Scripture moves away from "a cool objectivity that attempts to preserve scientific or theological truth by eliminating as far as possible any personal participation that might contaminate its meaning"; instead, eating requires the whole person to take "it all in, assimilating it into the tissues of our lives. Readers become what they read. If Holy Scripture is to be something other than mere gossip about God, it must be internalized."[75] Engaging Scripture thus requires intimate internalization, metabolized action, not only abstract cognition, as the angel in Rev 10 "does not instruct St. John to pass on information about God; he commands him to assimilate the word of God so that when he does speak, it will express itself artlessly in his syntax just as the food we eat, when we

---

69. Peterson, *Eat This Book*, 64.

70. Peterson, *Eat This Book*, 64.

71. Peterson, *Eat This Book*, 66. Wirzba also highlights that Christ sets the terms for his eaters: "To eat the 'bread of life' is not to absorb, and thereby abolish, this bread but to be altered by it." Wirzba, *Food and Faith*, 206.

72. For more on the Holy Spirit's operation regarding Scripture, see Peterson, *Eat This Book*, 17; and Feinberg, *Light in a Dark Place*, 107–8, 567–619.

73. Peterson, *Eat This Book*, 65.

74. Peterson, *Eat This Book*, 66.

75. Peterson, *Eat This Book*, 20.

are healthy, is unconsciously assimilated into our nerves and muscles and put to work in speech and action."[76]

In short, Scripture spiritually forms people. Its words "do something *in* us, give health and wholeness, vitality and holiness, wisdom and hope ... to our souls and body," testifying to the "gut-level necessity" of Scripture.[77] For John, Ezekiel, and Jeremiah, all of whom eat Scripture, their spiritual diet "issues in sentences of tensile strength, metaphors of blazing clarity, and a prophetic life of courageous suffering" that form and sustain God's people even in their most difficult days. Scripture still does the same for Christians today if they will read it "with [their] entire life, not just employing the synapses in [their] brain," taking it into their lives "in such a way that it gets metabolized into acts of love, cups of cold water, missions into all the world, healing and evangelism and justice in Jesus' name, hands raised in adoration of the Father, feet washed in company with the Son."[78] So readers should *experience* Scripture, not just think about it; it should lead not to big heads but to big hearts and bodies in service to God and others.

Such holistic, embodied reading entails habit and repetition. One must make time to open the Bible and have spiritual meals that assimilate God's words into one's being. These daily meals allow Scripture to shape everything one says and does. Peterson recognizes the all-encompassing nature of this simple yet difficult act; he states that eating Scripture "requires all of us, our muscles and ligaments, our eyes and ears, our obedience and adoration, our imaginations and our prayers."[79] As food, then, Scripture invites "participatory reading, receiving the words in such a way that they become interior to our lives, the rhythms and images becoming practices of prayer, acts of obedience, ways of love."[80] As food, Scripture is life-giving and life-forming. Its words are "intended, whether confrontationally or obliquely, to get inside us, to deal with our souls, to form a life that is congruent with the world that God has created, the salvation that he has enacted, and the community that he has gathered."[81] As food, Scripture operates deeply within people, transforming them from within into God's image by the Holy Spirit (cf. 2 Cor 3:18).

76. Peterson, *Eat This Book*, 21.
77. Peterson, *Eat This Book*, 21–22.
78. Peterson, *Eat This Book*, 10, 18.
79. Peterson, *Eat This Book*, xii, 10.
80. Peterson, *Eat This Book*, 10.
81. Peterson, *Eat This Book*, 4.

Eat the Bible

Norman Wirzba

While Norman Wirzba does not refer directly to food as a model of Scripture, his theological insights on food can enrich the model. In *Food and Faith: A Theology of Eating*, Wirzba reflects biblically and philosophically on the meaning of being creatures that eat. This reflection yields profound theological insights into human nature, especially regarding its dependence, embodiment, membership, fidelity, mortality, sacrifice, and celebration. As Wirzba points out, food is much more than "a bundle of nutrients that we simply need to get in the right quantities, variety, and proportion"; rather, food "*is God's love made nutritious and delicious, given for the good of each other.*"[82] Food thus speaks to "God's eternal communion-building life,"[83] just as Scripture builds and feeds communion by communicating God's love.

Wirzba identifies many of the wide-ranging implications of food for human life. Food "communicates your connection to a world beyond yourself" and "is a daily confirmation that you are never alone."[84] Food also implies risk. Unlike sight, which "assumes a safe distance between subject and object" and "establishes the independence and the freedom of the viewer" without requiring direct engagement, eating food precludes such objective detachment and entangles people in "intimate involvement with and need of others" that even puts people "at the mercy of the other."[85] Thus to "be" is to "be in relationship" and community, vitally dependent on others to provide life and nourishment, and eating "is the most fundamental means we know for understanding and appreciating the range and depth of creation's memberships."[86] Even one of the most basic foods, bread, requires that people "transform grain into flour, change the flour into dough, and then bake the dough at the right temperature for the right time to get something worth eating."[87] Food calls for focused participation and mutual cooperation, both of which entail hard work and humbling attentiveness. Food also requires that one take something from outside into oneself, "digest it, and incorporate it within. With an intimacy that rivals sexual union, the other's flesh and your flesh 'become one flesh.' The other does not stand

---

82. Wirzba, *Food and Faith*, xii, emphasis his.
83. Wirzba, *Food and Faith*, xviii.
84. Wirzba, *Food and Faith*, 1–2.
85. Wirzba, *Food and Faith*, 2–4.
86. Wirzba, *Food and Faith*, 5, 119.
87. Wirzba, *Food and Faith*, 52.

apart or alongside. Instead, when eaten, the other nurtures you, and thus reenergizes, refreshes, and revitalizes you from within."[88] Engaging food thus requires a deep level of intimacy.

Such observations carry far-reaching implications for "eating" Scripture. Like food, Scripture both is the product of community and invites readers into that community of intimate involvement with others. In this community, Christ "does not allow people to show partiality" and extends hospitality to everyone, made clear by Peter's vision of food in Acts 10.[89] Christ offers salvation to all and calls all to take his Word into themselves for nourishment. In fact, his Word reenergizes, refreshes, and revitalizes a person from within, not from a safe distance.

To be a faithful eater means to "make the sources of nurture the focus of their care, appreciation, and celebration."[90] Such fidelity moves away from a "world reduced to manipulable, mechanical bits" defined by "objectification and commodification of things" toward that of relationship, "care, and cherishing."[91] The faithful eater of Scripture, then, makes Scripture—the source of spiritual nurture—one's central concern and delight. Rather than a mere commodity used only for maintaining mechanical function, Scripture communicates and celebrates God's provision, sustenance, and nearness in covenant relationship, offering "the opportunity to see, receive, and taste the world with spiritual depth."[92] Such depth runs all the way to the grave.

Eating is "a daily reminder of creaturely mortality," as food reminds constantly of the nearness of death and the need for sacrifice to survive, "realizing that without the deaths of others—microbes, insects, plants, animals—we can have no food."[93] Food must die so that others can eat it and live; it thus points ultimately to "Christ's self-offering life," sacrificed so that any who eat of him will live in eternal communion with God.[94] Since Christ's sacrificial death and resurrection form the central message of Scripture, Scripture shapes Christians toward the same "cruciform self-giving" that makes "one's life into a gift that creates communion."[95] By pre-

---

88. Wirzba, *Food and Faith*, 6.
89. Wirzba, *Food and Faith*, 223.
90. Wirzba, *Food and Faith*, 19.
91. Wirzba, *Food and Faith*, 35–36, 39.
92. Wirzba, *Food and Faith*, 69.
93. Wirzba, *Food and Faith*, 156–57.
94. Wirzba, *Food and Faith*, 162.
95. Wirzba, *Food and Faith*, 177.

senting God's "self-offering way of being with the world," Scripture forms its readers not into self-centered consumers but "a living and holy sacrifice, acceptable to God" (Rom 12:1). Scripture thus empowers Christians to lay down their lives for each other, "turn themselves into food for others, and in so doing nurture and strengthen the memberships of life."[96]

Such sacrifice entails embodied service that resists "the Gnostic tendency to devalue creaturely, material life."[97] As God's provision of food affirms bodies as "the places and the means of God's creating and sustaining love,"[98] God's provision of Scripture stresses his intention to redeem and sanctify embodied living. Scripture is food not for some otherworldly realm but for this embodied life on earth. So Scripture should not just feed theories to the mind but empower "an embodied faith that seeks the care and the healing of bodies, and that strives to make the hospitable love of God incarnate in the mundane, unglamorous places of daily life."[99]

Mundane dailyness stresses that spiritual formation does not happen all at once but requires "slow, demanding care,"[100] a process of daily discipline and growth "under the influence of [Christ's] instruction and his way of being in the world. It is to submit to and let one's own life be guided by the concerns and priorities that define him."[101] Rather than succumbing to this "age of the spectacle" that experiences the world in "superficial and ephemeral ways,"[102] Christians' spiritual diet involves being "properly corrected, instructed, and trained by Christ" such that they become in Christ "the nutritious food that will heal and strengthen the world."[103] This process takes painstaking time and builds patience, which does not sit well in today's spectacle-addicted, fast-food culture; however, regular, sustained intake of and obedience to Christ's instruction in Scripture escapes such idols and "brings healing to creation and praise to God as the life of our life."[104] Food thus highlights the blessing of Scripture over time.

---

96. Wirzba, *Food and Faith*, 181, 204–5.
97. Wirzba, *Food and Faith*, 215.
98. Wirzba, *Food and Faith*, 227.
99. Wirzba, *Food and Faith*, 231.
100. Wirzba, *Food and Faith*, 310.
101. Wirzba, *Food and Faith*, 212.
102. Wirzba, *Food and Faith*, 245.
103. Wirzba, *Food and Faith*, 213.
104. Wirzba, *Food and Faith*, 268.

John Feinberg

Feinberg makes a second appearance here because even though he presents light as his main model of Scripture, he ends *Light in a Dark Place* by driving his key points home not so much with light as with food. Feinberg argues that Jesus's statement in Matt 4:4–that humanity "shall not live on bread alone, but on every word that proceeds out of the mouth of God"— implies the necessity, universality, accessibility, and power of Scripture.[105] Its necessity comes from the fact that human "life ultimately depends upon and should be lived in accordance with every word that comes from God's mouth," and since Scripture records those words from God's mouth, human life ultimately depends upon eating and exercising the teaching of Scripture.[106] Proclaiming and living according to Scripture, then, proves nothing less than "essential to sustaining and nurturing spiritual growth and health."[107] Moreover, Jesus's statement in Matt 4:4 quotes Deut 8:3, wherein Moses reminds the Israelites of God's provision of manna, "a nourishing but uninteresting food when that is all there is to eat every day."[108] This link between God's Word and the plain, daily bread of manna may imply a daily routine of relying on Scripture for sustenance. Like manna, Scripture may seem mundane, uninteresting, or "all there is to eat every day," yet it remains no less necessary and life-sustaining.

That every human life depends on this word also speaks to the accessibility and universality of Scripture. Not everyone gets a dream or vision, but "anyone can learn about God and his demands by reading Scripture. It is God's word, and it is written for everyone."[109] Moreover, since "following Scripture produces life, especially a spiritual life pleasing to God, it

---

105. Feinberg justifies treating God's words as Scripture by referencing how Jesus frequently quotes Scripture while attributing its words to God. See Feinberg, *Light in a Dark Place*, 154–67. In John 6:38–45, Jesus connects two passages to Scripture and teaching by God; he thus "intended his listeners to see that Scripture is God's word and that God's word points to him. At the very least, this passage links God's word with Scripture and with Jesus." Feinberg, *Light in a Dark Place*, 153–54. In John 17:7–8, Jesus speaks the words of God, and the Gospels record these words; therefore, Jesus's teachings in the Gospels are God's words. Feinberg thus concludes "that Jesus would likely, if asked directly, say that anything recording the words of Scripture, or recording words that will wind up as Scripture, is God's word and thus inspired." Feinberg, *Light in a Dark Place*, 154.

106. Feinberg, *Light in a Dark Place*, 673.
107. Feinberg, *Light in a Dark Place*, 662.
108. Feinberg, *Light in a Dark Place*, 153.
109. Feinberg, *Light in a Dark Place*, 673.

is indeed a powerful word!"[110] The ability of Scripture to give and sustain spiritual life testifies to its power.

Feinberg also employs the food model to elucidate spiritual growth and sanctification. Based on 1 Pet 2:2 ("like newborn babies, long for the pure milk of the word, so that by it you may grow in respect to salvation"), Feinberg reasons that "God doesn't want members of his family to remain in spiritual infancy; they need to grow in their faith," and Scripture constitutes God's appointed means for growing believers in spiritual maturity; to this end, "a casual and occasional glance at Scripture won't do. Rather, Peter likens Scripture to the mother's milk that an infant newly born through natural reproduction craves."[111] The milk metaphor conveys that spiritual growth requires frequency, enthusiasm, desperation, and exclusivity regarding Scripture. A newly born baby hungers quite frequently yet never tires of mother's milk; similarly, the Christian returns again and again to God's Word "with a commitment to 'nurse' frequently on it."[112] He does not "merely take a 'small taste' of [Scripture] for a half-hour each Sunday morning when his pastor preaches. He meditates on God's word both day and night."[113] One would not survive on a single meal per week; consequently, Feinberg asks, "Why, then, can't we see that there will be dire consequences if we limit our intake of God's word to once or twice a week—and some weeks to nothing?"[114] Food requires daily intake, and the same goes for Scripture.

Frequent intake of Scripture also guards against sin. Believers "should be eager to 'ingest' as much of God's word as quickly as possible. The more we internalize it, the better prepared we will be to fight temptation,"[115] as Jesus demonstrated in his wilderness temptations. Speaking positively, Feinberg also asserts that Scripture provides the means for sanctification: "As believers feast on God's word, learn it, and internalize it, they should become increasingly less enamored with sin and its temptations, and more determined to live a godly life."[116]

Milk also conveys enthusiasm, desperation, and a sense of exclusivity regarding Scripture. Babies "drink with abandon, as though tasting

---

110. Feinberg, *Light in a Dark Place*, 673.
111. Feinberg, *Light in a Dark Place*, 675.
112. Feinberg, *Light in a Dark Place*, 675.
113. Feinberg, *Light in a Dark Place*, 678.
114. Feinberg, *Light in a Dark Place*, 679.
115. Feinberg, *Light in a Dark Place*, 677.
116. Feinberg, *Light in a Dark Place*, 676.

something new each time," and Christians should "long for God's word with the same kind of enthusiasm. . . . Just as the newborn is totally dependent on its mother's milk, and couldn't survive without it, so Christians desperately need the milk of God's word."[117] As for exclusivity, mother's milk comprises the only food babies can digest, and Scripture "is the only food there is for spiritual growth."[118] While other spiritual books can supplement and enrich one's understanding of Scripture, one should accept no substitutes to Scripture; Scripture comprises the one necessary food staple sufficient for spiritual growth. As believers grow in understanding this singular food source, however, its words will become "a rich banquet with great variety, and all of it is useful in furthering our spiritual growth and maturity."[119] In short, Scripture will become both milk and meat (cf. 1 Cor 3:2), accessibly clear yet unfathomably delectable.

Scripture as food carries serious pastoral implications. Based his remarks on 1 Pet 5:2, "Shepherd the flock among you," Feinberg exhorts, "You don't have to be a shepherd to know that an essential duty of a shepherd is to feed his sheep. No matter what else a shepherd does for his sheep, if the sheep starve, the shepherd fails. Sheep must be well-fed, and it is the minister's, the preacher's, job to ensure that they are."[120] So the pastor must prioritize preaching Scripture to feed Christ's sheep, and his task "is not to entertain and/or amuse his audience. It is to present a banquet of spiritual food that the Holy Spirit can use to accomplish things in our lives that are for our best benefit and that brings the most glory to God."[121] Scripture, as food, is serious business. It empowers and transforms lives to the glory of God. A pastor must never lose sight of the fact that souls desperately need Scripture as nothing less than life-sustaining, spiritual food.

Feinberg closes his book with a food-centered personal testimony, praising God for the food of Scripture that "nourishes the soul along life's journey. It is a sad and even dangerous thing to be hungry and have no access to food. We need food for our physical bodies, and we also need food for our souls!" Personally testifying to the soul-nourishing power of Scripture, Feinberg tells the story of growing up in a family that prioritized eating Scripture every morning:

117. Feinberg, *Light in a Dark Place*, 675.
118. Feinberg, *Light in a Dark Place*, 675.
119. Feinberg, *Light in a Dark Place*, 676.
120. Feinberg, *Light in a Dark Place*, 679.
121. Feinberg, *Light in a Dark Place*, 679.

> No matter how busy anyone in the family was, all of us were expected to be together for breakfast. This was a time for a hearty meal, conversation about the events of the upcoming day, and something else. At some point during the meal, Mom would get her Bible and read a portion of it for that morning. We were expected to listen quietly and reverently, and we knew that no matter how busy we might be, we could not leave before this part of the meal ended. . . . After Mom read Scripture, Dad led the family in prayer, praying for each member of the family and about the events of the day. This had been their procedure every day of their marriage before I came along, and it was their practice for the rest of their lives.[122]

This daily routine of reading Scripture at breakfast instills in the young Feinberg that Scripture must form the staple diet of one's spiritual life and family. Feinberg's father would read ten pages in the OT and five in the NT every day, showing "clearly and constantly that Scripture is the foundation of every aspect of life."[123] For the Feinberg family, Scripture as food has proved much more than a good idea but a cherished, transformative, and life-giving practice.

To summarize, food has proven a rich model not only to church fathers like Athanasius, Origen, and Gregory but also to modern theologians like Eugene Peterson, Norman Wirzba, and John Feinberg. Reflecting on Rev 10, Peterson sees in the model an invitation to receive Scripture in an intimate and embodied way so that it becomes a visceral part of one's being, informing not only how one thinks but how one lives. Wirzba does not directly address the model but provides deep theological insights that enrich and deepen the implications of the model, including dependence, embodiment, membership, fidelity, mortality, sacrifice, celebration, and God's love communicated in daily, mundane life. Feinberg develops the food model from Matt 4:4 and 1 Pet 2:2 to find that food communicates the necessity, universality, and enjoyability of Scripture, which call readers to receive Scripture with desperation, frequency, enthusiasm, and a sense of exclusivity in accepting no substitutes. He also notes that pastors should prioritize preaching and embodying Scripture to feed Christ's sheep and nurture their spiritual growth.

---

122. Feinberg, *Light in a Dark Place*, 762.
123. Feinberg, *Light in a Dark Place*, 763.

Evaluating the Food Model

Evaluating the food model by the criteria of faithfulness, fittingness, and fruitfulness will show that, compared to the other models, "Scripture is food" safeguards more effectively, discloses more comprehensively, and renders more viscerally the nature of Scripture.[124]

Evaluating Faithfulness

FAITHFULNESS TO SCRIPTURE

The biblical survey at the beginning of this chapter gives ample evidence for the faithfulness of the food model to Scripture in both the OT and NT. While Scripture does not describe itself as a theatrical script or a musical score and only in a handful of places as light (cf. Ps 19:8; 43:3; 119:105; Prov 6:23; Job 29:3; 2 Pet 1:19), Scripture depicts itself as food with inescapable frequency. From the Pentateuch to the Psalms, the wisdom literature to the Prophets, and the Gospels to the Epistles, virtually every genre in Scripture presents unanimous and consistent support for treating Scripture as food. No other model, including light, comes across with such repeated emphasis. Scripture presents itself so decisively and unequivocally as food that one simply cannot doubt the support of Scripture for the model.

FAITHFULNESS TO TRADITION

As shown in the above section, "The Food Model in Theology," the recurrence of the model in both ancient and modern theology confirms its fidelity to church tradition. The food model finds support from church fathers like Athanasius, Origen, and Gregory the Great. It also finds contemporary proponents in Peterson and Feinberg, and it draws rich depth from Wirzba's theology of food. While other models, especially light, also have clear support from tradition, food remains one of the most enduring, universal, and accessible models from biblical times to the present, demonstrating its faithfulness to the long line of "eaters" who have ingested, digested, metabolized, and exercised Scripture in the history of the church's theological discourse.

---

124. The section on evaluating faithfulness will stay brief because the food model, as presented above, already demonstrates its faithfulness to Scripture and church tradition.

While the model of light certainly enjoys a longstanding legacy in historical theology that rivals that of food, the prominence of the food model in Scripture coupled with the urgent necessity of food at all points in human history ensures that the food model will stay forever relevant to theological treatments of Scripture.[125] One of the strongest proofs of the exceptional faithfulness of the food model comes from the fact that scholars who develop other models tend to fall back on food to make their points regarding the nature of Scripture. Feinberg closes his *Light in a Dark Place* not so much with light as with food. Vanhoozer, too, turns to food to express the "diet," or discipline, of growing in Scripture and doctrine: "The term *diet* derives from a Greek term, *diaita*: 'a way of life; to regulate oneself; a series of activities which form one's main concern, usually for a purpose; a course of life.' A diet is a regulated or disciplined way of living and thinking . . . a kind of obedient doing [of Scripture's teaching]."[126] So the food model proves so inevitable in Scripture and theology that Feinberg and Vanhoozer, while developing other models, return to food to illustrate key points in their doctrine of Scripture.

Evaluating Fittingness

Fittingness to the Subject

The food model most fittingly encapsulates the subject of Scripture. Such fittingness shows in the way the model captures inspiration, authority, necessity, sufficiency, clarity, and inerrancy.

---

125. Whidden laments that even the model of light has seemed to lose relevance in contemporary theology as "a dead metaphor," and Edison's invention of the light bulb as well as the impact of the Enlightenment has turned light into a mere commodity that humans have conquered, meaning that light no longer holds "a special place in our imaginations." He goes so far as to say that light has suffered a "real descent into theological oblivion." Whidden, *Christ the Light*, 2. Whidden thus seeks to reclaim a waning theological interest in light. See Whidden, 3. While the modern industrial complex threatens to do the same to food, the fundamental connection of food to daily life—the fact that absolutely everyone must eat to stay alive—keeps food from falling prey to such theological indifference.

126. Vanhoozer, *Drama of Doctrine*, 375–76.

Inspiration

Returning to Peterson's distinction between mere "reading" and "eating," Rev 10:8–11 provides a provocative picture of the process of inspiration. John "eats the book—not *just* reads it"; God's words get "into his nerve endings, his reflexes, his imagination" and become "metabolized into the book he wrote . . . the Revelation."[127] In terms of food, then, the process of inspiration involves more than hearing and repeating God's words, or, as Vanhoozer would have it, taking the Holy Spirit's promptings from below the stage.[128] Rather, metabolism entails that God's words enter the writer's gut, move through his bloodstream, and turn into his "muscle and gristle and bone" before becoming written down as Scripture.[129] In other words, the food model best captures the interactive process of dual authorship, beautifully depicting the authentic, personal contribution of the human author while necessitating the priority and enablement of the divine author, since the food of God's Word fundamentally enables the human authors to pen Scripture. The biblical writer not only hears but personally assimilates and embodies God's words into his very being and then renders that intimate ingestion into the words of Scripture. The food model thus shows how Scripture maintains the integrity of both the divine and human authors without violating the divine author's initiative and will nor the human author's personality and writing style. In fact, the divine author provides the very food necessary to empower the human authors to write in the fullness of their humanity and personality, and the divine author neither sidesteps nor reduces the human author to a mere mouthpiece. In Feinberg's words, "the human authors didn't take dictation from the Holy Spirit. Rather, using their own writing styles, vocabularies, and marks of personal interests, they composed the very words of Scripture that communicate exactly what God wanted them to say."[130] Food thus maintains what John Webster calls "the creatureliness of the text."[131] Though fully God's words, Scripture undergoes creaturely "metabolism" by the human author such that the words perfectly reflect what both authors intend to say. Food thus safeguards the co-authorship of Scripture by God and human beings while preserving the

---

127. Peterson, *Eat This Book*, 9.
128. Vanhoozer, *Drama of Doctrine*, 228.
129. Peterson, *Eat This Book*, 37–38.
130. Feinberg, *Light in a Dark Place*, 228.
131. Webster, *Holy Scripture*, 20.

nature and order of their respective contributions. Unlike the script and score, which need to be *qualified* to include this deep sense of divine enablement, the enablement and personal integrity of dual authorship prove *integral* to the food model.

The script and score can also account for this inspired dual-authorship if one conceives of the actors working with the original author to write the concerto or play. The intimacy and enablement involved in ingesting food, however, may better account for the formation of Scripture as the Word of God metabolized through human authors. The model of light, too, depicts clearly how the Holy Spirit's initiative provides the light that empowers human beings to write Scripture, but even light tends to emphasize God's agency to the point of erasing the human contribution. Light tends to be something seen and reflected "as is" rather than something embodied and disseminated through the complex process of intake, assimilation, transformation, and transmission necessary to convey the truly interactive, participatory nature of dual authorship. Light tends more to be reflected than transformed, so it would imply inspiration by way of dictation rather than genuine dual authorship. Given its history in Western philosophy as well, light may misconstrue Scripture as a cognitive and detached transmission of data rather than a fully embodied assimilation of God's Word communicated through the personalities and experiences of human authors. Food retains the same divine priority and enablement as light, but food also depicts the intimate and embodied process of the human authors as they metabolize God's words to produce inspired Scripture.

Authority

The script and score models highlight the authority of Scripture to command the church, but they posit an unhelpful dichotomy between participants and spectators, falling short of depicting the universal scope of God's authority over all people, not just those musicians and actors in the church. The model of light better conveys the universal scope of God's authority but does not have as natural a connection to the idea of command as a score or script. At the same time, art tends not to carry much authoritative force in and of itself, which poses a problem for the score and script.

The model of food carries the strengths of these models without the weaknesses. While even light does not prove entirely universal—as some people are blind from birth and never see light yet live full lives—absolutely everyone must eat or die. Food thus holds an unquestionably universal sway over all created life as one of the most fundamental needs of all living creatures; and since eating remains a nonnegotiable obligation and perpetual need, the one who controls the food wields incredible power. Revisiting Bavinck's definition of authority as "the power of a person who has something to say, the right to have a voice in some matter" in a relationship "between nonequals . . . a superior to his inferior,"[132] the most power often resides with the person who controls the food source.[133] The philosopher Confucius lists food as one of the three utmost requirements for maintaining government authority, and being richly fed is often "a mark of the aristocracy."[134] In Asian and other patronage cultures, the colloquial expression for a person's belly is "authority," since if "someone has the money to eat that much food, people assume he must be important! The extra weight communicates his social precedence over others—his substance and power."[135] So the "weighty" ones—those who wield power, authority, and influence—tend to be the people who hold sway over the food supply. Food thus denotes authority twice over, both in requiring all to submit to the need to eat and in securing power for those who control food production and distribution.

Scripture as food, then, denotes universal weight and authority. As food, Scripture has the power to enforce its demands. One simply cannot ignore its demands and survive, as one cannot survive without eating. If one ignores the obligation to eat, one will fall faint and die. So just as one lives by submitting to the demand to eat, one lives by submitting to the demands of Scripture. By designating his Word as food, therefore, God proclaims the authority of his Word over all life. Scripture carries a certain *gravitas* in that

---

132. Bavinck, *Reformed Dogmatics*, I.463.

133. Political elites in ancient China "established their authority by controlling intensive pig production as early as 4300 B.C.," and in early Mesopotamia, "state authority was involved in the organization of cattle keeping." Gade, "Hogs (Pigs)," 537; and Gade, "Cattle," 492; cf. Lih, *Bread and Authority in Russia*. Types of food also denote social status. Rachel Laudan writes of kitchens in ancient empires, "One section prepared high cuisines for the king and his immediate entourage, another made less prestigious dishes for the nobles, and yet another assembled humble fare for the manual workers in the palace. In creating the aura of power, the magnificence of high cuisine was as important as palaces and pyramids, purple linen and colorful silk." Laudan, *Cuisine and Empire*, 37.

134. Confucius says, "Provide people with adequate food, provide them with adequate weapons, induce them to have faith in their ruler." Confucius, *Analects*, 12.7.; cf. Keltenmark, *Lao Tzu and Taoism*, 52–53.

135. Georges and Baker, *Ministering in Honor-Shame Cultures*, 40.

while "many overlook and/or reject what Scripture teaches, . . . they cannot do so forever," and all will "finally realize that this is no ordinary book and that its contents matter supremely."[136] Just as all face serious consequences for their response to food, all face serious consequences for their response to Scripture. Its authority is inescapably universal, and one ignores it at one's peril.

Food also speaks to the relationship between "nonequals . . . a superior to his inferior."[137] Food communicates not only God's supreme authority but also the distinction between God's authority and all other authorities: It underscores the nonequality between Creator and creature, as God does not have to eat but human beings do (Ps 50:12–15). Food thus highlights how God's authority submits to no higher power. He alone need not eat but gives food to all at the proper time, opening his hand to satisfy the desire of every living thing (cf. Ps 145:15–16; Gen 1:30). Applied to Scripture, God alone gives all people his authoritative Word as food to satisfy their inbuilt hunger as his creatures, thus asserting his universal, yet benevolent, authority. Food also stresses that God's authority encompasses all creatures, not only the church, although the church uniquely recognizes and operates under that authority as God's covenant people (Jer 31:31–36; Mark 14:24; Heb 10:16–17).

Scripture as food also informs the place of church tradition by putting it firmly under the authority of Scripture. As food, Scripture is always prior: it empowers the church, not vice versa. So the food model disallows any vision of the church's authority as equal to that of Scripture. Rather, church authority receives its power from the words of Scripture, and church tradition simply means those who have eaten God's authoritative Scripture as their food by submitting to his Word, tasting of his goodness, and growing in the strength he provides. Scripture as food thus relegates church tradition to a position of perpetual humility beneath God's written Word; and "if Scripture and tradition conflict, Scripture as norm means that Scripture's teaching is correct and tradition is wrong."[138] The food model thus precludes tradition from being a second locus of authority alongside or above the word.[139] It also affirms that Scripture exerts ontological and not

---

136. Feinberg, *Light in a Dark Place*, 401.

137. Bavinck, *Reformed Dogmatics*, 1.463.

138. Feinberg, *Light in a Dark Place*, 404.

139. Vanhoozer points out that tradition itself has affirmed consistently the supreme authority of Scripture, making it ironic "that many of those today who speak up for

merely functional authority since its authority does not rest in its recognition or use by the church but in God as its divine source and author.[140]

Necessity

The above considerations for the authority of Scripture also apply to its necessity. Food is always necessary, and Scripture as food speaks to the church's need for its nourishment. So the church needs Scripture for the church's spiritual vitality, and Scripture as food speaks to how urgently people need to take in God's words to have spiritual life. The score and script models can also speak to people's need for the life-giving directions of Scripture, but food also includes the built-in sense of enablement necessary to complete those directions. Even the model of light does not convey such urgent necessity since the blind can live without light but not without food, and while light is necessary to see clearly, food is necessary to stay alive in the first place. Food thus models Scripture as "the source for life, . . . the authoritative source about how we should relate to God, others, our world, and ourselves."[141] Just as food is the source of all physical life, Scripture is the source of all spiritual life. Both are eminently and universally necessary.

Food also renders the necessity of Scripture most seriously and urgently since lives are at stake. A score or script does not naturally carry this sense of life-or-death gravity, and light proves significantly grave since lack of it brings blindness or the terror of darkness. Food, however, carries the highest level of gravity. With food, lives are immediately at stake. If people do not eat, they die. Food thus conveys the terror of death and the life-threatening consequences of lacking or disregarding Scripture. Food also locates the nature of Scripture firmly in the real world rather than in that of make-believe theater and entertainment. So food captures best God's kindness and severity surrounding his Word. While food does represent "*God's love made nutritious and delicious*,"[142] it also shows the nearness of God's judgment upon sin since all must eat frequently to stave off death. After all, Adam and Eve fall through eating forbidden food, and God's judgment on Adam regards difficulty in obtaining food (cf. Gen 3:1–19). Along with

---

tradition turn a deaf ear to what tradition has actually handed down." Vanhoozer, *Drama of Doctrine*, 165.

140. See Feinberg, *Light in a Dark Place*, 394–400.
141. Feinberg, *Light in a Dark Place*, 404.
142. Wirzba, *Food and Faith*, xii, emphasis his.

being a reminder of God's love, then, food can remind of God's judgment upon sin and of people's constant need for God's saving provision every day so that they do not starve to death. The food model, then, imbues Scripture with all these qualities as the revelation of God's kindness in love as well as his severity in judgment. The subject matter of Scripture is "not just of marginal or negligible import. Its topics are extremely important to life on earth and life thereafter."[143] Whatever "God reveals, we must believe and obey. Otherwise, there will be divine judgment."[144] Stressing these life-or-death stakes, the food model portrays Scripture as exceedingly necessary. As "God's answers to ultimate issues,"[145] Scripture sets before all people "life and prosperity, and death and adversity," that they may choose life (Deut 30:15, 19). The model also makes clear that the necessity of Scripture entails both divine blessings and curses—blessings to those who partake and curses to those who reject this spiritual food that God provides.

The ability of the food model to communicate the divine blessings and curses of Scripture also entails inescapability of Scripture no matter how humans respond to it. If humans obey it, Scripture is effective in blessing. If humans disobey or neglect it, Scripture is effective in judgment. Either way, people cannot escape the total effectiveness of Scripture: "Sooner or later you will bow the knee to what Scripture teaches. Given its truth, you can reject it, ignore it, and try to get around it, but you will ultimately have to yield to what it says! That's the nature of truth; it can't be ignored and avoided forever."[146] So food makes sense of the unavoidability of the necessity of Scripture.

Sufficiency

Food most readily depicts the sufficiency of Scripture to provide all that people need to know God and to do his will. Just as manna sustains God's people in the wilderness (Deut 8:3), Scripture sustains the church with the sufficient nourishment of God's Word throughout their earthly sojourn, and as food, Scripture upholds the church, not vice versa. While performance models like the script and score require human beings to uphold and "actualize" the life of these texts, the food model shows the opposite

143. Feinberg, *Light in a Dark Place*, 401.
144. Feinberg, *Light in a Dark Place*, 401.
145. Feinberg, *Light in a Dark Place*, 401.
146. Feinberg, *Light in a Dark Place*, 710.

to be the case with Scripture in that Scripture actualizes life in the people who eat it. Scripts and scores need actors and musicians to keep them alive, but food keeps the actors and musicians alive, thus highlighting the sole sufficiency of Scripture to feed God's people and complete the work for which God sent it (cf. Isa 55:11). Put another way, God does not need human words or deeds to sustain him; rather, humans need God's words and deeds to sustain them.

Scripture thus lacks nothing essential but rather fills up what is lacking in people, making them "adequate, equipped for every good work" (2 Tim 3:17). Scripture provides the sufficient nourishment to make God's people adequate for his service. Sufficiency, then, means that Scripture enables human performance rather than needs it; Scripture offers the "complete diet" to strengthen and shape God's people as they ingest, metabolize, and exercise it. Unlike a script or score, Scripture not only commands and directs; it gives the strength to do what it commands. As Origen suggests, Scripture profits a person like food: It nourishes one's better elements, banishes one's weaknesses, and strengthens one's faith and understanding over time through continual assimilation.[147] So people do not enable the power of Scripture; rather, people receive the power of Scripture as sufficient food for their daily needs. Food makes clear that the words of Scripture "are not primarily words, however impressive, that label or define or prove, but words that mean, that reveal, that shape the soul, that generate saved lives, that form believing and obedient lives."[148] As food, Scripture saves, feeds, and forms lives.

Food depicts the sufficiency of Scripture even better than light. Like light, the potency of food does not need humans to make it sufficient but provides the power to act in the first place. Both food and light thus carry a sense of priority, as they must come first to give the ability to perform other actions, like seeing. However, food entails an even more pressing and visceral priority than light because of its immediate, life-or-death urgency. Lacking light, one loses one's sight, but lacking food, one loses one's life. With food, the stakes could not be higher, as people require the sufficiency of Scripture for their very survival. If Scripture is not sufficient to sustain spiritual life, or if it remains insufficient until mediated by ecclesiastical tradition or human performance, people will be worse than the blind leading the blind (cf. Matt 15:14; Luke 6:39); they will die.

147. Origen, *The Philocalia*, 12.2.
148. Peterson, *Eat This Book*, 140.

So while light tends to stay dispassionately cognitive and abstract, leading to a merely intellectual conception of the sufficiency of Scripture, food gets to the very "muscle and gristle and bone" of this doctrine: as food, Scripture not only tells sufficient information but enables sufficient action, empowering one's obedience to God.[149] Scripture provides sufficient ability to receive, assimilate, and live by God's communication. So food reveals Scripture as not only cognitively or intellectually sufficient but existentially and experientially sufficient.

Clarity

Returning to how Thompson's defines the clarity of Scripture as *"that quality of the biblical text that, as God's communicative act, ensures its meaning is accessible to all who come to it in faith,"*[150] light readily portrays such accessibility and carries a sense of priority in that it enables one to see clearly. A score and script also entail clear communication through a system of musical notes and meaningful letters.

Like light, food also carries a sense of priority and enablement: as light enables one to see, food enables one to live. While light most naturally captures clarity by its very nature as that which illumines and thus clarifies, food conveys better the last part of Thompson's definition, that Scripture is clear "to all who come to it in *faith*." While light tends to be something one sees or does not see involuntarily, food always involves volitional trust and the risk of putting an object into one's mouth and swallowing it, allowing that object to become part of oneself. Food thus illustrates the trust necessary to grasp Scripture clearly; Scripture reveals its meaning to the one who trusts it enough to take it into oneself and metabolize it as one's spiritual food. In short, one must "let it in" to access its clear meaning. Scripture presents itself as eminently clear to the one willing to "taste and see that the LORD is good" (Ps 34:8).

Thompson's definition also asserts that Scripture manifests its clarity "to all who *come to it* in faith." Food reveals the nature of this "coming" as continual and ongoing. As Mark Reasoner says, Scripture cannot "be fully enjoyed at one meal. As one can enjoy and benefit from meals each day, so each interaction with Scripture can bring delightful, new sustenance."[151] In

---

149. Peterson, *Eat This Book*, 37–38.
150. Thompson, *A Clear and Present Word*, 169–70, emphasis his.
151. Reasoner, *Five Models of Scripture*, 266.

contrast, light tends to be on or off; one either sees it or not. Light, then, might give the wrong impression that Scripture must be immediately clear on the first reading; one either "gets it" or one does not. The food model, however, implies that the clarity of Scripture often involves a process. Digestion takes time; likewise, discerning the clear meaning and significance of Scripture may "require a good bit of our time and thought" in prayerful study, as not every part of Scripture will appear immediately clear.[152] This process of study requires patience in returning to the same passages again and again to eat, digest, and exercise the clear meaning of Scripture over time. Food thus depicts this gradual—and sometimes long-term—process better than light. As Origen attests, sometimes the clarity of Scripture may not be a matter of instantly "seeing the light" or immediately grasping the benefit of Scripture; rather, the reader gradually assimilates the nourishment that Scripture provides and thus gains clearer understanding in the process.[153]

Inerrancy

Since Scripture always tells the truth that corresponds to reality, such correspondence proves problematic for the script and score models, which tend to posit an unhelpful distance between reality and imagination. Such distance can fail to safeguard the rootedness of Scripture in the real world and confuse people into thinking that the biblical world differs from the real one.

The food model, however, requires no such distance from reality. Food ties directly to the most urgent and pressing need: feeding hunger in the real world. Rather than creating an extra layer of artifice inherent in stage performance, food speaks to the life-or-death struggle to survive in the real world. So while scripts and scores may reflect reality, eating food engages directly with reality, participating in "the first of the essentials of life."[154] Food thus undergirds the inerrancy of Scripture since Scripture provides the true food of God's Word, which proves literally a matter of life or death that alters "one's eternal destiny."[155] While music and theater remain optional luxuries, food renders Scripture as a nonnegotiable necessity. Food must be healthy, or it will kill; similarly, Scripture must be truthful, or people will die of spiritual hunger. Though food also remains delicious and

---

152. Feinberg, *Light in a Dark Place*, 708.
153. See Origen, *The Philocalia*, 12.2.
154. Belasco, "Future of Food: A History," 676.
155. Feinberg, *Light in a Dark Place*, 662.

pleasurable as humanity's "most frequently indulged pleasure," food also brings with it "considerable concern and dread" since people literally die without it.[156] So food depicts the words of Scripture as anything but flights of fancy or make-believe; rather, they tell the truth that lives depend on in the real world.

Food also illustrates the inescapability of scriptural truth. In short order, "everyone learns that we must live in accord with the truth, regardless of whether we want to or not. Truth, enforced by an almighty God, must be embraced, or we must sooner or later own up to the consequences."[157] So just as one must eat or soon face the consequences of ill health and death, one must live in accord with Scripture or also face such dire outcomes. One cannot ignore Scripture, as one cannot ignore food, without serious, life-threatening repercussions. As Athanasius points out, those repercussions for pastors even include facing God's judgment for failing to feed his flock the words of Scripture.[158] So food not only locates Scripture firmly in the context of reality, but it demonstrates the high stakes attached to the truth-telling words of Scripture. In other words, Scripture as food explains why inerrancy matters so much; people's very lives hang on such truth-telling words.

Food thus renders the inerrancy of Scripture more viscerally than light. While light serves well as a cognitive and intellectual metaphor for truth, food drives that truth straight to the stomach: food puts in full view the universal hunger and desperate need for God's truth to sustain life. Moving beyond the tendency of light to stay merely cognitive and intellectual, food makes clear that the truth of Scripture must not be held at arm's length but rather taken into oneself, incorporated into one's life, to do one any good. Such truth is not merely a detached, abstract system of coherent propositions; it is life-sustaining food.

Food also depicts Scripture as universal truth better than light. Once again, light is not entirely universal, as those born blind may never see physical light and yet live full lives without it, and not all life requires light to exist.[159] However, all life requires food. Absolutely everyone must eat to

---

156. Belasco, "Future of Food: A History," 676.

157. Feinberg, *Light in a Dark Place*, 661.

158. See Athanasius, "Letter 49: Letter to Dracontius," 558.

159. According to scientists at the University of California at Santa Barbara (UCSB), some deep-sea organisms that live near sea vents do not need the sun's light to survive: "They are so far down in the ocean that no sunlight reaches them and they get all of their energy from chemicals dissolved in the water near the vents." "Does Everything in the

survive. Food thus captures best the universality of God's truth and that all need to receive and abide by the truth of Scripture to live.

Food most fittingly conveys the inspiration, authority, necessity, sufficiency, clarity, and inerrancy of Scripture, not only encapsulating these attributes but stressing their vital importance. Even in terms of the clarity of Scripture, which light more readily depicts, the food model plays a key role in highlighting the trust and process involved in grasping the clear teaching of Scripture.

Fittingness to Current Culture

While the script and score models rightly promote corporate performance of the biblical text in the current context, they run the risk of portraying Scripture merely as disposable entertainment rather than indispensable truth, or as an escape from reality rather than engagement with reality. They also may mislead people into thinking that only the highly cultured or educated can understand the Bible, thus preventing children and the lesser educated from encountering its universally accessible truth. Even light, with its philosophical and scientific moorings in the current culture, can make Scripture seem too inaccessible or complicated, a subject limited to only those few, enlightened specialists who can understand such mysteries. Such limitedness applies not only socially but also situationally, as the script and score models tend to lose cultural relevance in certain situations, such as during times of war.

Food, however, speaks to everyone at all times, especially times of war when food is scarce. Since everyone eats, food presents Scripture as accessible to all, regardless of age, culture, geography, social class, or season. As food, Scripture holds relevance for all people in all cultures, not only the privileged few. Food thus communicates the necessity of Scripture to all, including children and those without education. All must intake and trust the truth of Scripture to live, especially its truth concerning the ultimate Word of God, Jesus Christ (cf. John 5:39). In fact, children may understand Scripture better than adults, as God delights in revealing his Word to children while hiding it from "the wise and intelligent" (Matt 11:25; cf. 18:3).

World Need the Sun to Survive?" *UCSB ScienceLine*, May, 26, 2016, http://scienceline.ucsb.edu/getkey.php?key=5412#:~:text=Most%20organisms%20either%20directly%20or,to%20make%20sugars%20and%20oxygen.

Eat the Bible

Food also avoids the unhelpful dichotomy between rehearsal and performance inherent in the script and score models. Rather than promoting a culture of performing one's spirituality only on Sundays and other church events, food fosters a culture that pays attention to the mundane, daily rhythms of eating meals and sharing community around the table. Here, one need not perform in any spectacular way, nor is one always rehearsing to perform an exhibition; instead, spiritual growth happens through consistent intake and disciplined exercise of Scripture in daily community. As food, Scripture simply becomes part of one's necessary habit in everyday life, carried and lived all the time rather than in sporadic performances. In this way, Scripture as food also precludes any dichotomy between performers and spectators. All must participate, as none can go without eating.

Pastors in particular can benefit from the food model. The model frees them from having to prepare a spectacular performance of a sermon every Sunday. While pastors should prepare to deliver the spiritual food of Scripture as best they can, concentrating on feeding rather than performing helps to see the real import of their calling as well as place their confidence rightly in God's Word rather than in human performance. In short, the pressure is off. One need not perform with food; one need only eat and share it, as Scripture will feed God's people regardless of the messenger or the packaging. Moreover, Scripture as food means that pastors themselves must continually eat and digest the Word to guard against burnout and gain the strength to endure through the many hardships and challenges of ministry (cf. 2 Cor 11:23–33). As Gregory the Great suggests, shepherds must keep eating the Word lest their flocks also starve.[160]

The food model thus depicts the mundanity and regularity involved in building a healthy culture around Scripture and corrects the current culture's addiction to the spectacular. Rather than seeking God only in the exciting and spectacular, the food model encourages people to seek God in the mundane and ordinary times of life, when reading the Bible may not prove exhilarating but remains no less nourishing and necessary. Sometimes the most ordinary practice turns out to be the most needed and profound, and the small decisions regarding one's routine end up making the biggest difference in the long term. Such is Scripture as food. Daily intake and exercise of Scripture may appear unglamorous and even boring at times, but it ends up quietly shaping the life of God's community and building a healthy culture nourished by God's truth.

---

160. See Gregory the Great, *Moralia in Job*, 1.21.29.

This gradual process inherent in food also helps to confront the current culture's impatience and its demand to get everything right away. In this sense, food offers a better model than light. Hearkening back to the discussion on the clarity of Scripture, light depicts immediate contrasts well—such as light and dark, on or off, seeing or blind—while food portrays better the sense of gradual development and repetitive process required for digestion, metabolism, and growth. So while light—especially the speed of light—may give the current culture the wrong idea that spiritual growth needs to happen quickly or all at once, food tempers this unrealistic expectation by counseling much-needed patience and the hope of gradual growth. Ellen F. Davis points out that such painstaking patience and trust have reflected the agrarian culture of God's people, especially in ancient Israel.[161] Patience in growing and harvesting food confronts modern culture concerning its approach to Scripture: Scripture cannot be hoarded or understood all at once; rather, one should expect spiritual growth to happen gradually, as one regularly hears and obeys Scripture in community with God and his people. In this humble, day-to-day way, food also helps the culture view engagement with Scripture as embodied and down-to-earth, not merely abstract or cognitive, as the philosophy of light may imply.

Light also does not readily depict cultural diversity, but such diversity abounds with food. For example, bread is a ubiquitous food found in every culture, but not every culture bakes bread the same way. The Jews have challah, the French have baguettes, the Ethiopians have injera, the Italians have focaccia, and the Chinese have shaobing.[162] Diversity resides in how bakeries in different cultures prepare their carbohydrates, yet this diversity does not render the bread ineffective. Similarly, "Scripture is food" carries implications for how biblical truth stays stable across all cultures yet is expressed legitimately across different cultures spanning diverse times, locations, and even denominational divides. The food model thus captures the unchanging universality of God's truth while encouraging creative and fresh expressions of that truth within distinct Christian communities. Thus "it is imperative that we listen carefully to interpretations of Scripture by Christians in contexts different from our own. We must remain open to the freedom of the Spirit who sheds new light on Scripture. . . . Unfamiliar

---

161. See Davis, *Scripture, Culture, and Agriculture*, 75–79.

162. See Abesamis, "What Bread Looks Like in 15 Places around the World," *Insider* online, March 11, 2019, https://www.insider.com/bread-around-the-world-2019-13.

voices can challenge and enrich scriptural interpretation."[163] Since no one culture holds the exhaustive interpretation of God's Word, Christians in all cultures should be open to deeper interpretation and correction. So the food model not only emphasizes the universal accessibility of God's Word to every culture but also invites believers in diverse cultures to enrich the church's understanding of Scripture.

Evaluating Fruitfulness

CONCEPTUAL FRUITFULNESS

The food model carries rich implications for one's conception of other doctrines in systematic theology. Examples include theological anthropology, soteriology, and ecclesiology.

Theological Anthropology

Scripts and scores depict humanity with too much power since these documents depend on humans to keep them alive, while light shows more clearly that humanity depends entirely on God to enable sight. The need for food, however, runs even deeper, emphasizing that humanity depends on God not only for sight but for life itself. Furthermore, food insists on the constant and continual nature of this dependence, as one needs daily bread to continue living. Food thus speaks to humanity's desperate need for God and roots their dependence on God at all points in life. From birth to death, humans need God to empower them daily to live on his Word as their very food. This perspective not only safeguards the Creator-creature distinction—since God does not need to eat but provides what humans need to eat—but it also highlights that God's agency in giving his Word does not violate or nullify human agency but rather enables it; God gives the food that enables humans to live as fully human agents. At the same time, humans never stop needing to rely on that food to "live and move and have [their] being" (Acts 17:28). In short, food binds humanity to God in radical dependence on God's provision. Such provision stands in stark contrast to the common view in the ancient Near East "that man was created to supply the gods with food."[164] Rather, God needs no food and yet designs his image

---

163. Migliore, *Faith Seeking Understanding*, 63.
164. Wenham, *Genesis 1–15*, 33.

to need him for food (cf. Acts 17:25). Food depicts humanity as hungry and needy, utterly dependent on God to provide the means to stay alive.

Soteriology

The food model makes inescapably clear that Scripture saves and preserves lives. While lives do not usually hang in the balance during a play or musical performance, food is a matter of life or death. A dance or drama can be aesthetically pleasing and enjoyable, but the enjoyment of food always includes the high level of seriousness that should accompany something as crucial and life-sustaining as God's Word. Such seriousness does reflect in the light model, which posits the need for salvation from the darkness of sin and demonic forces; but food captures this dire need even more viscerally and urgently since all people feel the pressing pangs of hunger every day, and many even die of malnourishment. So food discloses the salvific necessity of Scripture as more than light in a dark place but food for the starving.

Along with such gravity, food captures the enjoyability of Scripture better than any other model. Food is, after all, humanity's "most frequently indulged pleasure."[165] Just as eating constitutes one of the most enjoyable pleasures in life through flavor, satiety, and community around the table, partaking of the saving words of Scripture also brings life-giving richness, satisfaction, and association with others. So food depicts that while one must eat, one gets to eat. God's testimonies bring joy to the heart (Ps 119:111) and restore the joy of God's salvation to those weighed down by sin (cf. Ps 51:12). Theater, music, and light all bring their respective joys, but food remains the fundamental joy as it sustains life itself. Food thus entails both "the kindness and severity of God" (Rom 11:22), kindness to those who partake of his salvation and severity to those who reject it.

Food also captures the universal accessibility of God's salvation. God wants all to be saved (cf. 1 Tim 2:4) and offers his clear and accessible Word for all to eat and live (cf. Isa 55:1–4). Food features no steep learning curve as with music and theater; even children and the handicapped can and should partake. God offers his banquet to the naïve and simple (Prov 9:4–6). No social barriers inhibit participation either; God welcomes the poor and the unworthy, the lowly and despised, to his feast (cf. 1 Cor 1:26–29; Luke 14:13; Matt 15:30). He calls the foolish and ignoble to swallow his words and live, words that center on his ultimate Word, Jesus, since

---

165. Belasco, "Future of Food: A History," 1:676.

"there is no other name under heaven that has been given among men by which we must be saved" (Acts 4:12).[166]

Jesus highlights his accessibility to all people by calling himself bread. He could have called himself the lamb rack of life, but he instead calls himself bread—a universally accessible food to rich and poor alike—to underscore that his salvation lies within reach of anyone, so that "whoever believes in him shall not perish but have eternal life" (John 3:16). "Whoever" includes anyone from any culture, even the tribesmen of Papua New Guinea and those who do not have any access to theater, music, or definition of light. Food makes sense in every culture, reflecting God's desire to save all people. Scripture as food thus safeguards and bolsters the universal accessibility of the saving message of Scripture across all times, cultures, geographies, social strata, age groups, and even disabilities; it is especially good news to people who live with handicaps and cannot perform in any musical, theatrical, or eyesight-requiring capacity. Through Scripture, God invites all to taste and see his goodness (cf. Ps 34:8): to eat of his bread, drink of his wine, and be saved (cf. Prov 9:5–6). This food is not too difficult to obtain but is very near, in people's mouths and hearts, that they may observe it (cf. Rom 10:8; Deut 30:14).

Food even encompasses the story of salvation. At creation, God gifts humanity with food (Gen 1:29), but humanity falls into sin and death through eating forbidden food (Gen 3:1–19). God's resultant curse, along with bringing death, involves obtaining food (Gen 3:19), though he often shows his presence and grace through continually providing food (Exod 35:13; Ps 23:5; 36:8; 67:6; 78:24–25; 81:10, 16; Luke 1:53). God then marks his decisive acts of salvation with food through the Passover Meal and Lord's Supper (Exod 12; Matt 26). He sends his only Son as the "bread of life" to save the world by dying as an atoning sacrifice for sins so that people can eat him and live forever (cf. John 6:35, 50–51; Matt 26:26–29; 1 Cor 11:23–34; 1 Pet 3:18; 1 John 2:2). The church's first corporate controversy involves none other than "the daily distribution of food" (Acts 6:1), and God even depicts his salvation's multiethnic inclusiveness by giving Peter

---

166. As Wirzba points out, Jesus is the ultimate food to whom all food points: "Jesus is not simply the *provider* of bread. He is the full meaning of bread, the nurture that 'comes down from heaven and gives life to the world' (6:33). The bread that Jesus *is* is not simply a product like manna that can temporarily satisfy a physical hunger. It is food for the *healing, transformation*, and *fulfillment* of life rather than its mere continuation." Wirzba, *Food and Faith*, 206. Jesus thus constitutes the purpose of all food, and all food culminates in him.

a vision of food, thus showing Jewish-gentile relations "restored in the realm of the meal."[167] Food even displays humanity's final restoration in the Marriage Supper of the Lamb, where "a great multitude, which no one can count, from every nation and all tribes and peoples and tongues" will gather around the table at Christ's marriage feast (Rev 7:9; cf. 19:9; 22:2). So food fittingly and comprehensively tells the story of God's salvation rooted in the real world without resorting to the artifice of show business. Food comes with its own complete social imaginary that "brings together all the significant events of revelation—who God is and what he has done."[168] To describe Scripture as food thus recognizes Scripture as the life-saving narrative of God.

As God's life-saving narrative, Scripture ultimately does not call attention to itself but invites to the main meal: Jesus Christ, the bread of eternal life (cf. John 6:53–58). In other words, Scripture "effects transformation by pointing to Jesus as the only means by which fellowship with God becomes available to anyone, and beyond that, by calling into being that fellowship."[169] In John 5:39–40, Jesus rebukes the Jewish leaders: "You search the Scriptures because you think that in them you have eternal life; it is these that testify about me; and you are unwilling to come to me so that you may have life." Peterson puts it bluntly that "not everyone who gets interested in the Bible and even gets excited about the Bible wants to get involved with God."[170] To "eat" the Bible rightly, however, one must move beyond the propositions of Scripture to embrace the person of Christ revealed in Scripture. Scripture is thus not an end in itself; it is food that points to the true food and "bread of life" (John 6:35), which entails that right understanding of Scripture requires moment-by-moment dependence on Christ through prayer, dependence emphasized by people's need for food.

At the same time, food incorporates the necessity of sacrifice for salvation better than any other model. Even light does not naturally include sacrificial elements, but food makes clear that a price must be paid; food has to die for others to eat it and live. So Christ's sacrificial death, "far from being an unfortunate error or derailment of his purpose, was the willed

---

167. Radner, *A Time to Keep*, 215; cf. Acts 10:9–15; Gal 2:11–21.

168. Chan, *Spiritual Theology*, 115. The term "social imaginary" comes from Charles Taylor and consists of a complex of stories and root metaphors that shape a culture's worldview and plausibility structure. See Taylor, *A Secular Age*, 171–76.

169. Dharamraj, "On the Doctrine of Scripture," 57.

170. Peterson, *Eat This Book*, 30.

culmination of that life of self-giving for our good."[171] Similarly, Christ's word in Scripture calls all Christians to offer their lives as living and holy sacrifices for God and others (cf. Rom 12:1), which entails being a community willing to suffer to share his "words of eternal life" to the world (John 6:68).[172]

Ecclesiology

Food humbles church tradition under the primacy of Scripture. While tradition aids in understanding Scripture by showing how the previous community of eaters have digested and metabolized God's Word, they remain submissive eaters who desperately depend on that Word to enable and sustain their very lives. In no sense do they become a second locus of authority that completes or sustains the Word; rather, they always remain subject to the life-giving, inspired, necessary, sufficient, clear, and inerrant authority of the Word.[173] The church always "receives" rather than "uses" Scripture, and Scripture constitutes the church, never vice versa.[174]

Scripture thus brings together God's covenant community, and nothing draws community together like food. As Kaplan says, "Food pleasures are physical, mental, and cultural. Our tastes and enjoyments are about more than bodily urges and impulses but shared experiences and social practices."[175] Food always carries this shared and relational component, as even a newborn gets food only in relationship with the mother. So food fittingly models the nature of Scripture as a community-binding, covenant-preserving document. Eating God's Word establishes "a binding agreement, a covenant, among the eaters to abide by his word."[176]

The covenant feast, in which parties make a binding agreement by eating together, has a long and rich history in the OT.[177] The Hebrew word for

---

171. Rutledge, *The Crucifixion*, 31.

172. See Chan, *Spiritual Theology*, 113.

173. Ward claims that the authority of Scripture sums up all its attributes. See Ward, *Words of Life*, 129.

174. C. S. Lewis makes this distinction between "receiving" and "using" a text or artwork: "When we 'receive' . . . we exert our senses and imagination and various other powers according to a pattern invented by the artist. When we 'use' it we treat it as assistance for our own activities." Lewis, *An Experiment in Criticism*, 88; cf. Vanhoozer, *Drama of Doctrine*, 180.

175. Kaplan, *Food Philosophy*, 76.

176. Feeley-Harnik, *The Lord's Table*, 82.

177. Examples of covenant feasts include those between Isaac and Abimelech (Gen

covenant, *berith* (Gr. *diatheke*), could derive from *barah* meaning "to cut," *baru* meaning "to bind or bond," or another *barah* meaning "to eat." Thus,

> to set a meal before someone or to partake of a meal with them is equivalent to entering into a covenant with them.... The root idea may well be to "cut" a covenant or to break into two parts, but that has just as clear a reference to a meal, to the breaking of bread as the Hebrew idiom puts it, as to the cutting of sacrifice, and both involve the conception of covenant engagement.[178]

If *barah* means "to eat," that "would make the sacred meal the important feature of the covenant."[179] Thus food and covenant naturally go together (cf. Ps 111:5), making Scripture as food exceedingly appropriate as a model for the covenantal nature of Scripture: Scripture must be "eaten" by faith to enter into covenant with God and then continually eaten to maintain covenant fidelity. So Scripture never leaves the mouths of God's church but requires daily meditation and practice (cf. Josh 1:8; Ps 1:2).

Such practices include "*shared hospitality and table fellowship between God and his people*" that "necessarily results in and creates hospitality to others."[180] Hospitality is "the act or process whereby the identity of the stranger is transformed into that of guest,"[181] and Jesus enacts divine hospitality by providing food to the masses and observing open commensality, even with his enemies (Matt 9:10–13; Mark 2:15–17; Luke 5:29–32; 7:36–50). During his Galilean ministry, Jesus hosts a meal that feeds five thousand people (cf. Luke 9:10–17), thus demonstrating his "inclusive table, to which he invites sinners and the unclean."[182] His church, then, also should practice such welcome and hospitality, not only with its physical food but with the spiritual food of Scripture, "tangibly extending God's friendship to those who, in the eyes of others, are not righteous, have a low status, and are viewed as unworthy of friendship with God."[183] As the issue with feeding

---

26:30–31), Jacob and Laban (Gen 31:54), Jacob and Esau (Gen 32:13–21; 33:8–11), Israel's leaders and Jethro (Exod 18:12), God and Israel (Exod 24:11), the Gibeonites and Israel (Josh 9:3–15).

178. Torrance, *Atonement*, 12–13.
179. Morris, *The Apostolic Preaching of the Cross*, 67.
180. Jipp, *Saved by Faith and Hospitality*, 20, 177, emphasis his.
181. Jipp, *Saved by Faith and Hospitality*, 2.
182. Karris, *Eating Your Way through Luke's Gospel*, 52; cf. Jipp, *Saved by Faith and Hospitality*, 24–25.
183. Jipp, *Saved by Faith and Hospitality*, 23; cf. 12, 18, 20–27, 55–57, 87–93.

widows in Acts 6 makes clear, the church bears the responsibility to extend God's hospitality not only through sharing physical food but also through sharing God's Word (cf. Acts 6:4).

Jesus himself refers to the church as salt, a food preservative and flavor enhancer that carries covenantal overtones in the OT, mentioned three times (Lev 2:13; Num 18:19; 2 Chr 13:5) and twice within the Mosaic covenant. As a preservative, salt symbolizes perpetuity and durability. A "covenant of salt" thus refers to the "notion of an enduring covenant—one that *continues through the generations.*"[184] So God insists that his people remember the longevity of his covenant by seasoning every grain offering "with salt, so that the salt of the covenant of your God shall not be lacking from your grain offering" (Lev 2:13). In Num 18:19, God makes with Aaron a "covenant of salt," meaning "an unbreakable or permanent covenant."[185] Salt again appears in 2 Chr 13:5 to convey the permanence of David's dynasty: "Do you not know that the LORD God of Israel gave the rule over Israel forever to David and his sons by a covenant of salt?" The OT meaning of salt thus forms the backdrop of Jesus's words, "You are the salt of the earth" (Matt 5:13) and "Have salt in yourselves" (Mark 9:50), which may very well refer "to the covenant of salt, reminding his disciples of the importance of their loyalty and devotion to one another. This is particularly significant in light of the last part of the sentence, which says, 'and be at peace with one another' (Mark 9:50)."[186] Moreover, "the admonition in Colossians 4:6 ('Let your speech always be . . . seasoned with salt') may refer to the symbolic power of salt to create unity and harmony."[187] Christ thus could be referring to this covenantal use of salt to encourage his church to seek the unity enabled by his covenant.

These references to salt carry fruitful implications for the church, especially given that Scripture is food. As salt, the church is not the food but preserves it and enhances its flavor. Salt thus envisions the church as guarding the good deposit of God's "sound words" entrusted to it (cf. 2 Tim 1:13–14). At the same time, salt reminds the church of its new covenant with God, a covenant that is truly everlasting (cf. Isa 55:3; Jer 32:40; Ezek 37:26; Heb 13:20). So the church, as God's covenant partner, preserves the

---

184. Bernard, "A Covenant of Salt," Jewish Theological Seminary, March 27, 2020, https://www.jtsa.edu/torah/a-covenant-of-salt, emphasis his.

185. Juengst, *Breaking Bread*, 51.

186. Juengst, *Breaking Bread*, 52.

187. Juengst, *Breaking Bread*, 52.

food of God's Word in Scripture, enhances its flavor to the world by embodying its practices, and invites others to taste its life-giving goodness (cf. Heb 6:5; 1 Pet 2:3). This distinction between salt and food also highlights the church's secondary role underneath the primary role of God's Word; the Word does the work of ministering life and salvation, but the church eats, digests, metabolizes, embodies, and shares that saving Word to all.

Ultimately, the church cannot fail in this role because God's Word comes with the Holy Spirit (cf. John 6:63), who indwells and enables the church to understand the things of God (cf. 1 Cor 2:10-13). By the Spirit, the church instinctually knows—as a kind of spiritual reflex—how to digest and metabolize God's Word in Scripture, much like how the body reflexively knows how to digest and metabolize food.[188] Scripture gives believers the ability to understand it through continual reading, and this comprehension comes only because the church is "strengthened with power through [God's] Spirit in the inner man . . . able to comprehend with all the saints what is the width and length and height and depth, and to know the love of Christ" (Eph 3:16, 18-19). God's Spirit gives the church a new nature that reflexively "gets it": that knows what to do with God's Word in a mysterious yet nourishing way, just as the body mysteriously knows what to do to metabolize food.[189] As Barth says, this new nature frees the church to put her "whole joyful trust in this word and to become unreservedly obedient to what this announcement of God himself expresses about his love for the world, his people," and every individual.[190] So the Holy Spirit empowers the church to receive, digest, and exercise the teaching of Scripture so as to "live, think, and speak wholly and entirely freed from [ungodly] presuppositions . . . as a believing, loving, hoping, witness to the Word of God," Jesus Christ.[191] The

---

188. See Origen, *The Philocalia*, 12.2. Music also incorporates a level of "subconscious" power that renders instinctual response. Music can "set the mood" and affect people at subconscious levels, which Scripture also does for the church. Music thus "conveys an atmosphere" in a space. Boersma, *Violence, Hospitality, and the Cross*, 102. Both script and music form a world and atmosphere, but light and food do the same in a seemingly more real-world, survival-oriented way.

189. Of course, the interpretation and application of Scripture have their complications, complexities, and difficulties. Fundamentally, however, Christians have a Spirit-given, childlike instinct, rooted in a new nature, for metabolizing God's Word, "a sort of spiritual reflex requiring no more conscious effort on their part" so that they "know that something inside their hearts sees God." Tozer, *The Pursuit of God*, 112, 118.

190. Barth, *Evangelical Theology*, 101.

191. Barth, *Evangelical Theology*, 54-55.

Spirit not only inspires the writing of Scripture but ensures that the church will discern all "the things freely given to us by God" (1 Cor 2:12).

In addition, food envisions the church as a diverse community. All cultures eat, yet each culture prepares its food in a unique way. Similarly, the truth of Scripture stays universal and stable across all cultures, and yet the church in different cultures will express and apply that truth in legitimately contextualized ways. Such contextualization does not risk the loss of Christian identity or undermine commitment to objective truth; rather, as Migliore points out, such diverse appropriations of Scripture provide "an opportunity for understanding the message of the Bible that frequently remains hidden to those who insulate themselves" within only their own culture, which tends to limit the relevance or meaning of Scripture only to one's own personal history or locale.[192] At the same time, the church's diverse communities demonstrate a remarkable global unity in proclaiming that "Jesus Christ is alive, that we have not yet exhausted the riches of the gospel, that the Spirit brings forth new light from the Word of God, and that we are called to faithful discipleship here and now."[193] The church thus witnesses to "the continuing and surprising activity of the Spirit to deepen and correct our understanding of the message of Scripture through the voices of the people of God in different times and places," which testifies to the scriptural vision of Christ's church as a diverse "multitude that no one could count, from every nation, tribe, people and language, standing before the throne and before the Lamb" (Rev 7:9). Light, with its tendency to remain uniform, typically does not express diversity across cultures; food, however, naturally lends itself to diverse expressions across cultural contexts. Food, then, fittingly portrays the diverse ways that Scripture speaks into different cultures and manifests God's purposes in every cultural context worldwide, thus nourishing, enriching, and even at times correcting the church's understanding of God's Word.

Food also gives the church an anticipatory orientation. In the OT, God repeatedly describes the promised land as a land "flowing with milk and honey" (cf. Exod 3:8, 17; 13:5, 33:3; Lev 20:24; Num 13:27; 14:8; 16:13–14; Deut 6:3; 11:9; 26:9; 26:15; 27:3; 31:20; Josh 5:6; Jer 11:5; 32:22; Ezek 20:6; 20:15). Isaiah recasts this future hope in a vision of an eschatological feast shared not only with Israel but with all people who have covenanted with God (Isa 25:6–9), an event that Juengst describes as "a coronation feast

---

192. Migliore, *Faith Seeking Understanding*, 64.
193. Migliore, *Faith Seeking Understanding*, 64.

celebrating God's rule throughout the whole world. By recognizing God as king and by participating in table fellowship, all nations are brought into fellowship with God and with one another."[194]

In the NT, Jesus tells his disciples at the Lord's Supper that he will not drink wine again until the fullness of God's kingdom comes (cf. Matt 26:29), and Scripture ends with a wedding feast that awaits the church in the eschaton (Rev 19:6–9). Food thus helps the church ground its hope in God's promise of a blessed future, despite all the challenges the church currently faces. So the church certainly does not operate in an "empty space" but rather a starving space filled with dying sinners who desperately need the food of Scripture, which God's Spirit-filled church preserves, flavors, shares, and distributes to give life to the world. So the church is never the "main course" but rather the humble flavoring agent that preserves and commends the main course of God's Word so that hungry people can eat Jesus, the bread of life, and live forever (cf. John 6:51). The church is not the food but those who themselves need to feed on God's Word to feed others. The food model thus provides a clear answer to the all-important question many a child has asked, "Why do we go to church?" We go to church to feed on God's Word and thus draw near to God within his covenant community.[195]

The church's feeding on Scripture shapes her identity. As Brillat-Savarin says, "Tell me what you eat, and I shall tell you what you are," which also holds true for people who eat God's words in Scripture.[196] People who eat Scripture come to embody its message, especially concerning God's kindness and severity. So just as food forms the body, Scripture forms the church into a letter of Christ "written not with ink but with the Spirit of the living God, not on tablets of stone but on tablets of human hearts" (2 Cor 3:3), a living letter that testifies not only to God's mercy and grace but also to his wrath and judgment on sin.

---

194. Juengst, *Breaking Bread*, 91–92.

195 A child might reply, "Why can't we feed on the Bible at home, as a family? Why do we need to go to church for it? After all, we don't have to go to a restaurant to eat. We can eat at home." My response would be, "It is true that we can eat the Bible at home, but eating the Bible involves not just taking it in but exercising it so as to be healthy. If we exercise the words of the Bible, it instructs us to participate in the church body for a healthy spiritual diet. So if we claim to eat the Bible's words at home and not at church, it's doubtful we're really eating the Bible's words at home."

196. Brillat-Savarin, *The Physiology of Taste*, 15.

Eat the Bible

Practical Fruitfulness

Faith

Food renders faith better than the other models. While the score and script models call for concrete action through creative improvisation and noncoercive persuasion to respond to God's word in Scripture, they fall short in capturing the necessity, universality, and truth of Scripture. By promoting improvisation in particular, these models tend to encourage faith in one's own creative abilities rather than the sufficient enablement of Scripture, which can lead to merit-based rather than grace-based motivations for behavior. These models also tend to narrow the function of Scripture only to that of instruction while missing its crucial, antecedent function of nourishment and sustenance. While the model of light avoids these implications of merit-based salvation, stressing instead the need to depend continually on the enablement of Scripture, light falls short of portraying faith as embodied and lived, not just cognitively accepted.

The food model, however, robustly nurtures faith as an embodied practice while strengthening the weaknesses of the other models. First, food renders faith as full dependence on the sufficiency of Scripture, not on one's performance. As food, Scripture requires that one's existence be "oriented to and kept open by God's promise of abundant and abiding life that . . . can only be received as a gift again and again."[197] One vitally depends on God's continual gift of food, both physical food and the food of his Word. Jesus teaches such dependence in his model prayer "Give us this day our daily bread" (Matt 6:11). This prayer recognizes that one's life and well-being are "not [one's] own, but are merely derived from the being of God."[198] Scripture as food thus promotes the practice of desperate and ongoing dependence on God's sustaining Word, which issues in the daily intake and exercise of that Word accompanied by thankful, humble, and expectant prayer. In these ways, the food model renders faith as continual reliance on God's sufficient power through Scripture, placing one's trust not in oneself but in God's Word that will never pass away but unfailingly accomplish all that God purposes (cf. Matt 24:35; Isa 55:11).

Second, food stresses faith as grace-based, not merit-based. Like swallowing food, faith is trust in another's ability, not in one's own. Faith trustingly swallows God's provision of his Word, thus finding that Scripture, as

---

197. Migliore, *Faith Seeking Understanding*, 152.
198. Davison, *Participation in God*, 70; cf. Wirzba, *Food and Faith*, 167.

spiritual food, is the *source* of one's theological energy, not just the *space* in which to create one's own formulations or the blind *stuff* one uses to build whatever systems one wants. Rather, God's Word carries God's agency; it always succeeds in the thing for which he sends it (cf. Isa 55:11). Jesus likens this Word to seed sown on different soils (Matt 13:3–23); the Word acts within people in ways beyond their control. It implants itself in their hearts and saves them (Jas 1:21), just as ingested food sustains life. Like food, Scripture graciously effects health in the mind, body, and soul of the one who swallows it in faith (cf. 1 Thess 2:13). People do not gain merit for eating; they simply must eat to survive. Just as they must eat to live, they must believe in the Lord Jesus to be saved (cf. Acts 16:31; cf. Rom 10:13). This immediacy in salvation yields thankfulness and peace as people simply entrust their lives to God's unmerited grace revealed through Scripture, no matter their merits or demerits.

Such merit-free salvation proves especially good news to people who live with physical, mental, or social disabilities that impair them from playing a score, performing a script, or even seeing light. Food commends faith as meritless participation; it precludes any merit-based system while rightly portraying faith as surrender of one's life to God by swallowing his Word and letting it shape one's life. Food thus highlights human weakness and neediness while exalting God's grace and enablement; therefore, no one can boast (cf. Eph 2:8–9). Food also renders faith in such a way that everything people do is only what God enables since he provides the food that empowers the ability to do any work at all. Food thus eliminates all pride and humbles all human achievement, unlike music and theater, which tend to foster pride in the best and most recognized celebrity performers. In short, food forms eaters, not celebrities, and humbles rather than puffs up.

Third, faith entails a choice: people must choose to swallow or not. They must appropriate those kernels of spiritual energy. To do them good, the Word must not stay external or theoretical; rather, they must open their mouths wide, that God may fill them (cf. Ps 81:10). In other words, they must make time to open and hear Scripture. They must create the space to eat a spiritual meal of listening carefully to God's words. They must assimilate those words into their being to live and participate in God's salvific agency throughout the world. This assimilation means, in Peterson's words, "letting Another have a say in everything we are saying and doing. It is as easy as that. And as hard."[199] Thus Scripture cannot remain merely informa-

---

199. Peterson, *Eat This Book*, xii.

tional but become "'incardiate,' transform[ing] the one taking it to heart."[200] Food also depicts faith as having an individual, volitional component, since no one can eat for another; each must eat for him or herself. At the same time, food reveals faith as having a communal component. Just as food draws community together to eat, Scripture draws the church community together to feast on God's Word.

Food thus portrays faith as intensely personal. People can study food all they want, but if they do not eat, they die. In the same way, Scripture can and should be studied with historical-critical, grammatical, literary, and theological methods, but such study must not stay theoretical but become personal because if people do not eat God's Word, they die. So the church must become interested not just "in knowing more but in becoming more,"[201] since it is entirely possible "to come to the Bible in total sincerity, responding to the intellectual challenge it gives, or for the moral guidance it offers, or for the spiritual uplift it provides, and not in any way deal with a personally revealing God who has personal designs on you."[202] People can approach Scripture as a rewarding science, but their interest in Scripture must not stop there lest they spiritually starve to death. Faith in Scripture means they must each ingest the Bible as their spiritual food, choosing to take in its "personally revealing God who has personal designs" on their lives.

Such personal faith entails intimacy. Faith, understood as swallowing God's Word in Scripture, engages in a profoundly intimate encounter with God. Barth describes his own unsettlingly intimate—even risky—encounter with Scripture:

> Certainly, he never knew beforehand what a risk he was taking, and he will certainly never fully grasp this risk. But at any rate he has taken this step. He is a theologian because he finds himself confronted by this object. . . . This object [that is God] disturbs him—and not merely from afar, the way a lightning flash on the horizon might disturb one. This object seeks him out and finds him precisely where he stands, and it is just *there* that this object has already sought and found him. *It met, encountered, and challenged him.* It invaded, surprised, and captured him. It assumed control over him.[203]

---

200. Dharamraj, "On the Doctrine of Scripture," 56.
201. Peterson, *Eat This Book*, 59.
202. Peterson, *Eat This Book*, 30.
203. Barth, *Evangelical Theology*, 75–76, emphasis his.

In other words, experiencing Scripture proves uncomfortably personal. It involves risk, much like the risk involved in putting food in one's mouth and swallowing it.[204] Such risk-taking "requires trust in others," and "trust always involves the risk of dangers."[205] Just as eating food means one cannot remain detached from the object that one eats, one's encounter with God through Scripture does not allow one to remain detached, but Scripture "invades" and compels the whole person's devotion to God's control and concerns, involving nothing less than "*the whole man. It concerns even what is most private in the private life.*"[206] So food informs the nature of faith as "putting one's life in God's hands." Food highlights the risk involved in this all-too-personal encounter with the living God; yet food also makes clear that the risk, once taken, gives way to deeply satisfying devotion that lives on God's sustaining sufficiency. Therefore, a Christian "may and should be a pleased or satisfied man . . . who also spreads satisfaction and pleasure throughout the community and world."[207] In short, faith is like *swallowing*: Intimately swallowing God's Word, living on it, being satisfied by it, and helping others be satisfied by it.[208]

Fourth, food insists on faith's necessity and priority as nourishment before action. As Raymond Boisvert says, "I eat, therefore I think."[209] In other words, people must incorporate the saving nourishment of Scripture through faith before they can take any other action, since "without faith it is impossible to please God" (Heb 11:16).[210] While not everyone likes music (surprisingly), and not everyone goes to the theater, everyone *must* eat.

---

204. Kaplan observes that such risk "involves partial, incomplete knowledge: enough is known about a situation to know that not enough is known about its probable outcome." Kaplan, "Introduction," 5. At the same time, "risk taking often requires trust in others; trust always involves the risk of dangers. . . . Food consumption is an exercise in the epistemology of trust." Kaplan, "Introduction," 5–6.

205. Kaplan, "Introduction," 5.

206. Barth, *Evangelical Theology*, 84; cf. Kaplan, "Introduction," 6.

207. Barth, *Evangelical Theology*, 95.

208. Such intimacy in *swallowing* the word also informs the Christian's union with Christ and his statement that "apart from me you can do nothing" (John 15:5). Food makes clear that at no point is faithfulness to God self-sustained; it is enabled by Christ, who, like food, is united to believers and strengthens them to live the Christian life.

209. Boisvert, *I Eat, Therefore I Think*, front cover.

210. Dawn points out that faith also plays an epistemically prior role in hermeneutics: "Do you think the people around Isaiah understood Isaiah? Did the folks with Jesus understand Jesus? Isn't the gap rather between those who believe and those who don't?" Dawn, "Practiced Theology–Lived Spirituality," 145.

As people's stomachs need food to live, so their souls need God's Word to live. The Word is not an optional add-on to one's day but "the fundamental source of life itself," as "God's commandments are God's enablements."[211] Food keeps the people alive. In the same way, Scripture as food requires people's real faith, which means "complete dependence on the word of God and God's ability and faithfulness to provide our essential needs."[212] This dependence implies that one's initial choice to eat Scripture does not stop there but issues in a life of continual eating. Just as people never outgrow their need for food, believers never outgrow their dependence on God's Word. Daily and repeatedly, they must satisfy their spiritual hunger by continually listening to, meditating on, and living out Scripture, just as they satisfy their physical hunger by eating food. This continual dependence then leads to growth in sanctification as they repeatedly turn away from eating poisonous idols to be "constantly nourished on the words of the faith and of the sound doctrine" (1 Tim 4:6). Food thus captures not only the instantaneous salvation of justification by faith but also the ongoing process of sanctification as believers repeatedly return to intake and exercise God's Word for spiritual growth. When they first have faith and "swallow" God's Word in the gospel, it immediately saves them, but they never just eat once; they must continue to eat and be transformed by that Word for the rest of their lives.

Fifth, food includes dangers that threaten faith. The models of score and script do not adequately account for the deceptiveness of heresy, which fatally substitutes the real thing with a fake. Even light does not readily portray the many forms that heresy might take since nothing can look like light without being light. With food, however, harmful substitutes abound: fast food, junk food, even poison. In fact, one might even view heresy as trans-fats: manmade substitutes that taste great but will kill a person over time. Food thus comes with an important sense of particularity in that what people eat matters, and the food they choose can either kill them or give them life. In this way, food precludes the idea that all purported claims to truth are as good as each other because people must eat from the right source of Scripture, the written Word of God, to have life. Some people's spiritual diet consists only of books and sermons on theology or Christian living that rarely, if ever, refer to the Bible, and some so-called "spiritual" books the apostle Paul would call "doctrines of demons" (1 Tim 4:1). Food

---

211. Christensen, *Deuteronomy 1:1—21:9*, 174.
212. Christensen, *Deuteronomy 1:1—21:9*, 175.

thus stresses the need for repentance and conversion, turning away from poisonous food to eat the healthy food of God's Word. Food also insists on continual growth in discernment and holiness since a small bit of poison taints the purity of otherwise good food and makes a healthy meal fatal, in the same way that a little heresy can entirely ruin good doctrine. So a healthy spiritual diet will accept no substitutes but return repeatedly and primarily to eat from the God-given source of spiritual health: the Bible, the written Word of God.

Sixth, food speaks to the universality of faith. All need the Bible, including children and adults. Food helps to explain how both can approach Scripture with confidence that God will speak to them. As milk, Scripture can be understood by a child. As meat, Scripture never will be exhausted by adults, no matter how advanced their biblical and theological training (cf. 1 Pet 2:2; 1 Cor 3:2). May the church never scare her children away from reading Scripture because of overcomplicated hermeneutical rules or methods. Instead, like the children to St. Augustine, let her always encourage whoever will to "Pick up and read! Pick up and read!"[213] Pastors should encourage their congregations to do and then decipher, to listen constantly to the Bible and grow in skill in interpreting it over time.

Seventh, faith, like food, is mundane. Skill in reading Scripture grows through daily, mundane routine. As Chan suggests, "If our aim is to go beyond acquiring facts to letting the truth speak to us, then we need to read slowly, savoring every word, mulling over it and digesting it, so that it begins to affect the heart deeply."[214] This daily routine should include a complete diet of Scripture that takes in the "less palatable," "negative," or "boring" parts of the Bible. Physically, one cannot live on bread alone but also on vegetables, fruits, and proteins to have a healthy, balanced diet. Similarly, the Bible is chock-full of different genres necessary to provide for the spiritual health of God's church. The church should make sure its diet of Scripture includes ingredients from all these to foster the full health of its members. Not everybody likes every food group; many children do not like Brussels sprouts or broccoli, but parents nonetheless make them eat these vegetables for nutritional value. In the same way, not every genre or portion of the Bible is fun to eat—such as genealogies, law codes, and judgments—but they are good for people to read, even though their spiritual

---

213. Augustine, *Confessions*, 152. Chan suggests, "At the beginning be concerned with reading it diligently; understanding will come later." Chan, *Spiritual Theology*, 171.

214. Chan, *Spiritual Theology*, 163.

value may not be readily apparent. So one must eat a balanced diet, the whole Bible, not just the parts one tends to like. Not everything in the Bible is immediately exciting, but all of it is profitable and necessary for spiritual life and growth as the Christian longs daily for God's "habitual presence."[215] The habitual reading of Scripture thus becomes "a traditioning process.... It is in reading and listening that the Word addresses us afresh and draws us into a living relationship with God and with one another. This is the basic theology of Scripture reading."[216] This daily routine of living by faith thus walks with God through the many mundane moments of life and guards against seeking God only through spectacular and emotional events. Food does allow for a spectacular or exceptional feast from time to time, but the church must not get caught up in the spectacularism of this age. Eating sometimes proves mundane or boring but always necessary.

Eighth, food captures both the "gut-level necessity" and the daily delight of faith.[217] Joy accompanies hearing from God, engaging with God, and tasting the sweetness of his Scripture (cf. Ps 119:103). The food model captures this joy of access to God but also grave danger since those who refuse to eat will not live eternally but die eternally. Food thus conveys the necessity of faith as the linchpin to either God's kindness or severity (cf. Rom 11:22). So sinners—who have forsaken God, "the fountain of living waters, to hew for themselves cisterns, broken cisterns that can hold no water" (Jer 2:13)—should come to Christ not just for superficial help or aesthetic reflection but for desperate salvation. Faith means to swallow God's Word for one's very survival, since to lack God's Word brings the horror of starvation and death. Food thus shows that participation in faith is mandatory; just as one must eat or die, one must swallow God's words or perish.

Ninth, food depicts faith as embodied action, not merely intellectual assent. In stark contrast to gnostic misconceptions of the material body as evil or a prison that the soul must escape, Scripture presents an emphatically positive view of the body as God's good gift and the site of incarnate delight, made especially clear in God's gift of food (cf. Gen 1:29; 9:3). As Wirzba says, food is God's visceral way of saying "I love you,"[218] and "the most prominent image used in Scripture for the eschaton is that of a great banquet, a eucharistic feast of carnal delight. Not a whiff of disembodied or

---

215. Allen, *Spiritual Theology*, 2.
216. Chan, *Spiritual Theology*, 116.
217. Peterson, *Eat This Book*, 21.
218. Wirzba, *Food and Faith*, xii; cf. 1 Cor 6:13–14.

ghostly existence is contained in that image."[219] So God creates and approves of the body, and he himself becomes embodied through the incarnation of Jesus Christ (John 1:14). It should come as no surprise, then, that God means for faith to be embodied and lived, not just mentally accepted. As both Jesus and James make clear, faith includes doing God's will since "faith without deeds is worthless" (Jas 2:20; cf. John 4:34), and food construes faith as embodied obedience rather than abstract agreement. As Peterson notes, eating Scripture

> takes it all in, assimilating it into the tissues of our lives. Readers become what they read. If Holy Scripture is to be something other than mere gossip about God, it must be internalized. Most of us have opinions about God that we are not hesitant to voice. But just because a conversation (or sermon or lecture) has the word "God" in it, does not qualify it as true. The angel does not instruct St. John to pass on information about God: he commands him to assimilate the word of God so that when he does speak it will express itself artlessly in his syntax just as the food we eat, when we are healthy, is unconsciously assimilated into our nerves and muscles and put to work in speech and action.[220]

In other words, the food model calls for faith that embodies God's Word by first swallowing, internalizing, and assimilating it, which then enables one to exercise it through obedient speech and action. While the score and script models depict an embodied faith better than light, food gives the most complete picture of faith by not skipping straight to performance but insisting on the crucial first step of drawing nourishment from Scripture, construing faith as fully embodied while balancing output with intake, thus guarding against both ministerial laziness and burnout.

So faith includes not only intake but also exercise. This crucial balance of intake and exercise of Scripture takes seriously James's injunction to become "doers of the word, and not merely hearers who delude themselves" (Jas 1:22). Food carries an inherent balance between intake and expense, lest the eater become unhealthy; and to be spiritually healthy, people must exercise the Word and not just hear it.

Such balance avoids spiritual anorexia, obesity, and bulimia. Spiritual anorexia happens when people do not take in the Word at all. Spiritual obesity occurs when people take in the Word but do not obey it or put it to

---

219. Corcoran, *Rethinking Human Nature*, 15; cf. 97.
220. Peterson, *Eat This Book*, 20–21.

EAT THE BIBLE

action. Spiritual bulimia results when Christians take in Scripture only to "vomit" it out at others in the name of ministry rather than metabolizing that Scripture for themselves, such as pastors who study Scripture only to write sermons while failing to apply these truths in their own lives. Just as diet must go with exercise to be physically healthy, hearing the Word must go with doing it to be spiritually healthy. So faith, according to food, is not only swallowing the Word of God but *doing* it, which involves surrender to its truth, personal risk, spiritual growth and intimacy, and embodied intake and exercise.

Hope

The food model kindles real and universal hope better than the other models. While the score and script models can inspire a feeling of hope by imagining a better or more beautiful world, they remain limited by their distance from daily life and their subtle implication that the biblical world differs from the real one. They also tend to ground hope only in spectacular experiences or in human performance, which—given human sinfulness—offers no hope at all.

The light model avoids these weaknesses and seems a natural model of hope since it signals the end of darkness. For example, hopeful phrases tend to employ light, such as "light at the end of the tunnel" and "I see the light." Light fails, however, to be entirely universal since not all people can see light, and those born with this handicap may find themselves unable to grasp the hope the model seeks to offer.

The food model, however, offers universal, real-world hope that rests in God, not humanity. Food insists that the crucial matter is not entertaining people but feeding them so that they can live. Theater and music aim at evoking imaginative emotion and pathos, but food provides hope of survival in the face of death and mortality. Food thus provides real, life-saving hope as seen in refugee ministries. In this way, the food model engages directly with reality and provides such solid hope to people who take in its message of the real God who actually saves. Scripture as food thus grounds hope in God's objective truth that does not change regardless of human belief or opinion. No matter how one feels about food, its truth is unavoidable: one must eat it or die. Scripture as food, then, proclaims most clearly that the only hope comes from ingesting God's Word and swallowing it by faith. All must take it in to live, which testifies to the universality of food. Absolutely everyone eats, but the blind cannot see light. Food thus speaks hope to absolutely everyone, using the most universal and accessible framework to communicate the hope of eternal life found in eating Scripture. Moreover, food expresses the hope of Scripture in terms of this real-world system, not some other world posited by theater or imagination.

Hope grows even during the daily grind of life, not just the spectacular events that are few and far between. Through the food of his Word, God provides daily sustenance in his hope, which calls for the needed practice of memorization. As Chan urges,

> we need to recover the lost art of memorizing Scripture. Once reading and listening to Scripture was accompanied by memorizing and reciting Scripture.... Memorization was very much the foundation of learning in an oral-aural culture. But in a world where information can be recalled almost instantly and just as quickly become obsolete, memorization has become a lost art.... In its place are bits and pieces of the story distilled into simplistic principles and formulas for meeting life's various exigencies: the four spiritual laws for becoming a Christian, five biblical keys to a successful marriage and so on.[221]

While the four spiritual laws, five biblical keys, and so on may serve as effective tools for evangelism or introductory "snacks" of Scripture, they cannot substitute for the solid hope of digesting full meals of memorizing large portions of God's Word. The "fast food" of a quick verse here and there will not do; people must chew on and memorize meaty sections of Scripture to metabolize its hope. By thus abiding in God's Word, they become set free by its hope-giving truth (cf. John 8:31–32). Scripture provides real and stable hope that rests not on human performance or ability but on God's immutable character and the assurance of his salvation (cf. Ps 112:8). Jesus is the healthy food amidst the junk food of the world's "varied and strange teachings" (Heb 13:8–9). By rooting believers firmly and daily in the unfailing ability of Christ (cf. Heb 4:15), Scripture enables the ability to stay stable and steadfast in hope, unshaken by the instability of this fallen world (cf. Col 1:23; Eph 4:14; Jas 1:6).

This unshakable hope grows through daily discipline and ritual. Food entails a daily ritual of eating and thus captures daily routine and regularity better than the other models. As creatures of habit, people practice hope by eating Scripture as a daily routine, not just in spurts or sporadic

---

221. Chan, *Spiritual Theology*, 118.

performances. Instead, hope increases steadily through the consistent, mundane discipline of taking in Scripture as one's daily bread. Scripture as food thus informs the hope that comes from persistent spiritual formation. Whereas the performance of a score or script may remain just an external role people put on from time to time, and light tends to remain external as well, food gets into people constantly, transforming them from the inside and shaping them in ways they may not have intended or realized. In the same way, Scripture gets inside people and transforms them over time through a mysterious process that they may not yet understand (cf. Luke 13:18–21). Just as they may not fully understand the process of digestion and metabolism, the food of Scripture requires patience and endurance in the hope it provides.

Scripture requires exercise, just like food. If people eat but do not exercise, they grow obese and unhealthy. They must not only consume food but "do the will of him" who gives the food (John 4:34). Food conveys this necessary balance better than other models, which informs how hope grows and strengthens through the daily rhythms of intake and exercise of Scripture. Exercising the Scripture eaten thus produces character, and character produces hope, hope that "does not disappoint, because the love of God has been poured out within our hearts through the Holy Spirit who was given to us" (Rom 5:4–5). The Spirit, through Scripture, acts like water to the soul, refreshing the Christian in God's love, comfort, and hope through even the hardest of times (2 Cor 1:3–11). The food model thus conveys hope even amid darkness, where there is no light; even in those situations, the hope of Scripture sustains Christians' lives with God's provision of his Word. The regularity of food also denotes Scripture as hope for all times, good and bad, not only in moments of crisis or emergency. Scripture as food fosters the practice of hope on a daily basis.

As food, Scripture also carries an anticipatory function, pointing to the hope of a final, heavenly banquet: the Marriage Supper of the Lamb (Rev 19:6–9). The food model thus entails a hope that lasts to the end of time. While theater and music grow quickly outdated, the hope provided by food remains utterly relevant forever, which speaks to God's provision of lasting hope through Scripture. Such hope never ceases. As people feed on its "words of eternal life" (John 6:68), they can only grow in hope since they "will not die but live, and tell of the works of the Lord," all the way to the eschaton. So hope, according to Scripture as food, is based in the real world, rests in God, grows daily, and lasts till the very end.

Love

When asked about the greatest commandment in God's law, Jesus replies, "'You shall love the Lord your God with all your heart, and with all your soul, and with all your mind.' This is the great and foremost commandment. The second is like it, 'You shall love your neighbor as yourself.' On these two commandments depend the whole Law and the Prophets" (Matt 22:37–40). Scripture as food cultivates this holistic love for God and neighbor more accessibly and tangibly than the other models.

While Scripture as a script or score communicates God's love as noncoercive and invites the audience to participate in the drama or music of divine love, the entertainment context of these models may relegate God's love to the realm of the ideal and not the real. This distance from the real world may mythologize God's love as utopian fantasy rather than insist on its actuality in Christ's historical death and resurrection (cf. Rom 5:8; 1 Cor 15:17). Moreover, the score and script models easily construe love as merely an emotion rather than active commitment and covenantal fidelity, and love in music and theater tend to stay limited to people who appreciate the art form rather than embracing everyone in that love.

Light connects to love by symbolizing moral action that overcomes the darkness of corruption, and the conceptual connection between light and illumination by the Holy Spirit reflects how the Spirit loves readers by disclosing the meaning of Scripture to them. Yet light tends to remain disembodied and cognitive, which may mischaracterize God's love as merely abstract or intellectual rather than embodied and tangible. Through this philosophical lens, light also tends to stay singular rather than communal, stressing individual enlightenment rather than communal engagement and interaction. Scripture then becomes merely the medium of propositions about God's love rather than the vital provision of his love that saves lives, and Bible study can become dry, intellectual exercises that fail to translate to loving action in everyday life.

Scripture as food, however, treats Bible study as life-giving and hunger-satisfying feasts of God's Word that empower active love for God and others. People often show love by providing food, and food identifies Scripture as God's love in feeding people's acute spiritual hunger. Without this food, they would die. Food thus removes the danger of treating God's love as mere fantasy or emotion. In providing Scripture, God demonstrates his intimate concern for people's most urgent needs in the real world. Since food also plays a covenantal function of binding two parties in agreement, such that even the Hebrew word for covenant, *berith*, could derive from *barah*, meaning "to eat,"[222] eating God's Word constitutes "a binding agreement, a covenant, among the eaters to abide by his word."[223] Scripture as food thus calls for active commitment and covenant fidelity inherent in a loving relationship with God, making clear that love is much more than an emotion but an ongoing commitment between God and his people.

Food also invites all people to have a seat at God's table rather than just those interested in a certain hobby or art form; food is love that everyone understands and needs. So food encompasses love from God, for God, and for others in the most universally accessible and visceral way. Food is love *experienced*, which makes the food of Scripture the way to experience God's love daily. God's love through Scripture thus becomes, to borrow Søren Kierkegaard's words, not just "a doctrine, but an existential communication."[224] Participating in God's love means to receive the food of his Scripture and then share that food with others for their life, friendship, and joy.

Food also highlights the deep intimacy of God's love, entailing the trust, commitment, and surrender that God requires to know him. Food cannot remain a detached, disinterested, or abstract issue; to engage with food means to eat it, and eating requires the risk of coming up close, putting it in one's mouth, and swallowing it. In the same way, God's loving provision of Scripture as food means that one cannot receive it from a distance but only up close; to experience God's love, his Word must be "very near you . . . in your mouth and in your heart so you may obey it" (Deut 30:14; cf. Rom 10:8). Scripture as food thus reflects God's heart to abide close to his people and erases the artificial distance or "steep learning curve" implied by other models like the script, score, or light. Rather than seeing God from a distance, food speaks of God *in* us, closer than our skin, and empowering our life such that "in him we live and move and have our being" (Acts 17:28). Eating God's Word thus participates in God's intimate love at the visceral, gut level so that "it is God who is at work in [us], both to will and to work for his good pleasure" (Phil 2:13). Through his Scripture as food, God's love literally enters the bones and sinews of people's bodies and transforms them from the inside into his "image from glory to glory" (2 Cor 3:18). God, through Scripture, thus shapes people into his holy image over time.

222. See Torrance, *Atonement*, 12–13.
223. Feeley-Harnik, *The Lord's Table*, 82.
224. Kierkegaard, *Concluding Unscientific Postscript*, 339.

Scripture as food also entails love in community better than the other models. Nothing invites community like food, and nothing brings together the church community like Scripture. As the church gathers regularly, she partakes of the covenant meal of God's Word to submit to her Lord's leadership, receive his good will, and be satisfied by his presence. The food model encompasses this participation, satisfaction, and surrender to Christ, as his Word binds together his covenant community. Since Christ remains the host of his banquet, the congregation must submit to his house rules and intentions stated in Scripture. Scripture as food thus becomes a way for the church to image God's unifying love in a corporate manner. Not only does the church gather regularly to observe the Lord's Supper and generously share their meals with anyone in need (cf. Acts 2:45–46; 6:1), but they invite all to partake in the most necessary food of God's Word (cf. Luke 10:42; Acts 6:2, 4). As Migliore observes, living in love means to be "created for life in community with others. . . . As the eternal triune love makes room for others, so human beings in the image of God are called to discover true personhood in relationship with others."[225] At the same time, this community hospitably invites others to join the table, since, at its best, "eating is a sharing and welcoming movement that makes room for others. Insofar as people learn to live in hospitable ways with each other and within their places, they participate in the eternal, hospitable ways of God that daily create, sustain, and fulfill life."[226] In the same way, sharing the food of Scripture images God's love by drawing together a community that shares in God's kindness, generosity, enjoyment, and cooperation.

Living life as God's community thus helps to avoid insularity, parochialism, and selfishness. The church images God by practicing generous hospitality toward others in need, especially when that need is food (Jas 2:15–17; Matt 25:35; 1 John 3:17). Providing food "is just where churches have most frequently expressed their ministries: soup kitchens, basement meals, celebrations, and, of course, peculiar liturgical actions."[227] In the same concrete way, the church serves all people the food of Scripture to show God's hospitality, proclaiming his universal invitation to "Come, buy and eat . . . without money and without cost" (Isa 55:1).

Food also entails a healthy balance between self-care and care for others. Reflecting Jesus's command "You shall love your neighbor as yourself"

---

225. Migliore, *Faith Seeking Understanding*, 149, 151.
226. Wirzba, *Food and Faith*, xi.
227. Radner, *A Time to Keep*, 212.

(Mark 12:31), the food model calls for "self-love [as] the basis of love for one's neighbor. We are to love our neighbor with the same degree of zeal and consistency with which we love ourselves. And since there is no practical limit to the claims of self-love, there is no practical limit to our duty toward a neighbor."[228] One first must eat to help others eat, and the same goes for Scripture: one must feed on Scripture regularly as much as seek to feed others. Food thus calls for self-care in maintaining one's regular diet of God's Word without entailing any merit or pride since one simply must eat to live. At the same time, such self-care does not focus on the self but on God and his Word; the Christian recognizes that all power to love others comes only from God, who provides his sufficient Word as food out of his love for all people. So Scripture as food not only humbles all people with their dependence on God's Word, but it also safeguards gospel ministers with the reality that they themselves must be nourished by God's Word as they nourish others.

Through this balance of self-care and community care, the food model helps to correct the imbalance that can happen when individual ministers nourish only themselves (leading to spiritual gluttony) or when they nourish others but not themselves (leading to weakness and burnout). The model therefore comes with built-in responsibilities to God, oneself, and others regarding eating and sharing Scripture as spiritual food. These responsibilities prove especially crucial for pastors, but they apply to all believers since pharisaical pride or hypocrisy can arise when one does not digest the Word for oneself before trying to help others. At the same time, food reminds people of their shared need as a community; it speaks to their intimate and interdependent connections to others since to eat "is to know that we are bound to others in a shared and common fate. For our shared fate to be good and beautiful, we must learn to cultivate the forms of fidelity that promote mutual nurture and wellbeing."[229] In other words, one should not feed only oneself but love others by nurturing their well-being with the food of God's Word. This others-oriented concern means that Scripture should be read and interpreted together with God's community so that the church ingests, metabolizes, and practices God's love together.

Furthermore, the food model readjusts spiritual expectations and reinforces that "love is patient" (1 Cor 13:4). Food nourishes people over time through regular feeding, and change often does not happen right away. In

---

228. Carnell, "Love," 333.
229. Wirzba, *Food and Faith*, xvi.

the same way, growth in God's love through Scripture proves a long-term process. Christians should not give up meeting together but continually encourage one another, especially with God's love in Scripture (cf. Heb 10:25). In short, Scripture as food depicts love as a way of life.

As food always remains a pressing moral issue, the food model also entails the ethical function of Scripture by forming holy readers in a holy community. First and foremost, Scripture presupposes moral faithfulness to God, who makes "himself known to us as the faithful Lord of the covenant."[230] As food, Scripture continually reminds people of God's loving provision for their lives as the source of their survival and joy. Scripture also binds the covenant community together under its loving Lord, who not only provides food but is the food that feeds his people eternally (cf. John 6:35–38). So the food model captures the need for personal holiness since even a little poison makes a whole dish fatal. In other words, a little heresy can corrupt otherwise good doctrine, so Christians should accept no substitutes to Scripture and beware of false teachings that can harm their digestion of Scripture. As a community bound to covenant fidelity under God's loving reign, the church should remain a word-saturated culture, fed and shaped by God's Word in Scripture rather than social media, television, movies, other books. At the same time, the church should remain a diverse community that invites and listens to all voices around the table, ready

> at all times to understand the other person's point of view, to regard them in Christ, to listen to what Christ has to say to us through them, and to rethink our own views in the light of what we thus learn. The Christian way of thinking is always open to the thinking of other Christians, and is always ready to repent, to revise and reconstruct its own ways in order to become more and more conformable to Christ.[231]

In other words, Christians should remain open to how other Christians, especially those from other cultures, digest and apply Scripture in other contexts since such openness might glean wisdom and insight for applying Scripture to their own context.

Such diverse, communal feedings of God's Word should ensure that no member of Christ's body goes hungry but experiences God's love. After all, babies cannot feed themselves milk but require extra help. Similarly, new Christians require much more attention and instruction in reading

---

230. Ward, *Words of Life*, 134.
231. Torrance, *Atonement*, 377.

and interpreting Scripture from more mature Christians. In these ways, the community shows love even to its most vulnerable members. Unlike the contexts of a concert or theater, which tend to direct people's love mostly toward the music, the art form, or the performers on stage, food spreads the love equally and directly to all people since everyone's life depends on eating. Even when an audience does show love to actors or musicians, such love may treat them as merely objects of self-gratification rather than real people; but serving food shows love by providing persons with their basic need.

Food is thus a more universal and tactile symbol of love's bond within a community and makes central Jesus's golden rule of love: "Treat others the same way you want them to treat you" (Luke 6:31). Jesus, quoting Prov 25:21, even ties such love to providing food for one's enemy: "But if your enemy is hungry, feed him, and if he is thirsty, give him a drink; for in so doing you will heap burning coals on his head" (Rom 12:20). So food not only conveys love but also carries ethical force that can shame enemies into understanding God's love for them. Food makes clear how to love as one needs to be loved, and it does so more universally, deeply, and viscerally than any other model, even light. So while theater and music tend to operate only among friends, Jesus's use of food entails forgiveness and reconciliation even with enemies around his table. Food also informs the nature of Scripture as universally loving, viscerally tangible, and urgently necessary for survival, and Scripture even provides a way for enemies to reconcile since it leads people to the ultimate reconciler and covenantal bread, Jesus Christ.

Such reconciliation around God's table reflects in Jesus's practice of open commensality. As Jesus eats with "tax collectors and sinners" (Matt 9:10–11; 11:19; Mark 2:16; Luke 5:29; 15:1–2), he enacts one "of the most important consequences of the change in the role of the Law [in] that Jewish Christians could eat with gentile Christians without defilement. . . . This removal of all barriers between Jew and gentile has been called a 'sociological miracle.'"[232] This "sociological miracle" appears again in Peter's rooftop vision and subsequent welcome of the gentile Cornelius (cf. Acts 10:9–16), and Paul also makes this miracle central to living out the gospel (cf. Gal 3:27–28). By inviting all to God's table, then, Jesus has broken down all social division between peoples and given them "an essential unity in Christ."[233] The food of Scripture draws together this essentially united yet

---

232. Allen, *Spiritual Theology*, 40.
233. Allen, *Spiritual Theology*, 40.

diverse community from all over the world, inviting all to join in God's hospitality "without money and without cost" (Isa 55:1).

So the food model includes an undeniable evangelistic thrust as well. Just as Christ describes his death on the cross as both giving his flesh as bread for the world (cf. John 6:51) and drawing all people to himself (cf. John 12:32), his Scripture draws people to constitute God's redeemed community until heaven celebrates "a great multitude, which no one can count, from every nation and all tribes and peoples and tongues" (Rev 7:9a) gathered around the table at Christ's marriage feast (cf. Rev 19:9; cf. Matt 8:11). So Scripture as food makes clear that God means for his Word to spread to all people, not create sectarian cliques that hoard the food for themselves.[234]

Food also speaks to the urgency of the evangelistic mission. It recognizes that hunger remains a reality from which many die every day, and Scripture as food recognizes that reality of those spiritually starving to death from lack of the life-giving and life-sustaining food that is God's Word (cf. Amos 8:11-13). Food thus envisions the church as a spiritual food bank for all, feeding all people the "words of eternal life" (John 6:68). This vision guards the church from becoming a "country club" for its members, closed off to the rest of the world, since Scripture, like food, should not remain merely insular, parochial, tribal, or even denominational but inviting, universal, and bonding, even toward one's former enemies. Food also makes clear that this invitation must remain *inviting*; the church cannot force-feed the food to people since they must swallow voluntarily and not spit it out. While the church can point out to people their spiritual hunger, they cannot force them to eat. Forcible evangelism simply does not work. Food thus makes clear that God's offer of his Word remains loving and invitational but not forced.

Furthermore, food gives an accessible way to reach native tribes with a universally applicable point of contact. Theater, music, and even light may prove difficult to translate to unreached peoples who have no written language or word for "light," but food speaks to everyone in every context since all eat, providing an accessible bridge to convey God's love in Scripture. "Scripture is food" tells everyone just how important its teachings

---

234. Webster notes that the Gospel of John in particular stresses eating "to describe the way in which believers are to respond: they are to feed others. This notion is introduced gradually throughout the Gospel," culminating in Simon Peter being "instructed to feed Jesus' sheep (21:15-17), even to the point of death (21:18-19). Throughout the Gospel . . . the ingesting motif is used as a vehicle to communicate the role of the disciples in feeding others." Webster, *Ingesting Jesus*, 150.

are and just how much their lives depend on partaking of its central food, Jesus. More than any other model of Scripture, food makes clear that God loves with a universal scope. God truly wants all people "to be saved and to come to the knowledge of the truth" (1 Tim 2:4).

Finally, food leads to doxology. God has "filled the hungry with good things" (Luke 1:53), and all people feast on the abundance of his house as he gives them to drink from the river of his delights (cf. Ps 36:7–8). Naturally, then, food elicits praise. Many give thanks and "say grace" for their food at each meal, and God deserves praise not only for providing food as a necessity but for infusing in food such joys as flavor, texture, and beauty.[235] Truly, food shows that God loves people, and this love accompanies every meal all the way to the final marriage supper in heaven.[236]

The same goes for Scripture as food. That God has given humanity Scripture should elicit not only daily "meals" of listening to it together but also constant praise for his provision that staves off death and brings life to whoever swallows it by faith. Scripture as food thus renders obedience as more than utility; obedience means enjoying God, praising God, experiencing his empowerment and sustenance, and even singing to God in response to the deliciousness of his presence. At the same time, food speaks to the seriousness of this joy. If heaven is a wedding banquet, hell is forever hungering outside that banquet with a teeth-gnashing, unsatiated emptiness filled with regret for rejecting the bread of life (cf. Matt 25:1–13). Food thus conveys the highest of stakes: everlasting joy or everlasting starvation. It also affirms, in the strongest of terms, humanity's creaturely dependence on God and their need for salvation from the sin of forsaking God, the fountain of living waters, to hew out for themselves "cisterns, broken cisterns that can hold no water" (Jer 2:13). Yet God deserves praise, for he has continued to sustain their lives with food (cf. Acts 14:17) and has given his Word as their food for eternal life (cf. John 6:68). This food does not lie outside anyone's grasp but is near, such that they can take it into their mouth and heart by faith and live (cf. Rom 10:8; Deut 30:14). Such is God's love, that he has given his inspired, authoritative, necessary, sufficient, clear, and inerrant Word as food that leads to Jesus, the ultimate bread of life, so that all who partake of him live forever (cf. 5:40).

So according to Scripture as food, God expresses his love to all people by providing his Word to meet their desperate need and save their lives.

---

235. See Wirzba, *Food and Faith*, 236ff.
236. See Wirzba, *Food and Faith*, xii.

This scriptural food also bonds people in everlasting, covenant community with God and his church. In his love, God invites anyone and everyone to take and eat his Scripture as food so that they may not die but live, "to the praise of his glorious grace" (Eph 1:6).

In summary, the model of "Scripture is food" describes the nature of Scripture better than the models of score, script, and light. According to the criteria of faithfulness, fittingness, and fruitfulness, the model of food safeguards more effectively, discloses more comprehensively, and renders more viscerally the nature of Scripture.

4

Doing the Dishes

Objections and Rejoinders

I HAVE ARGUED THAT metaphorical models play an essential role in conveying the nature of Scripture and that according to the criteria of faithfulness, fittingness, and fruitfulness, the model "Scripture is food" communicates that nature more adequately than the other models of a score, script, or light. To strengthen my argument, I raise and answer possible objections below. I confront three types of objections: (1) objections to models in general, (2) theological objections to the food model; and (3) practical objections to the food model.

Objections to Models in General

Four objections regard the general use of models. I term these objections as the "just a metaphor" objection, the "metaphors are dangerous" objection, the "many models" objection, and the criteria objection.

The "Just a Metaphor" Objection

This objection reflects Hobbes and Locke's attitude that models represent an "abuse of language" and "are for nothing else but to insinuate wrong ideas, move the passions, and thereby mislead the judgment; and so indeed are perfect cheats . . . wholly to be avoided."[1] This view remains prevalent today, which treats literal language "as primary and proper, while any propensity for metaphoric usage is deemed parasitic and deviant, alien to 'normal' communication and only acceptable to the extent that it can be paraphrased into the standard vocabulary of the dominant context."[2] Such objectors would claim that any serious treatment of the nature of Scripture should avoid metaphorical models entirely and stick to literal descriptors.

I answer that, given the historical survey in chapter 1, metaphorical models have proven useful and necessary in science and theology. Moreover, chapter 3 has shown that Scripture itself uses metaphorical models to describe its own nature, such as food, light, sword, et cetera. To avoid using these models, then, would amount to denying the testimony of Scripture about itself.

As for models in general, Richards and McFague have argued persuasively that one cannot avoid using models, as people inevitably think by metaphors and models. Thought itself thus exhibits a kind of "metaphoricity" that cannot help but form powerful, system-shaping models. These models constitute "comprehensive ways of envisioning reality" that even "control the ways people envision both human and divine reality."[3] Models thus shape how people view reality itself; they are not "just a metaphor" but affect and shift the way people view the nature of things in the real world. Andrew Louth even points out that metaphor reflects a culture's grasp of reality by exposing its implicit assumptions. In this sense, metaphors and models can serve as keys to understand history itself and one's connection to it.[4] So models do not move away from reality but are precisely how science, theology, and even history make sense of the real world and truth. Therefore, models should not be avoided but employed and improved.

The "Metaphors Are Dangerous" Objection

This objection advises against using metaphors in theology since they dangerously tend to lead to heterodox views. As McFague points out, "good metaphors shock, they bring unlikes together, they upset conventions, they

---

1. Locke, *Essay*, 372–73; cf. Hobbes, *Leviathan*, 29.
2. Fiumara, *Metaphoric*, 52.
3. McFague, *Metaphorical Theology*, 25; cf. Richards, *Philosophy of Rhetoric*, 92.
4. Louth, *Discerning the Mystery*, 19–20.

involve tension, and they are implicitly revolutionary."[5] Metaphorical theology thus finds favor among liberals and feminists like Dale Martin and Sallie McFague, who seem to want to "upset" orthodoxy and shift it toward their own special interests.[6] In answer, I repeat my response to the previous objection that one cannot avoid using metaphors, though one should use them cautiously and employ criteria like the ones I propose in chapter 1 to evaluate the biblical faithfulness, fittingness, and fruitfulness of the metaphors one chooses. Since metaphors do wield immense power in shaping one's theological system and even become models that both reveal and conceal elements within that system, metaphors certainly come with dangers. However, these dangers should not lead one to try to avoid metaphors—as if that is even possible—but rather to use them responsibly, critically, and prayerfully.

The "Many Models" Objection

This objection avers that I do a disservice by setting one model over against others since "*many* metaphors and models are necessary" and "a piling up of images is essential, both to avoid idolatry and to attempt to express the richness and variety of the divine-human relationship."[7] Since all models have limitations and weaknesses, any one model can be stretched too far in its application given "the limited scope of the metaphor."[8] Since one needs

---

5. McFague, *Metaphorical Theology*, 17.

6. Martin tends to treat Scripture as an open text that depends on a community's interpretation to mean anything, and he also endorses homoerotic and transgender readings. See Martin, *Pedagogy of the Bible*, 60, 66, 78. McFague pushes for acceptance of feminist models that refer to the world as God's body and to God as "Mother" as much as "Father." She also moves away from biblical models like God as a "rock" or monarch, the latter of which she deems "dangerous in our time." McFague, *Models of God*, 69; cf. 70–87; *Metaphorical Theology*, 24.

7. McFague, *Metaphorical Theology*, 20; cf. 144.

8. Boersma, *Violence*, 107. According to Soskice, "*all* paramorphic models are qualified; if they were not they would be, not models, but replicas of the modelled subject. By the same token, no paramorphic models can be pushed too far without consequent absurdity; Christian presuppositions make it absurd to extend the model of God's fatherhood so far as to say that he has a wife; scientific presuppositions make it absurd to push the billiard ball model for gas molecules so far as to suppose that gas molecules might be composed of plastic." Soskice, *Metaphor and Religious Language*, 116. Since all models have limits, Ramsey warns against theologizing based on only one model: "A picture theology which is too taped and too cut and dried is self-condemned—leaving no place for the mystery and transcendence of God, leaving no place for wonder and worship.

insights from many models, setting any model against others proves unhelpful and misguided.

I agree that one should integrate the best insights from multiple models to gain the most comprehensive understanding of a subject. For example, integrating the many models of atonement, rather than setting them at odds, provides the most balanced understanding into the meaning of Christ's saving work.[9] On the other hand, not every model proves equally helpful or central, nor should a model receive serious consideration if it fails the criteria. Regarding the specific models in this book, I have not called the models of Scripture as score, script, and light unhelpful or wrong, as each stands up to the criteria as faithful, fitting, and fruitful to the subject of Scripture in its respective ways. I thus maintain full support for each of these models as legitimate, valuable, and deserving of serious discussion.

At the same time, the legitimacy of these models does not preclude that some models demonstrate greater faithfulness, fittingness, and fruitfulness than others. Evaluated by these criteria, better models should take more prominence in one's understanding of their subject, as I have shown in chapter 3 with "Scripture is food." Still, "Scripture is food" should not remain the only model but be supplemented with other excellent models, especially biblically derived ones like "Scripture is light." Scripture provides many models of itself for a reason, and I agree that a multiplicity of models helps to grasp Scripture more deeply and guard against misconstruing its nature by viewing it through the lens of only one model.

The Criteria Objection

One might grant the use of models but still take issue with the criteria of faithfulness, fittingness, and fruitfulness by which I have evaluated the models in this book. This objector might accuse me of selecting criteria that favor the food model, whereas a different set of criteria would lead to a different outcome wherein the food model might turn out weaker than other models.

I grant that these criteria are not exhaustive and remain open to critique. I have gleaned these criteria, however, not from personal preference but from the history of metaphors and models with an aim toward

---

We can, indeed, be altogether too articulate about the Father-Son relationship and finish with rank heresy." Ramsey, *Models and Mystery*, 7.

9. For one such integration, see Crisp, *Approaching the Atonement*.

evaluating models as objectively as possible. Historically, the criteria of faithfulness, fittingness, and fruitfulness have received repeated affirmation, and I welcome suggestions of further criteria that would have similar support. Nevertheless, the criteria I have used remain fairly neutral and do not privilege any particular model. These criteria thus persist as viable categories by which to analyze models more or less objectively.

Theological Objections to the Food Model

"Scripture is food" may raise objections that pertain to theological problems that the food model might imply. I answer eleven of these possible objections below.

The Lord's Supper Objection

This objection alleges that I have taken the food model too far since *Christ himself*, not the words of Scripture, constitutes the food of eternal life that Christians ingest through the Lord's Supper, or Eucharist. I answer that however one views Christ's presence in the Supper, even the Gospel of John remains "vague about what it actually means 'to eat' Jesus and 'to drink his blood,'" and in John 6:60–70, "the possibility arises that a believer 'eats' Jesus by internalizing his words, hearing and obeying, and passing on the words of Jesus."[10] While eating the Supper and eating Scripture remain distinct actions, they both involve eating Jesus and thus mutually complement and bolster one another rather than contradict one another.

After all, engaging in one form of eating without the other threatens the meaning of both. Eating the Lord's Supper without "eating" Scripture threatens the meaning of the Supper, since Scripture provides clear teaching about how and why the Supper should be celebrated (Matt 26:26–29; Mark 14:22–25; Luke 22:19–20). Paul even records an instance in which eating the Supper causes people to fall ill and even die by eating it in "an unworthy manner" (1 Cor 11:27), a manner that contradicts the Lord's teaching now written in Scripture (cf. 1 Cor 11:23–30). "Eating" Scripture without eating the Lord's Supper also violates Christ's clear teaching of Scripture to remember him through the Supper until he comes (cf. Luke 22:19). So these two forms of eating must go together and mutually support one another.

---

10. Webster, *Ingesting Jesus*, 153.

The Bibliolatry Objection

According to this objection, the model "Scripture is food" puts too much emphasis on Scripture itself and not on its function of pointing to Christ, thus overemphasizing Scripture as an idol or "paper pope."[11] After all, Jesus rebukes the Jewish leaders in John 5:39–40, "You search the Scriptures because you think that in them you have eternal life; it is these that testify about me; and you are unwilling to come to me so that you may have life." In response to this objection, I reaffirm that Scripture does not ultimately point to itself but to Christ as the ultimate authority from whom Scripture derives its authority, and I reiterate that Scripture "effects transformation by pointing to Jesus as the only means by which fellowship with God becomes available to anyone, and beyond that, by calling into being that fellowship."[12] So to "eat" the Bible rightly, one must move beyond the propositions of Scripture to embrace the person of Christ revealed in Scripture and live in moment-by-moment dependence on him. At the same time, however, one expresses this dependence by ongoing intake and exercise of Scripture, just as Christ does throughout his earthly ministry. As John Wenham shows decisively in his *Christ and the Bible*, the avalanche of evidence points to the fact that Jesus himself teaches "the God-givenness of Scripture" and that his many allusions and quotations of the OT gives the total impression that "the mind of Christ is saturated with the Old Testament . . . [which] was the teaching of the living God."[13] In other words, Christ sets the example for how Christians should treat Scripture, and Christ regards Scripture as God's Word that saturates and sustains him throughout his earthly ministry. Therefore, one should not bifurcate Jesus as God's incarnate Word from the Bible as God's written Word. These two mutually reinforce one another; to follow Jesus as God's Word entails following Scripture as God's Word and vice versa.

The Holy Spirit Objection

This objection alleges that the food model leaves out the Holy Spirit, especially his ministry of illuminating Scripture. I answer that, on the contrary,

---

11. Bavinck notes that Luther's critics accuse Luther of delivering from the human pope but setting up the Bible as a "paper pope." Bavinck, *Reformed Dogmatics*, I.381.
12. Dharamraj, "On the Doctrine of Scripture," 57.
13. Wenham, *Christ and the Bible*, 36, 43–44.

the Spirit has everything to do with the model. He gives the new nature that can discern the meaning of Scripture (cf. 1 Cor 2:13–14), and he is the living water that comes with Jesus as the living bread (cf. John 7:38–39). So according to my definition of food as both solid and liquid, the Spirit's role as living water thus fits coherently within the food model of Scripture, and the model even helps to displays the trinitarian roles of the Son as the bread, the Spirit as the water, and the Father as the gardener or banquet host, thus highlighting how much people depend on God for their basic needs. Although a full treatment of the Spirit's role belongs more in the systematic category of pneumatology than bibliology, I fully affirm with Feinberg that "the theme of Scripture's power must include teaching about both word *and* Spirit. Without the Spirit's ministry in the lives of the readers and hearers of Scripture, the power of God's word will remain dormant,"[14] not to mention the Spirit's indispensable role in inspiring Scripture through the process of dual authorship. So no treatment of Scripture should go without reference to the Holy Spirit, the third Person of the Trinity, who "has used and uses [Scripture] to breathe life into our souls."[15] The food model depicts the Spirit's role as essential to the nature of Scripture.

The Church Authority Objection

Some may object that, given the church's agency in producing Scripture, the church stands as a second locus of authority. As I state in the above sections on ecclesiology and inspiration, however, the food model places the priority squarely with the divine agency in providing the Word to sustain the church, not vice versa. God's Word empowers the church as its food, and the church then receives the power to produce Scripture. So the food model, rather than precluding human agency in the production of Scripture, actually enables that production; and church tradition consists of believers who have eaten and metabolized God's Word, which then becomes written down as Scripture. The food model thus restricts tradition from being a second locus of authority alongside or above the Word. Instead, Scripture holds ultimate authority with God as its primary source and author, while its human authors rely on the Holy Spirit's enablement as he carries them along to write Scripture (cf. 2 Pet 1:21).[16]

14. Feinberg, *Light in a Dark Place*, 678.
15. Peterson, *Eat This Book*, 11.
16. See Feinberg, *Light in a Dark Place*, 394–400.

The Scriptural Passages Objection

Some verses in Scripture seem indirectly to oppose the food model, such as Paul's statements in Rom 14:17, 1 Cor 8:8, and Phil 3:19. In Rom 14:17, Paul says, "For the kingdom of God is not eating and drinking, but righteousness and peace and joy in the Holy Spirit." He says in 1 Cor 8:8 that "food will not commend us to God; we are neither the worse if we do not eat, nor the better if we do eat," and in Phil 3:19, he condemns those whose "end is destruction, whose god is their appetite, and whose glory is in their shame, who set their minds on earthly things." One thus might think that these verses disparage focusing on food in relation to God's kingdom, which would then discourage using the food model for Scripture. In the first two passages, however, Paul refers only to physical foods, and in Phil 3:19 he speaks of an appetite for sinful and worldly passions. An appetite for Scripture, however, Paul heartily affirms, as he does to Timothy by encouraging him to be "constantly nourished on the words of the faith and of the sound doctrine which you have been following" (1 Tim 4:6). Paul even treats physical food very seriously in 1 Cor 8, where he instructs the Corinthians on food sacrificed to idols. So while food can become an idol used for deception and temptation (cf. Esau in Gen 25:27–34; Heb 12:16), food remains a serious subject fitting as a theological model for Scripture.

The Transcendence Objection

This objection accuses the food model of stressing the immanence of God's Word to the neglect of its transcendence. According to this objection, food remains too rooted in mundane, earthly life and thus skews the nature of Scripture by highlighting immanence as a word for humans but downplaying its transcendence as the Word of God. So this objection holds that food does not take adequate account of God's holiness and otherness, thus promoting a view of Scripture that fosters too much familiarity with God, which may breed contempt or disrespect toward him.

I answer that food does capture the holiness of God and his Word, since God does not have to eat but humans do. So food maintains the Creator-creature distinction and upholds God as entirely set apart from humans, even as he also makes himself intimately accessible to humans through Scripture. At the same time, food remains mysterious as the key to the survival of all living things. As Jesus points out, a seed sprouts and grows, though people know not how (cf. Mark 4:27). In the same way, the ground mysteriously produces food, and the way food nourishes bodies remains equally mysterious yet universal. Therefore, food transcends humanity's understanding and reminds them that they do not make the rules; they must obey the rules of Another and eat to live, thus yielding to God's transcendent purposes enacted through his Word.[17]

The Deification Objection

This objection alleges that the food model implies too much of a theosis or divinization of human nature. Since people become what they eat, how does one avoid the implication that eating God's Word makes one into God? I answer that this same objection appears in discussions on the Eucharist, and while Christians are biblically commanded to take and eat Christ (Matt 26:26; 1 Cor 11:24), Christians do not claim that they thus become God; instead, they *partake* of the divine nature but do not become identical with it. A similar defense would apply to the food model: so long as Christians regard *partaking* of the divine nature through Scripture as distinct from *identifying* as the divine nature, the model does not violate the Creator-creature distinction and thus steers clear of saying that human beings can become God.

The Violence Objection

This objection accuses the food model of depicting Scripture—and thus evangelical theology—as inherently violent since all food must die so that others may eat it and live. So the model enshrines violence at the very center of the Bible and Christianity. I answer that the same objection tends to appear regarding Christ's atonement, and such objections tend to overlook that Christ's work centers not on violence but on sacrifice, especially self-sacrifice.[18] Therefore, sacrifice, not violence, sits at the center of Christianity, and the food model thus highlights Christ's self-sacrifice as both the

---

17. Not only does food describe the nature of Scripture but also the nature of God. According to Scripture, food models God's trinitarian life, with the Son as bread (cf. John 6:25–59), the Spirit as water (cf. John 4:15; 7:38–39), and the Father as the gardener or banquet host (Gen 2:8; Matt 22:2–14). By using these fundamental elements of food, God emphasizes people's basic need for him, which correlates well with their basic need for his Word.

18. See Boersma, *Violence, Hospitality, and the Cross*.

center of Scripture's narrative of redemption and its prime example for Christian living (cf. Gal 6:14–15; Rom 12:1; 1 Pet 2:20–22; 1 John 3:15–16).

The Legal Objection

According to this objection, food fails to account for the legal categories of Scripture and thus depicts its narrative of salvation too naturalistically: rather than guilty sinners in need of God's forgiveness, humanity becomes merely innocent, hungry creatures in need of God's natural sustenance. The food model thus presents a deficient view of sin and its legal consequences.

I answer that any honest reading of Scripture, especially its references to food, shows quite the opposite: the food model includes a robust view of sin that includes its legal consequences and that by no means depicts humanity as innocent or just naturally hungry creatures. After all, Adam and Eve fall through eating forbidden food, which incurs God's judgment upon them and their children (cf. Gen 3:1–19). This situation thus implies the legal category of guilt for breaking God's injunction while also making clear that human sinfulness runs even deeper than breaking the law; sin reflects the madness of trying to live while turning away from the food that gives life: God and his Word (cf. Gen 2:16–17; Jer 2:13). Jesus also includes food when speaking in legal terms of the final judgment (cf. Matt 25:31–46), and when the condemned ask, "Lord, when did we see you hungry, or thirsty, or a stranger, or naked, or sick, or in prison, and did not take care of you?" Jesus answers, "Truly, I say to you, to the extent that you did not do it to one of the least of these, you did not do it to me" (Matt 25:44–45). So the food model not only does well in depicting humanity's natural need and dependence on God, but it speaks to the categories of guilt and innocence, even explaining people's mortality better than any other model. People die because they have sinned and turned away from the food that gives them life; at the same time, God continues to provide his Scripture as food to turn people back to him through his "words of eternal life" (John 6:68). The food model discloses this reality more viscerally than any other model. It shows the heaviness, tragedy, and nearness of sin and death on a daily basis, but it also points to God's gracious provision that meets such tragedy head-on and reverses its effects through Christ as "the bread which comes down out of heaven, so that one may eat of it and not die" (John 6:50). Thus the food model does not sidestep the legal categories of sin but includes them and goes further, highlighting the madness of sin and the urgency of humanity's need for salvation.

The Born-Again Objection

This objection alleges that the food model is not radical enough because it does not highlight that one must be born again to be saved (cf. John 3:3), not merely improved through diet and exercise of the Scriptures. Salvation, such objectors might say, requires not merely eating but a rebirth. How can food capture such a stark transformation?

I answer that all these models find difficulty in capturing this notion of being born again, including the score, script, and light. In comparison to these, food still would convey rebirth best because of its close ties to bodily transformation and the intimacy required in engaging God's Word in Scripture. Rebirth speaks of a drastic change from within that involves the entirety of a person's body and spirit, and the food model helps to convey such an intimate and life-altering change that God enacts within a person through Scripture.

The Boundaries Objection

This objection accuses the food model of lacking proper hermeneutical boundaries to differentiate heresy from orthodoxy since it does not delineate how to tell the difference between valid and invalid ways of preparing and eating the food of Scripture. One also might call this the relativism objection. Since all cultures prepare the same ingredients in vastly different and yet equally valid ways, how does the food model avoid collapsing into relativism and "experiential-expressivist" theories of biblical interpretation wherein truth becomes whatever a particular culture or community deems as true?[19]

This problem of proper boundaries confronts all the models, not just food. Regarding food, a possible answer to this objection comes from nutritional science. Nutritional science appeals to a long history of research and data to differentiate between healthy and unhealthy diets, and not every type or combination of food proves healthy to any given culture. In other words, not everything goes; nutrition shows that a healthy approach to

---

19. The term "experiential expressivist" comes from Lindbeck, *The Nature of Doctrine*, 19–20, 24–25, 31, 34, 42, 51, 126.

food does not allow for people to eat whatever they want, but they must discover healthy choices and patterns of eating.[20] Applied to Scripture as food, the church must practice careful exegesis and look to its history to discern which spiritual recipes have led to death rather than life. When Scripture is taught faithfully and truly, the church body should evidence signs of vitality rather than decay and be safeguarded from the poison of heresy. Like physical food, spiritual food requires careful discernment so that one does not ingest poison or an unhealthy combination of ingredients.

So while delineating specific hermeneutical principles for such discernment lies outside the scope of this book, food does posit a framework for setting proper boundaries rather than degenerate into mere relativism. While food does reflect specific cultures, these cultures cannot simply choose anything as their food; they rather discover these healthy, God-given ingredients that stay stable over time. In the same way, God's truth in Scripture stays stable throughout time, but it can carry various applications for specific cultures. At the same time, food can bring people together to build a new culture, and Scripture builds a godly culture as the church gathers to partake of it together. Moreover, food is a matter of life and death, so one must get it right; one cannot simply pick and choose what one wants to eat in Scripture and discard the rest, nor should one discard how others in history have eaten and metabolized Scripture. To do so would lead almost certainly to eating the poison of heresy.

Practical Objections to the Food Model

The food model might raise objections related to faulty practices that the model allegedly engenders. I address here ten possible objections.

The Consumer Objection

This objection protests that "Scripture is food" overly stresses "taking in" while neglecting "giving out" God's Word, thus fostering a "consumerist" approach to the word that results in self-centered, spiritual obesity that does not account for doing God's will through active obedience to Scripture. The

---

20. Excellent books on food and nutritional science include Perkins, ed., *Food Microbiology*; Verene, *The Science of Cookery*; Coultate, *Food: The Chemistry of Its Components*; and Campbell, *The Future of Nutrition*.

food model thus would fail to account for the self-denial that Jesus requires of his disciples (Matt 16:24; Mark 8:34).

I answer that the food model does no such thing. In fact, the model comes with an implicit balance of intake and exercise. If one eats without exercising, one gets obese. If one exercises without eating, one gets anorexic and weak. Either way, food comes with an in-built balance rather than backing a merely consumerist paradigm. Rather, a healthy approach to food requires exercise. In the same way, a healthy approach to Scripture requires exercising its teaching to do God's will, which Jesus implies when he says in John 4:34, "My food is to do the will of Him who sent me, and to accomplish His work."

Nevertheless, food can become an idol. One can love eating food to the point of gluttony and obesity, failing to balance intake with exercise. This objection thus brings up a very important point that one must not make food an end in itself but rather a means to a greater end. Both physical food and the spiritual food of Scripture should not serve as a terminal point lest one become gluttonous and unhealthy; both should serve to advance God's will revealed in his Word, and both should lead to faithful exercise that seeks to glorify his name. In short, the food model promotes moderation, not excess, and thus guards against the idolatry, carnality, and worldliness that can come from misappropriating God's good gift of food. The model thus protects against the epicurean idolization of selfish pleasure as well as the overly ascetic thinking that refuses to rejoice in God's material gifts. Such wise balance reflects that of Agur, who prays to have only so much food as promotes his faithfulness to God: "Feed me with the food that is my portion, that I not be full and deny you and say, 'Who is the Lord?' or that I not be in want and steal, and profane the name of my God" (Prov 30:8–9). Such balance fosters a more holistic practice of spirituality and promotes more unity between the mind and body when approaching Scripture.

The Force-Feeding Objection

This objection states that God, by requiring that everyone eat his Word to live, does actually force-feed everyone his Word under the threat of death. So rather than being hospitable and inviting, God forces people to participate or die. One thus cannot say that God does not force-feed anyone.

I answer that God truly does not force-feed anyone, but that very truth comprises a reason for why hell exists. To say that one wants to live but not eat forms a nonsensical impossibility; in the same way, to say one wants to live eternally but not eat the food God provides for such life violates reality as well. Reality shows that to deny food means death; likewise, to deny the food of heaven means hell, complete with the painful "gnashing of teeth" while others eat at God's banqueting table (cf. Matt 8:11–12). So God's hospitality and invitation do not deny the facts of reality, and the food model highlights just how serious God's hospitality really is.

The Eternal Security Objection

This objection fears that the food model allows for possible loss of salvation. The objector asks, If a person is "once-saved-always-saved," can this person lose their salvation if they stop "eating," or continually believing in, God's Word in Scripture?

While all models would find difficulty with this objection, I respond that all true Christians never would stop eating God's "words of eternal life" because they have Jesus as their Good Shepherd, from whose hand none can snatch them out (cf. John 10:28). They are also "sealed in [Jesus] with the Holy Spirit of promise" (Eph 1:13), who has given them "the mind of Christ" complete with spiritual discernment (cf. 1 Cor 2:14–16). Therefore, these sheep never ultimately fall away but have a new nature, "which in the likeness of God has been created in righteousness and holiness of the truth" (Eph 4:24). In short, they cannot lose their salvation, and their new nature will never stop feeding on God's Word. While Heb 6:4–5 does speak of people who have "tasted of the heavenly gift and have been made partakers of the Holy Spirit, and have tasted the good word of God and the powers of the age to come, and then have fallen away" (Heb 6:4–5), this reference does not speak of true believers but of people who experience God's nourishing gifts through his church but never truly believe. One might say that such people have "tasted" but never "swallowed." They have not surrendered control to God's Word.

The Utilitarian Objection

One might object that the food model reduces one's relationship with God to one of mere utility rather than a personal relationship. In other words, food does not capture adequately that God is more than food but is a person, so food demeans God as merely fuel and leads to theology that uses God for self-sustenance rather than engaging him relationally as a person.

I suggest three possible answers to this objection. First, one could argue that food does not reduce but rather amplifies personal relationship with God because food proves an even deeper, more pressing, and more primal model because of its immediate connection to life-or-death survival. Jesus thus calls people to such intimate relationship with himself that they eat his flesh and drink his blood, drawing their very life sustenance from him (cf. John 6:56). The intimacy of such a relationship requires much more than conversation but penetration and vital dependence on him. Second, food is always relational in immediately requiring people's dependence on God and interdependence on one another. The most relational moments often come while eating together at meals. A third response points out that Scripture itself describes relationship with God in terms of food, even calling the Son "bread" and the Spirit "water" (cf. John 6:25–59; 7:39). Since Scripture unabashedly employs these terms, Christians should too.

The Vogue Objection

This objection avers that the food model only reflects the current vogue of talking about food and diet. The model thus falls victim to a fad that will fade in a short time. In Vanhoozer's view, the current North American fads are health, diet, and fitness.[21] He critiques what he calls "the cult of food" and specifically "fad diets" like that from Robert Atkins for their false promises of holistic wellness through group identity and the substitution of religion for food habits.[22] These have become "big business" and offer shortcuts to physical and spiritual growth, and Vanhoozer thus exhorts the church to "resist the temptation to become a fast-food holy nation" that seeks cheap shortcuts rather than biblical growth and discipleship.[23] Recognizing this danger, one may object that the food model simply reinforces the current idolization of food. One also might object that the food model succumbs to the current culture's faddish "food cults" and thus will soon pass away with these gimmicks.

I answer that, on the contrary, food is not a passing fad but is a perennially serious issue, and ignoring it also proves serious. The reality of food

---

21. Vanhoozer, *Doers and Hearers*, 16–42.
22. See Vanhoozer, *Doers and Hearers*, 25–27.
23. Vanhoozer, *Doers and Hearers*, 28, 32.

has nothing gimmicky about it, although current culture's renderings of food may miss God's intentions for food expressed in his word. Biblically speaking, food remains so foundational that it actually challenges current trends in philosophy and theology, promoting a habitual, patient, and balanced approach to God and his Word that guards against the current culture's addiction to the spectacular and immediate. As chapter 3 above has shown, food carries with it lasting and profound implications for how one rightly approaches God's written Word faithfully, fittingly, and fruitfully. So while Vanhoozer's insights are well taken, the food model, rightly conceived, does not fall prey to current food fads. As for the danger of reinforcing food as an idol, one always must guard against this danger since anything less than God can become an idol; however, "Scripture is food" makes clear that food is not an end in itself but points ultimately to God, his Word, and Jesus as the Bread of Life. The food model thus has in-built safeguards against idolizing food.

The Modern Life Objection

This objection brings up that while the food model may speak wonderfully to premodern people, people today live in a culture of convenience that removes them from the agricultural source of their food, which hurts the ability of the model to speak effectively to the current culture. For example, people in the modern West will tend to think of steak as a shrink-wrapped, sterile piece of meat in the supermarket rather than a cow that has been slaughtered, and so this distance between people and their source of food creates difficulty in seeing that food comes with notions of death and sacrifice.

I answer that this objection is precisely why people need the food model today. People need to get in better touch with the land and the source of their food, and their distance from their food source encourages people toward more selfishness and alienation from the realities of life and survival. The food model has the added effect of encouraging people to think about the source of their food and the serious necessities of death and sacrifice to eat. The model also promotes conceiving of Scripture in these serious terms, viewing the Bible as the source of spiritual survival rather than optional additive to one's life.

The Vegan Objection

This objection points out that food divides as much as it unites, as people particularize their diets ranging from solely carnivorous to entirely vegan and even gluten-free. Food tends to bring up strong opinions, so according to this objection, the food model does not unite community as much as further divide it. The model thus falls short at being uniting and universal, and it also may cause people to be picky with the parts of the Bible they like while ignoring what they do not like.

I answer that food, scripturally conceived, avoids possible problems with particularities like veganism and instead proves universal to all people, as even Jesus's choice of metaphor for himself as "bread" speaks to his universal applicability and accessibility to all people. Jesus could have called himself the "lamb rack of life," but that would have implied that only the rich could access his salvation. As bread, however, Jesus speaks to his accessibility to people of all cultures and classes. Regarding people's tendency to pick and choose only what they like, this problem arises with any model, but the food model can help to bring more balance since it implies a "complete diet" of Scripture to be healthy. Just as one cannot eat only what one likes and remain physically healthy, one cannot accept only the parts of Scripture that one likes and be spiritually healthy. One needs the whole, balanced diet, complete with exercise.

The Automaticity Objection

This objection alleges that the metaphor between food and Scripture falls apart since digesting food is mostly automatic while digesting Scripture is not. Food features a kind of "automaticity" in that people's bodies seem subconsciously to know what to do with ingested food. A much different situation arises with Scripture, however, since one actively must reflect and mull over the Word; one cannot simply digest Scripture subconsciously. Unlike food, the Bible must be intentionally and sometimes even painstakingly interpreted.

I answer that while this objection makes sense on the surface, it may overlook a kind of "automaticity" that Scripture has by the power of the Holy Spirit. As Origen indicates, God's Word has an ability to enable one to understand it over time, and this ability is a divine, Spirit-given mystery.[24]

---

24. See Origen, *The Philocalia*, 12.2.

So perhaps Christians should be open for God's Word to have a kind of "automatic" or subconscious element in nourishing them. Besides, the capacity to take in and understand words seems built into humanity. Moreover, food is not something that people have full control over; they must eat trusting that what they are eating is healthy and strengthening. Similarly, reading the Bible is not something people have full control over, but they must trust that listening to it is healthy and strengthening.

At the same time, this element does not preclude careful preparation and active study of the Word, just as people should exercise active wisdom in choosing and preparing their food so as not to ingest poison or harmful substances. Food comes with important intentional considerations, such as what to eat, the amount eaten, and exercise. Food also speaks to the patience and time necessary to progress in learning to eat, digest, and exercise the food. So just as with food, approaching Scripture has both automatic and non-automatic elements.

The Fasting Objection

According to this objection, the food model ignores the long history of contemplative theology that has valued fasting over feasting. Since church history and the patristic fathers tend to valorize fasting and speak against eating, the food model does not reflect enough faithfulness to church tradition and neglects the importance of fasting that tradition upholds.

I answer that the food model does no such thing. In fact, the model shows the importance of fasting by highlighting just how important food is for humanity's survival. For humanity to fast, therefore, means to refrain from the necessity of food both to seek the God who gives the food and also to exercise the food one has taken in. So connecting Scripture to food does not neglect fasting but rather highlights the importance of exercising the Scripture that one knows so as not to become spiritually obese. As Scripture teaches, fasting certainly proves important and instructive to one's spiritual diet (cf. Dan 10:3; Ezra 8:21–23; 1 Sam 7:6; 1 Kgs 19:4–8; Esth 4:16; Matt 4:1–2; 6:16), but fasting by no means contradicts the importance of food but rather reinforces it. So humanity's vital connection to food is what gives fasting its powerful meaning. Since people depend on God's provision of food to live, their choice to fast can proclaim an even deeper dependence on God (cf. Job 23:12).

Scripture speaks much more of food and feasting than of fasting; and though Christ does command Christians to fast, this command does not preclude that eating is much more normative in knowing the goodness and love of God since the "children of mankind . . . feast on the abundance of your house, and you give them drink from the river of your delights" (Ps 36:7–8). The food model points out that just as God provides this physical food to sustain physical life, he provides the spiritual food of Scripture to sustain spiritual life.

The Prayer Objection

This objection accuses the food model of neglecting the centrality of prayer that should accompany the Word. I answer that, on the contrary, the food model includes prayer better than all the other models, as prayer often naturally goes before, during, and after meals. Before meals, Christians pray, "Give us this day our daily bread" (Matt 6:11). At meals, Christians give thanks around the table. After meals, Christians bless the Lord for their satisfied stomachs (cf. Deut 8:10). So the biblical patterns for food all include prayer, and food often brings thanksgiving and long conversation around the table. The current culture's addiction to fast-food and convenience tends to keep people from seeing these prayerful elements of communing with God that should accompany food, and the food model helps to correct this misconception as well as encourage Christians to saturate their diet of Scripture with prayer, thus demonstrating the dependence and thankfulness befitting God's amazing gift of his Word as food.

In sum, the model "Scripture is food" withstands these general, theological, and practical objections. It thus remains a faithful, fitting, fruitful, and robust model of God's written Word.

Conclusion

IN THIS BOOK, I have argued that metaphorical models play an essential role in conveying the nature of Scripture but that current models, though helpful, have fallen short of communicating that nature adequately. I thus proposed a biblically derived model, "Scripture is food," to safeguard more effectively, disclose more comprehensively, and render more viscerally the nature of Scripture. In chapter 1, I traced a history of metaphor to demonstrate how metaphors turn into system-shaping models and to glean criteria to evaluate models. These criteria included faithfulness, fruitfulness, and fittingness. In chapter 2, I surveyed three current models for Scripture—Anthony Thiselton's "Scripture is a musical score," Kevin Vanhoozer's "Scripture is a theo-dramatic script," and John Feinberg's "Scripture is light"—and I employed the criteria from chapter 1 to evaluate these models. This evaluation found these models useful but lacking in ways that called for a better model. I thus proposed, in chapter 3, a biblically derived model of "Scripture is food" and developed this model from Scripture and theologians ancient and modern. Then using the same criteria from chapter 1, I evaluated the food model over against the other three models to demonstrate that the food model better communicates the nature of Scripture. In chapter 4, I defended the food model against general, theological, and practical objections that may threaten the legitimacy or effectiveness of the model in conveying the nature of Scripture. Despite these "contra-factors," the model has proven robust.[1]

Yet this book only begins to plumb the depths of the fruitfulness of the food model. Further study can delve into implications of the model for scriptural interpretation, especially for the developing discipline of

---

1. For more on "contra-factors," see McFague, *Metaphorical Theology*, 139.

theological interpretation of Scripture (TIS).[2] Specifically, one can explore the theological, spiritual, and philosophical connections between hearing, reading, and eating. One can develop specific hermeneutical principles for how to "eat" the Bible in terms of exegetical practices and theological method. Further research also can explore specific ways that the food model informs the agency of Scripture, or as Feinberg calls it, the "animation" of Scripture.[3]

More study can delve into how the food model informs theological anthropology, especially its implications for humanity's ontology. For instance, Rowan Williams points out that much "popular scientific literature these days encourages us to think of the mind as a machine or the brain as a computer."[4] The food model renders such mechanistic models extremely problematic or even untenable. Machines and computers do not eat, but people do, which may carry profound implications for the nature of human persons both individually and collectively.

Further study could delve into implications of the model for soteriology, especially the ways in which the model may restructure how theologians approach the idea of merit. Food may transform or even remove the system of merit altogether, since eating saves lives without requiring any such system. Exploring how the food model interacts with any system of merit may prove fruitful and illuminating for understanding God's salvation more accurately. One also may develop the food model in ways that encourage people to go to God not only for forgiveness but for life itself on a daily basis.

Areas of further study also could include implications of the food model for apologetics, preaching, and church growth. For example, one might pay special attention to how Scripture as food commends God's Word to unbelievers or to how Scripture nourishes the apologist and sets the appropriate framework for apologetic discussions. After all, apologetics

---

2. Specifically defining the theological interpretation of Scripture (TIS) proves elusive. Putman helpfully distills TIS into four common points of concern: (1) to interpret the Bible through the lens of Christian theological discourse; (2) to go beyond historical-critical method as the dominant hermeneutical paradigm of biblical interpretation; (3) to reconcile the long-estranged disciplines of biblical studies and systematic theology; and (4) to employ insights from the philosophy of language and contemporary hermeneutical theory in biblical interpretation. Putman, *In Defense of Doctrine*, 52–56; cf. Treier, *Introducing Theological Interpretation of Scripture*.

3. See Feinberg, *Light in a Dark Place*, 661–79.

4. Williams, *Being Human*, viii.

must appeal not only to the mind but also the gut, reminding people of their spiritual hunger so that they can "taste and see that the LORD is good" (Ps 34:8). Pastorally, one might study sermons as differently prepared meals, specifically delineating how and why some may be better prepared or more delicious than others. Further research can employ the model to develop ways to guard against pastoral burnout.

More study can go into implications of the model for spirituality and Christian living. Such study can highlight ways that approaching Scripture as food helps to live out one's "immediate calling" within the "sacrament of the present moment" rather than succumbing to the current culture's addiction to the exciting or the spectacular.[5] Further research can explore ways in which food can help Christians influence a richer "social imaginary" that centers on thankful dependence on God.[6] Such study can uncover how food fosters a more fully embodied and mundane theology that balances intake and exercise as well as self-care and care for others. Food also may hold further insights into corporate memory and covenant fidelity, especially in meals like the Passover and Lord's Supper. Additional study would illuminate these connections between Scripture, memory, and community.

Further research can explore how "Scripture is food" informs ecclesiology and missions, highlighting specific ways in which the model fosters a more diverse and global theological discourse that includes the contributions of Christians from multiple cultures and age groups. Food may open doors for more effective ministry to children and more inclusion of children in theological conversations since children must eat Scripture as well as adults, and Jesus declares that God's kingdom belongs to people who receive it like children (cf. Matt 19:14; Luke 18:16). More study also could delve into the connection between Scripture and covenant, especially Scripture as a covenant document.

The possibilities are endless. Food remains a universal, comprehensive, and vital model that powerfully informs the nature of Scripture and opens countless vistas of fruitful research into the meaning of knowing and walking with God and others. As Charles Spurgeon has said, "Visit many good books, but live in the Bible."[7] I heartily agree but would only add, "Live *on* the Bible" as one's necessary, life-giving food.

---

5. Chan, *Spiritual Theology*, 234.

6. For more on the "social imaginary," see Taylor, *A Secular Age*, 171–76.

7. "Live in the Bible," Reasonable Theology, https://reasonabletheology.org/live-bible/.

Bibliography

Aaron, David H. *Biblical Ambiguities: Metaphor, Semantics, and Divine Imagery.* Boston: Brill, 2001.

Abba, Raymond. *The Nature and Authority of the Bible.* London: James Clarke, 1958.

Abernethy, Andrew T. *Eating in Isaiah: Approaching the Role of Food and Drink in Isaiah's Structure and Message.* Boston: Brill, 2014.

Abesamis, Abigail. "What Bread Looks Like in 15 Places around the World." *Insider* online. March 11, 2019. https://www.insider.com/bread-around-the-world-2019-13.

Abraham, William J. *Canon and Criterion in Christian Theology: From the Fathers to Feminism.* Oxford: Clarendon, 1998.

Abraham, William J., Jason E. Vickers, and Natalie B. Van Kirk, eds. *Canonical Theism: A Proposal for Theology and the Church.* Grand Rapids: Eerdmans, 2008.

Abraham, William J., and Frederick D. Aquino, eds. *The Oxford Handbook of the Epistemology of Theology.* Oxford: Oxford University Press, 2017.

Achtemeier, Paul J. *Inspiration and Authority: Nature and Function of Christian Scripture.* Grand Rapids: Baker Academic, 1999.

Adam, A. K. M., Stephen E. Fowl, Kevin J. Vanhoozer, and Francis Watson. *Reading Scripture with the Church: Toward a Hermeneutic for Theological Interpretation.* Grand Rapids: Baker Academic, 2006.

Adams, Marilyn McCord. *Christ and Horrors: The Coherence of Christology.* New York: Cambridge University Press, 2006.

Ahn, Jumsik. "Contextual Theology as Related to Ch'i: An Assessment on the Theology of Jung Young Lee." PhD diss., Trinity Evangelical Divinity School, 2002. UMI Microform (3047809).

Aichele, George. *Sign, Text, Scripture: Semiotics and the Bible.* Sheffield, UK: Sheffield Academic Press, 1997.

Albaba, Ken, and Trudy Eden, eds. *Food and Faith in Christian Culture.* New York: Columbia University Press, 2011.

Alexander, Denis R. "Creation and Evolution." In *The Blackwell Companion to Science and Christianity*, edited by J. B. Stump and Alan G. Padgett, 233–45. Malden, MA: Blackwell, 2012.

Allen, Dave. "'Who Are My Congregants?' Identifying Strategies for Church Growth in Our Community." DMin diss., Drew University, 2017. ProQuest (10267136).

Allen, Diogenes. *Spiritual Theology: The Theology of Yesterday for Spiritual Help Today.* Lanham, MD: Cowley, 1997.

Allen, Leslie C. *Ezekiel 1–19*. Word Biblical Commentary 28. Dallas, TX: Word, 1994.

Allen, Paul L. *Theological Method: A Guide for the Perplexed*. London: T&T Clark, 2012.

Allhoff, Fritz, and Dave Monroe. "Setting the Table: An Introduction to Food & Philosophy." In *Food & Philosophy: Eat, Think and Be Merry*, edited by Fritz Allhoff and Dave Monroe, 1–10. Malden, MA: Blackwell, 2007.

Altmann, Peter. *Festive Meals in Ancient Israel: Deuteronomy's Identity Politics in Their Ancient Near Eastern Context*. Boston: de Gruyter, 2011.

Ambrose, Glenn P. "Eucharist as a Means for 'Overcoming' Onto-Theology? The Sacramental Theology of Louis-Marie Chauvet." PhD diss., Graduate Theological Union, 2001. UMI Microform (3007727).

Arbib, Michael A., and Mary B. Hesse. *The Construction of Reality*. Cambridge: Cambridge University Press, 1986.

Arcadi, James M. *An Incarnational Model of the Eucharist*. New York: Cambridge University Press, 2018.

Aristotle. *Nicomachean Ethics*. Translated by Terence Irwin. Indianapolis, IN: Hackett, 1985.

———. *The Rhetoric and the Poetics of Aristotle*. Translated by W. Rhys Roberts and Ingram Bywater. New York: Random House, 1984.

Arjona-Mejia, Ruben. "Hoagies and Tacos: Food and Men's Unquenchable Hunger." *Pastoral Psychology* 64.3 (2015) 297–310.

Armstrong, Karen. *The Lost Art of Scripture: Rescuing the Sacred Texts*. Eldon, MO: Knopf, 2019.

Astell, Ann W. *Eating Beauty: The Eucharist and the Spiritual Arts of the Middle Ages*. Ithaca, NY: Cornell University Press, 2006.

Asumang, Annang. "Be Filled with the Spirit and Not with Wine: Echoes of the Messianic Banquet in the Antithesis of Ephesians 5:18." *Conspectus: The Journal of the South African Theological Seminary* 5 (2008) 21–38.

Athanasius. "Letter 7. Easter 335." In *Nicene and Post-Nicene Fathers*. Vol. 4, *Athanasius: Select Works and Letters*, edited by Philip Schaff and Henry Wace, 523–27. Peabody, MA: Hendrickson, 2004.

———. "Letter 49: Letter to Dracontius, Written A.D. 354 or 355." In *Nicene and Post-Nicene Fathers*, Vol. 4, *The Letters of Athanasius*, edited by Philip Schaff, 495–581. Peabody, MA: Hendrickson, 2004.

Augustine. *Confessions*. In *Nicene and Post-Nicene Fathers*, Vol. 1., edited by Philip Schaff, 27–207. Peabody, MA: Hendrickson, 2004.

———. *Confessions*. Translated by Henry Chadwick. New York: Oxford University Press, 1991.

———. *On the Trinity*. In *Nicene and Post-Nicene Fathers*, edited by Philip Schaff, 1–228. Peabody, MA: Hendrickson, 2004.

Aumann, Jordan. *Spiritual Theology*. June 1, 1980. http://www.traditio-op.org/biblioteca/Aumann/Spiritual-Theology-by-Jordan-Aumann-OP.pdf.

Austin, Benjamin M. *Plant Metaphors in the Old Greek of Isaiah*. Septuagint and Cognate Studies. Atlanta: SBL Press, 2019.

Austin, J. L. *How to Do Things with Words: The William James Lectures Delivered at Harvard University in 1955*. London: Oxford University Press, 1962.

Avieli, Nir. *Food and Power: A Culinary Ethnography of Israel*. Oakland, CA: University of California Press, 2018.

Avis, Paul. *God and the Creative Imagination: Metaphor, Symbol and Myth in Religion and Theology*. London: Routledge, 1999.

Ayres, Jennifer. *Good Food: Grounded Practical Theology*. Waco, TX: Baylor University Press, 2013.

Bacote, Vincent, Laura Miguelez Quay, and Dennis L. Okholm, eds. *Evangelicals & Scripture: Tradition, Authority, and Hermeneutics*. Downers Grove, IL: IVP, 2004.

Bahnson, Fred. "The Salvation of the City: Defiant Gardens in the Great Northern Feedlot." In *Wendell Berry and Religion: Heaven's Earthly Life*, edited by Joel James Shuman and L. Roger Owens, 98–114. Lexington, KY: University Press of Kentucky, 2009.

———. *Soil and Sacrament: A Spiritual Memoir of Food and Faith*. New York: Simon and Schuster, 2013.

Baillie, John. *The Sense of the Presence of God*. New York: Scribner's Sons, 1962.

Baker, Matthew, and Mark Mourachian, eds. *What Is the Bible?: The Patristic Doctrine of Scripture*. Minneapolis, MN: Fortress, 2016.

Bakhtin, Mikhail. *Art and Answerability: Early Philosophical Essays*. Edited by Michael Holquist and Vadim Liapunov. Austin, TX: University of Texas Press, 1990.

———. *Speech Genres and Other Late Essays*. Translated by Vern W. McGee. Austin, TX: University of Texas Press, 1986.

Balthasar, Hans Urs von. *Theo-Drama: Theological Dramatic Theory*. 5 vols. Translated by Graham Harrison. San Francisco: Ignatius, 1988–98.

Barbour, Ian G. *Myths, Models and Paradigms: A Comparative Study in Science and Religion*. New York: Harper & Row, 1974.

———. *Religion and Science: Historical and Contemporary Issues*. New York: HarperCollins, 1997.

———. *Religion in an Age of Science: The Gifford Lectures, 1989–1991*. Vol. 1. New York: HarperCollins, 1990.

Barnhill, Anne, and Tyler Doggett, eds. *The Oxford Handbook of Food Ethics*. New York: Oxford University Press, 2018.

Barrois, Georges A., ed. *The Fathers Speak: St. Basil the Great, St. Gregory of Nazianzus, St. Gregory of Nyssa*. Translated by Georges A. Barrois. Crestwood, NY: St. Vladimir's Seminary Press, 1986.

Barth, Karl. *Church Dogmatics I.2. The Doctrine of the Word of God, Sections 19–21*. Study ed., edited by G. W. Bromiley and T. F. Torrance. London: T&T Clark, 2010.

———. *Church Dogmatics I.2. The Doctrine of the Word of God, Sections 22–24*. Study ed., edited by G. W. Bromiley and T. F. Torrance. London: T&T Clark, 2010.

———. *Evangelical Theology: An Introduction*. Grand Rapids: Eerdmans, 1963.

Bartholomew, Craig G., and Heath A. Thomas, eds. *A Manifesto for Theological Interpretation*. Grand Rapids: Baker Academic, 2016.

Bartholomew, Craig G., and Ryan P. O'Dowd. *Old Testament Wisdom Literature: A Theological Introduction*. Downers Grove, IL: IVP, 2011.

Barton, John, ed. *The Cambridge Companion to Biblical Interpretation*. New York: Cambridge University Press, 1998.

Basil the Great. *Exegetic Homilies*. Washington, DC: Catholic University of America Press, 2003.

Bass, Dorothy C. "Eating." In *The Wiley-Blackwell Companion to Practical Theology*, edited by Bonnie J. Miller-McLemore, 51–60. Malden, MA: Blackwell, 2012.

Bavinck, Herman. *Reformed Dogmatics*, Vol. 1, *Prolegomena*. Translated by John Vriend. Grand Rapids: Baker Academic, 2003.

BIBLIOGRAPHY

Baxter, Margaret. *The Formation of the Christian Scriptures*. Philadelphia: Westminster, 1988.
Beardsley, Monroe C. *Aesthetics from Classical Greece to the Present: A Short History*. Tuscaloosa, AL: University of Alabama Press, 1966.
Beaudoin, Tom, ed. *Secular Music and Sacred Theology*. Collegeville, MN: Liturgical, 2013.
Begbie, Jeremy S. *Theology, Music, and Time*. New York: Cambridge University Press, 2000.
Begbie, Jeremy S., Daniel K. L. Chua, and Markus Rathey, eds. *Theology, Music, and Modernity: Struggles for Freedom*. New York: Oxford University Press, 2021.
Belasco, Warren. *Food: The Key Concepts*. New York: Bloomsbury Academic, 2008. Kindle.
———. *Meals to Come: A History of the Future of Food*. Berkeley, CA: University of California Press, 2006.
Benitez Riley, Siobhan Christine. "Table of Sacrifice, Table of Plenty: Toward a Sacramental Family Food Ethic." PhD diss., Catholic University of America, 2019. ProQuest (13426744).
Bennett, Kyle David. "Involved Withdrawal: A Phenomenology of Fasting." PhD diss., Fuller Theological Seminary, 2013. UMI Microform (3565377).
Benson, Bruce Ellis, and Norman Wirzba. *Words of Life: New Theological Turns in French Phenomenology*. New York: Fordham University Press, 2010.
Berger, Peter L., and Thomas Luckmann. *The Social Construction of Reality: A Treatise in the Sociology of Knowledge*. New York: Doubleday, 1966.
Berghuis, Kent D. "Christian Fasting: A Theological Approach." PhD diss., Trinity International University, 2002. UMI Microform (3068014).
Berkhof, Louis. *Systematic Theology*. 4th ed. Grand Rapids: Eerdmans, 1959.
Berkouwer, G. C. *Holy Scripture*. Grand Rapids: Eerdmans, 1975.
Bernard, Tim Daniel. "A Covenant of Salt." Jewish Theological Seminary. March 27, 2020. https://www.jtsa.edu/torah/a-covenant-of-salt.
Berry, Wendell. *The Art of the Commonplace: The Agrarian Essays of Wendell Berry*. Edited by Norman Wirzba. Berkeley, CA: Counterpoint, 2002.
———. *The Unsettling of America: Culture & Agriculture*. San Francisco: Sierra Club, 1986.
———. *The World-Ending Fire: The Essential Wendell Berry*. Berkeley, CA: Counterpoint, 2017.
Berthrong, John H., and Evelyn Nagai Berthrong. *Confucianism: A Short Introduction*. Oxford: Oneworld, 2000.
Beyers, Jaco. "How Scientific Is Theology Really? A Matter of Credibility." *HTS Teologiese Studies/Theological Studies* 72.4. http://dx.doi.org/10.4102/ hts.v72i4.3449.
Bhaskar, Roy. *Reclaiming Reality: A Critical Introduction to Contemporary Philosophy*. London: Routledge, 2011.
Bhatia, S. C. *Food Biotechnology*. New Delhi: Woodhead, 2016.
Billings, J. Todd. *The Word of God for the People of God: An Entryway to the Theological Interpretation of Scripture*. Grand Rapids: Eerdmans, 2010.
Billington, Ray. *Understanding Eastern Philosophy*. London: Routledge, 1997.
Bird, Michael. *Evangelical Theology: A Biblical and Systematic Introduction*. 2nd ed. Grand Rapids: Zondervan Academic, 2020.
Bittman, Mark. *Animal, Vegetable, Junk: A History of Food, from Sustainable to Suicidal*. Boston: Houghton Mifflin Harcourt, 2021.

Black, Max. *Models and Metaphors: Studies in Language and Philosophy*. Ithaca, NY: Cornell University Press, 1962.

———. "More about Metaphor." In *Metaphor and Thought*, edited by Andrew Ortony, 19–41. 2nd ed. New York: Cambridge University Press, 1993.

Bloesch, Donald G. *Holy Scripture: Revelation, Inspiration, & Interpretation*. Downers Grove, IL: IVP, 1994.

Blomberg, Craig. *Contagious Holiness: Jesus' Meals with Sinners*. New Studies in Biblical Theology 19. Downers Grove, IL: IVP Academic, 2005.

———. "Matthew." In *Commentary on the New Testament Use of the Old Testament*, edited by G. K. Beale and D. A. Carson, 1–109. Grand Rapids: Baker Academic, 2007.

Blowers, Paul M. *Drama of the Divine Economy: Creator and Creation in Early Christian Theology and Piety*. Oxford: Oxford University Press, 2012.

Blowers, Paul M., and Peter W. Martens, eds. *The Oxford Handbook of Early Christian Biblical Interpretation*. New York: Oxford University Press, 2019.

Bockmuehl, Klaus. *The Unreal God of Modern Theology—Bultmann, Barth, and the Theology of Atheism: A Call to Recovering the Truth of God's Reality*. Translated by Geoffrey W. Bromiley. Colorado Springs, CO: Helmers & Howard, 1988.

Bockmuehl, Markus, and Alan J. Torrance, eds. *Scripture's Doctrine and Theology's Bible: How the New Testament Shapes Christian Dogmatics*. Grand Rapids: Baker Academic, 2008.

Boersma, Hans. *Scripture as Real Presence: Sacramental Exegesis in the Early Church*. Grand Rapids: Baker Academic, 2017.

———. *Violence, Hospitality, and the Cross: Reappropriating the Atonement Tradition*. Grand Rapids: Baker Academic, 2004.

Boff, Leonardo. *Cry of the Earth, Cry of the Poor*. Maryknoll, NY: Orbis, 2008.

Boffey, Matthew. "7 Key Elements of the Doctrine of Scripture." The Logos Bible Software Blog. March 23, 2018. https://blog.logos.com/2018/03/7-key-elements-doctrine-scripture/.

Boggs, Alli Voorhees. "A Christian Hermeneutic of Simplicity: A Holistic Perspective on Lifestyle and Environmental Decisions." ThM thesis, Anderson University School of Theology, 2016. ProQuest (10115700).

Boisvert, Raymond D. *I Eat, Therefore I Think: Food and Philosophy*. Lanham, MD: Fairleigh Dickinson University Press, 2014.

Boisvert, Raymond D., and Lisa Heldke. *Philosophers at Table: On Food and Being Human*. London: Reaktion, 2016.

Bonhoeffer, Dietrich. *The Communion of Saints*. Translated by Ronald Gregor Smith. New York: Harper & Row, 1963.

Booker, Hilary B. "A Poetics of Food in the Bahamas: Intentional Journeys through Food, Consciousness, and the Aesthetics of Everyday Life." PhD diss., Antioch University New England, 2017. ProQuest (10626774).

Boothe, Charles Octavius. *Plain Theology for Plain People*. Bellingham, WA: Lexham, 2017.

Bordo, Susan. "Anorexia Nervosa: Psychopathology as the Crystallization of Culture." In *Cooking, Eating, Thinking: Transformative Philosophies of Food*, edited by Deane W. Curtin and Lisa M. Heldke, 28–55. Indianapolis: Indiana University Press, 1992.

Borghini, Andrea. "Philosophy of Food." ThoughtCo (Feb. 16, 2021). http://thoughtco.com/philosophy-of-food-2670489.

Bowker, John. *Problems of Suffering in Religions of the World*. New York: Cambridge University Press, 1970.
Braaten, Carl E., and LaVonne Braaten. *The Living Temple: A Practical Theology of the Body and the Foods of the Earth*. Eugene, OR: Wipf and Stock, 2016.
Brady, Emily. "Smells, Tastes, and Everyday Aesthetics." In *The Philosophy of Food*, edited by David M. Kaplan, 69–86. Berkeley, CA: University of California Press, 2012.
Brakke, David. *Athanasius and the Politics of Asceticism*. New York: Oxford University Press, 1995.
Braxton, Brad. "Preaching, Politics, and Paul in Contemporary African-American Christianity." In *The Oxford Handbook of the Reception History of the Bible*, edited by Michael Lieb, Emma Mason, and Jonathan Roberts, 556–75. New York: Oxford University Press, 2011.
Brillat-Savarin, Jean Anthelme. *The Physiology of Taste, or Meditations on Transcendental Gastronomy*. Translated by M. F. K. Fisher. New York: Heritage, 1976.
Brook, Peter. *The Empty Space*. London: MacGibbon and Kee, 1968.
Brooke, John Hedley. *Science and Religion: Some Historical Perspectives*. New York: Cambridge University Press, 2014.
Brown, David. *God and Mystery in Words: Experience through Metaphor and Drama*. New York: Oxford University Press, 2008.
Brown, Jeannine K. *Scripture as Communication: Introducing Biblical Hermeneutics*. Grand Rapids: Baker Academic, 2007.
Brown, William P. *Sacred Sense: Discovering the Wonder of God's Word and World*. Grand Rapids: Eerdmans, 2015.
Brueggemann, Walter. *The Bible Makes Sense*. Rev. ed. Winona, MN: Saint Mary's, 1997.
———. *The Book That Breathes New Life: Scriptural Authority and Biblical Theology*. Minneapolis, MN: Fortress, 2005.
———. *Texts under Negotiation: The Bible and Postmodern Imagination*. Minneapolis, MN: Fortress, 1993.
———. *Truth Speaks to Power: The Countercultural Nature of Scripture*. Louisville, KY: Westminster John Knox Press, 2013.
Brumberg-Kraus, Jonathan. "'Bread from Heaven, Bread from the Earth': Recent Trends in Jewish Food History Writing." In *Writing Food History: A Global Perspective*, edited by Kyri W. Claflin and Peter Scholliers, 121–39. New York: Berg, 2012.
Brümmer, Vincent. *The Model of Love: A Study in Philosophical Theology*. New York: Cambridge University Press, 1993.
Buckholtz, Thomas J. *Models for Physics of the Very Small and Very Large*. Amsterdam, Netherlands: Atlantis, 2016.
Bulthuis, Kyle T. "Food for Thought, Food for Action: An Historical Analysis of Latter-Day Saint and Seventh-Day Adventist Dietary Laws." MA thesis, Utah State University, 2000. UMI Microform (1402659).
Buschart, W. David, and Kent Eilers. *Theology as Retrieval: Receiving the Past, Renewing the Church*. Downers Grove, IL: IVP, 2015.
Byrne, Peter, and Leslie Houlden, eds. *Companion Encyclopedia of Theology*. London: Routledge, 1995.
Cagney, Michael F. "The Problem of 'Big Food' and the Response of an Integrated Catholic Ecological Ethic." PhD diss., Boston College, 2016. ProQuest (10194987).
Cajes, Prisco A. "*Anitism* and *Perichoresis*: Towards a Filipino Christian Eco-Theology of Nature." PhD diss., Graduate Theological Union, 2002. UMI Microform (3047770).

Calvin, John. *Commentary on the Book of Psalms*, Vol. 5. Translated by James Anderson. Edinburgh: Calvin Translation Society, 1849.

———. *Commentaries on the Epistle of Paul the Apostle to the Hebrews*. In *Calvin's Commentaries*, Vol. 22. Grand Rapids: Baker, 2005.

———. *Commentary on the Holy Gospel of Jesus Christ according to John*. In *Calvin's Commentaries*. Vol. 18. Grand Rapids: Baker, 2005.

Camille, Alice. "Famines, Fasts, and Feasts: A Close Look at Scripture Shows the Importance of Food throughout Human History." *U.S. Catholic* 82.6, June 2017, 47–49.

Campbell, T. Colin. *The Future of Nutrition*. Dallas, TX: BenBella, 2020.

Capon, Robert Farrar. *Food for Thought: Resurrecting the Art of Eating*. New York: Harcourt Brace Jovanovich, 1978.

———. *The Supper of the Lamb: A Culinary Reflection*. New York: Smithmark, 1996.

Carnell, Edward John. "Love." In *Baker's Dictionary of Theology*, edited by Everett F. Harrison, Geoffrey W. Bromiley, and Carl F. H. Henry, 332–33. Grand Rapids: Baker, 1960.

Carson, D. A. *Christ and Culture Revisited*. Grand Rapids: Eerdmans, 2008.

———. *Collected Writings on Scripture*. Wheaton, IL: Crossway, 2010.

———, ed. *The Enduring Authority of the Christian Scriptures*. Grand Rapids: Eerdmans, 2016.

Carson, D. A., and John D. Woodbridge, eds. *Scripture and Truth*. Grand Rapids: Baker, 1992.

Carter, Craig. A. *Interpreting Scripture with the Great Tradition: Recovering the Genius of Premodern Exegesis*. Grand Rapids: Baker Academic, 2018.

Castello, Daniel, and Robert W. Wall. *The Marks of Scripture: Rethinking the Nature of the Bible*. Grand Rapids: Baker Academic, 2019.

Cantalupo, Charles. "Hobbes' Use of Metaphor." In *Restoration: Studies in English Literary Culture, 1660–1700* 12.1 (1988) 20–32.

Chafer, Lewis S. *Systematic Theology*, Vol. 1. Dallas, TX: Dallas Seminary Press, 1974.

Chai, Ch'u, and Winberg Chai. *Confucianism*. Woodbury, NY: Barron's Educational Series, 1973.

Chan, Simon. *Spiritual Theology: A Systematic Study of the Christian Life*. Downers Grove, IL: IVP, 1998.

Chan, Wing-Tsit, trans. *A Source Book in Chinese Philosophy*. Princeton: Princeton University Press, 1963.

Chapman, Emily Stimpson. *The Catholic Table: Finding Joy Where Food and Faith Meet*. Steubenville, OH: Emmaus Road, 2016.

Chard, Robert L. "Rituals and Scriptures of the Stove Cult." In *Ritual and Scripture in Chinese Popular Religion: Five Studies*, edited by David Johnson, 3–54. New Haven, CT: Chinese Popular Culture Project, 1995.

Charles, Marilyn. *Constructing Realities: Transformations through Myth and Metaphor*. New York: Rodopi, 2004.

Charry, Ellen T. *By the Renewing of Your Minds: The Pastoral Function of Christian Doctrine*. New York: Oxford University Press, 1997.

Cheng, Chung-Ying. "Chinese Metaphysics as Non-Metaphysics: Confucian and Taoist Insights into the Nature of Reality." In *Understanding the Chinese Mind: The Philosophical Roots*, edited by Robert E. Allinson, 167–208. Oxford: Oxford University Press, 1989.

BIBLIOGRAPHY

Chester, Tim. *A Meal with Jesus: Discovering Grace, Community & Mission around the Table*. Wheaton, IL: Crossway, 2011.

Chignell, Andrew, Terence Cuneo, and Matthew C. Halteman. *Philosophy Comes to Dinner: Arguments about the Ethics of Eating*. London: Routledge, 2016.

Childs, Brevard S. *Biblical Theology of the Old and New Testaments: Theological Reflection on the Christian Bible*. Minneapolis, MN: Fortress, 1993.

Ching, Julia. *Chinese Religions*. Maryknoll, NY: Orbis, 1993.

Chong, Hwa Young. "Toward a Theology of *Maum*: The Broken Body of God and the Broken Bodies of Comfort Women." PhD diss., Garrett-Evangelical Theological Seminary, 2009. UMI Microform (3356206).

Christensen, Duane L. *Deuteronomy 1:1—21:9*. Rev. ed. Word Biblical Commentary 6A. Nashville: Thomas Nelson, 2001.

Ciraulo, Jonathan Martin. "The Eucharistic Theology of Hans Urs von Balthasar." PhD diss., University of Notre Dame, 2018. ProQuest (13836133).

Civitello, Linda. *Cuisine and Culture: A History of Food and People*. Hoboken, NJ: Wiley and Sons, 2008.

Claassens, L. Juliana M. "The God Who Feeds: A Feminist-Theological Analysis of Key Pentateuchal and Intertestamental Texts." PhD diss., Princeton Theological Seminary, 2001. UMI Microform (3006838).

Clark, David K. *To Know and Love God: Method for Theology*. Foundations of Evangelical Theology. Wheaton, IL: Crossway, 2003.

Cohen, Martin. *I Think, Therefore I Eat: The World's Greatest Minds Tackle the Food Question*. Nashville, TN: Turner, 2018.

Cohen, Ted. *Thinking of Others: On the Talent for Metaphor*. Princeton: Princeton University Press, 2008.

Coin, John Ross. "Assisting Anchor Baptist Church of Grand Rapids, Michigan, with Engaging the Celiac Community with the Gospel." DMin thesis, The Southern Baptist Theological Seminary, 2014. UMI Microform (3669658).

Cole, Graham. *Faithful Theology: An Introduction*. Wheaton, IL: Crossway, 2020.

Combs, Gene, and Jill Freedman. *Symbol, Story, and Ceremony: Using Metaphor in Individual and Family Therapy*. New York: Norton, 1990.

Confucius. *The Analects*. Translated by David Hinton. New York: Counterpoint, 1998.

———. *Analects, with Selections from Traditional Commentaries*. Translated by Edward Slingerland. Indianapolis, IN: Hackett, 2003.

Conley, Thomas M. *Rhetoric in the European Tradition*. Chicago: University of Chicago Press, 1990.

Coolman, Boyd Taylor. "Spiritual Apprehension: The Spiritual Senses and the Knowledge of God in the Theology of William of Auxerre." PhD diss., University of Notre Dame, 2001. UMI Microform (3001482).

Cooper, David E. *A Philosophy of Gardens*. New York: Oxford University Press, 2006.

Corcoran, Kevin J. *Rethinking Human Nature: A Christian Materialist Alternative to the Soul*. Grand Rapids: Baker Academic, 2006.

Corey, Judith L. *Light from Light: Cosmology and the Theology of the Logos*. Minneapolis, MN: Fortress, 2016.

Corley, Bruce, Steve W. Lemke, and Grant I. Lovejoy. *Biblical Hermeneutics: A Comprehensive Introduction to Interpreting Scripture*. 2nd ed. Nashville, TN: B&H, 2002.

Cornish, Richard. *Brain Food: A Culinary Cornucopia of Questions*. Melbourne: Melbourne University Press, 2017.
Cortez, Marc. *Resourcing Theological Anthropology: A Constructive Account of Humanity in the Light of Christ*. Grand Rapids: Zondervan, 2017.
———. *Theological Anthropology: A Guide for the Perplexed*. London: T&T Clark International, 2010.
Cotter, David W. *Genesis*. Berit Olam Series. Collegeville, MN: Liturgical, 2016.
Coultate, T. P. *Food: The Chemistry of Its Components*. 4th ed. Cambridge: The Royal Society of Chemistry, 2002.
Cowan, George A., David Pines, and David Meltzer, eds. *Complexity: Metaphors, Models, and Reality*. Reading, MA: Addison-Wesley, 1994.
Craigie, Peter C., Page H. Kelley, and Joel F. Drinkard Jr. *Jeremiah 1–25*. Word Biblical Commentary 26. Nashville, TN: Thomas Nelson, 1991.
Craigo-Snell, Shannon. *The Empty Church: Theater, Theology, and Bodily Hope*. New York: Oxford University Press, 2014.
Crane, Jonathan K. *Eating Ethically: Religion and Science for a Better Diet*. New York: Columbia University Press, 2018.
Crawford, Nathan. *Theology as Improvisation: A Study in the Musical Nature of Theological Thinking*. Boston: Brill, 2013.
Creel, H. G. *Chinese Thought from Confucius to Mao Tse-tung*. London: Eyre & Spottiswoode, 1954.
———. *Confucius and the Chinese Way*. New York: Harper and Brothers, 1949.
Crisp, Oliver D. *Approaching the Atonement: The Reconciling Work of Christ*. Downers Grove, IL: IVP, 2020.
———. *Divinity and Humanity: The Incarnation Reconsidered*. New York: Cambridge University Press, 2007.
Crisp, Oliver D., and Fred Sanders. *The Christian Doctrine of Humanity: Explorations in Constructive Dogmatics*. Grand Rapids: Zondervan, 2018.
Crisp, Oliver D., and Fred Sanders. *The Voice of God in the Text of Scripture*. Grand Rapids: Zondervan, 2016.
Crush, Jonathan. *The Food Insecurities of Zimbabwean Migrants in Urban South Africa*. Oxford: Southern African Migration Programme, 2016.
Csikszentmihalyi, Mark. "Confucius." *Stanford Encyclopedia of Philosophy*. March 31, 2020. https://plato.stanford.edu/entries/confucius/index.html#ref-1.
Cunningham, Conor. *Genealogy of Nihilism: Philosophies of Nothing and the Difference of Theology*. London: Routledge, 2002.
Cunningham, Mary B., and Elizabeth Theokritoff, eds. *The Cambridge Companion to Orthodox Christian Theology*. New York: Cambridge University Press, 2008.
Curtin, Deane W., and Lisa M. Heldke. "Introduction." In *Cooking, Eating, Thinking: Transformative Philosophies of Food*, edited by Deane W. Curtin and Lisa M. Heldke, xiii–xvii. Indianapolis: Indiana University Press, 1992.
Dailey, Erik W. "The Fit Shall Inherit the Earth: A Theology of Sport and Fitness." PhD diss., Fuller Theological Seminary, 2017. ProQuest (10272711).
Danielewicz, Joe. *Models, Metaphor, and Meaning: How Models Use Metaphors to Convey Meaning*. Seattle, WA: Kindle Direct, 2020.
Daniell, Anne M. "Incarnating Theology in an Estuary-Carnival Place: New Orleans in the Pontchartrain Basin." PhD diss., Drew University, 2005. UMI Microform (3199670).

Danielson, Robert A. "Earthly Food at the Heavenly Banquet: A New Model for an Evangelical Protestant Inculturation-Contextualization of Holy Communion in Global Mission." PhD diss., E. Stanley Jones School of World Mission and Evangelism, 2005. UMI Microform (3179534).
Davis, Ellen F. *Scripture, Culture, and Agriculture: An Agrarian Reading of the Bible.* Cambridge: Cambridge University Press, 2008.
Davison, Andrew. *Participation in God: A Study in Christian Doctrine and Metaphysics.* New York: Cambridge University Press, 2019.
Dawn, Marva. "Practiced Theology—Lived Spirituality." In *For All the Saints: Evangelical Theology and Christian Spirituality*, edited by Timothy George and Alister McGrath, 137–54. Louisville, KY: Westminster John Knox, 2003.
Dawson, Raymond. *Confucius.* Oxford: Oxford University Press, 1981.
D'Costa, Gavin. *Theology in the Public Square: Church, Academy, and Nation.* Malden, MA: Blackwell, 2005.
Deane-Drummond, Celia E., and David Clough. *Creaturely Theology: God, Humans and Other Animals.* London: Hymns Ancient & Modern, 2009.
DeBenedictis, Nicole. "Food, the Body, and Experience in Boccaccio's *Decameron*." PhD diss., Stanford University, 2019. http://purl.stanford.edu/ns831bh2608.
Dennis, S. Yael. *Edible Entanglements: On a Political Theology of Food.* Eugene, OR: Cascade, 2019.
Dentith, Simon. *Bakhtinian Thought: An Introductory Reader.* London: Routledge, 1995.
Detisch, Scott P. "Paul VI's *Mysterium Fidei*: Bridging the Objective and the Subjective Dimensions of Eucharistic Real Presence." PhD diss., Duquesne University, 1997. UMI Microform (9623860).
Devitt, Michael, and Kim Sterelny. *Language and Reality: An Introduction to the Philosophy of Language.* 2nd ed. Oxford: Blackwell, 1999.
DeWolf, L. Harold. *A Theology of the Living Church.* New York: Harper & Brothers, 1953.
Dharamraj, Havilah. "On the Doctrine of Scripture: An Asian Conversation." In *Asian Christian Theology: Evangelical Perspectives*, edited by Timoteo D. Gener and Stephen T. Pardue, 39–59. Carlisle, UK: Langham Global Library, 2019.
Dionysius the Areopagite. *Ecclesiastical Hierarchy.* In *The Works of Dionysius the Areopagite*, translated by John Parker, 35–156. Houston, TX: Veritatis Splendor, 2013.
———. *On Divine Names.* In *The Works of Dionysius the Areopagite*, translated by John Parker, 35–156. Houston, TX: Veritatis Splendor, 2013.
Diven, Rene, Roslyn Frank, and Martin Putz, eds. *Cognitive Models in Language and Thought: Ideology, Metaphors and Meanings.* New York: de Gruyter, 2003.
Dixon, Thomas. *Science and Religion: A Very Short Introduction.* New York: Oxford University Press, 2008.
"Does Everything in the World Need the Sun to Survive?" *UCSB ScienceLine*, May, 26, 2016. http://scienceline.ucsb.edu/getkey.php?key=5412#:~:text=Most%20organisms%20either%20directly%20or,to%20make%20sugars%20and%20oxygen.
Doriani, Daniel M. "Take, Read." In *The Enduring Authority of the Christian Scriptures*, edited by D. A. Carson, 1119–54. Grand Rapids: Eerdmans, 2016.
Dostoevsky, Fyodor. *The Brothers Karamazov.* Translated by Richard Pevear and Larissa Volokhonsky. New York: Vintage Classics, 1992.
Dotson, Don Wade. "The Science of God: Philosophy of Science and the Search for Theological Foundations." PhD diss., The Union Institute, 1997. UMI Microform (9804164).

Dube, Jimmy G. "Towards a Theology of the Excluded: A Socio-Political Agenda for 21st Century Zimbabwean Methodism." PhD diss., Drew University, 2005. UMI Microform (3166957).

Duby, Steven J. *God in Himself: Scripture Metaphysics, and the Task of Christian Theology.* Downers Grove, IL: IVP, 2019.

Dufresne, Mary. "Our Bodies Are Not Our Own: A Theology of Food and the Body." MA thesis, Ave Maria University, 2020. ProQuest (27959270).

Dulles, Avery. "The Eucharist as Sacrifice." In *Rediscovering the Eucharist: Ecumenical Conversations*, edited by Roch A. Kereszty, 175–87. Mahwah, NJ: Paulist, 2003.

———. *Models of Revelation.* Garden City, NY: Doubleday, 1983.

Duvall, J. Scott, and J. Daniel Hays. *Grasping God's Word: A Hands-On Approach to Reading, Interpreting, and Applying the Bible.* 4th ed. Grand Rapids: Zondervan Academic, 2020.

East, Brad. *The Doctrine of Scripture.* Eugene, OR: Cascade, 2021.

Eberhart, Timothy Reinhold. "Rooted and Grounded in Love: Joining God's Feast of Holy Communion in the Global Market Economy." PhD diss., Vanderbilt University, 2012. UMI Microform (3533788).

Ebrey, Patricia. "The Liturgies for Sacrifices to Ancestors in Successive Versions of the *Family Rituals*." In *Ritual and Scripture in Chinese Popular Religion: Five Studies*, edited by David Johnson, 104–36. New Haven, CT: Chinese Popular Culture Project, 1995.

Eco, Umberto. *From the Tree to the Labyrinth: Historical Studies on the Sign and Interpretation.* Translated by Anthony Oldcorn. Cambridge, MA: Harvard University Press, 2014.

Ehrman, Bart D., Michael F. Bird, and Robert B. Stewart. *When Did Jesus Become God? A Christological Debate.* Louisville, KY: Westminster John Knox, 2022.

Ellis, A. C. "Academic Theology and Christian Growth: An Exploration into the Use and Potential of Theology as a Resource in Christian Faith and Living." PhD diss., University of Manchester, 1980. ProQuest (28115407).

Emory, Gilles, and Matthew Levering, eds. *The Oxford Handbook of the Trinity.* New York: Oxford University Press, 2011.

Enns, Peter. *The Bible Tells Me So: Why Defending Scripture Has Made Us Unable to Read It.* New York: HarperCollins, 2014.

Epstein, Heidi. "The Nature of the Relationship between Music and Theology according to Oskar Söhngen and Oliver Messiaen." MA thesis, McGill University, 1990. https://escholarship.mcgill.ca/concern/theses/7h149q943.

Erickson, Millard J. *Christian Theology.* 3rd ed. Grand Rapids: Baker, 2013.

Eschliman, Carley. "Let's Grab a Bite: The Intersection of Eating and Community." *Claritas: A Journal of Christian Thought* 5 (Fall 2017) 9–11.

Eustace, Tanya Marie. "Experiencing God Together: A Practical Theology for Ministry with Children." PhD diss., Garrett-Evangelical Theological Seminary, 2014. UMI Microform (3645732).

Fagerberg, David Wilson. "What Is Liturgical Theology? A Study in Theological Method." PhD diss., Yale University, 1991. UMI Microform (9221331).

Fan, Lizhu, and James D. Whitehead. "Spirituality in a Modern Chinese Metropolis." In *Chinese Religious Life*, edited by David A. Palmer, Glenn Shive, and Philip L. Wickeri, 13–29. Oxford: Oxford University Press, 2011.

Farkasfalvy, Denis. "The Eucharistic Provenance of New Testament Texts." In *Rediscovering the Eucharist: Ecumenical Conversations*, edited by Roch A. Kereszty, 27–51. Mahwah, NJ: Paulist, 2003.

———. *Inspiration & Interpretation: A Theological Introduction to Sacred Scripture*. Washington, DC: Catholic University of America Press, 2010.

———. *A Theology of the Christian Bible: Revelation, Inspiration, Canon*. Washington, DC: Catholic University of America Press, 2018.

Farris, Joshua R. *Introduction to Theological Anthropology*. Ada, OK: Baker Academic, 2020.

Faulkner, Gregory C. "Return to the Eucharist: The Eucharistic Ecclesiology of Alexander Schmemann's Liturgical Theology and Its Methodological Implications for a Reformed Liturgical Theology." PhD diss., Princeton Theological Seminary, 2001. UMI Microform (3006830).

Feeley-Harnik, Gillian. *The Lord's Table: The Meaning of Food in Early Judaism and Christianity*. Washington, DC: Smithsonian Institution, 1994.

Feibleman, James K. *Understanding Oriental Philosophy: A Popular Account for the Western World*. New York: New American Library, 1976.

Feinberg, John S. *Light in a Dark Place: The Doctrine of Scripture*. Wheaton, IL: Crossway, 2018.

———. *No One Like Him: The Doctrine of God*. Wheaton, IL: Crossway, 2001.

Feinberg, Margaret. *Taste and See: Discovering God among Butchers, Bakers, and Fresh Food Makers*. Grand Rapids: Zondervan, 2019.

Ferguson, Priscilla Parkhurst. *Word of Mouth: What We Talk About When We Talk about Food*. Berkeley, CA: University of California Press, 2014.

Fernandez, Jennifer. "Theology of Bread and Roses: A Feminist Relational Theology Embracing Women's Social Movements as Divine In-Breaking." PhD diss., Graduate Theological Union, 2020. ProQuest (28149210).

Ferrara, Massimo. "Food, Migration, and Identity: Halal Food and Muslim Immigrants in Italy." MA thesis, University of Kansas, 2011. UMI Microform (1494287).

Fick, Gary W. *Food, Farming, and Faith*. Albany, NY: State University of New York, 2008.

Fiddes, Nick. *Meat: A Natural Symbol*. London: Routledge, 1991.

Fieldhouse, Paul. *Food, Feasts, and Faith: An Encyclopedia of Food Culture in World Religions*. Santa Barbara, CA: ABC-CLIO, LLC, 2017.

Fields, Leslie Leyland, ed. *The Spirit of Food: 34 Writers on Feasting and Fasting toward God*. Eugene, OR: Cascade, 2010.

Fingarette, Herbert. *Confucius—The Secular as Sacred*. New York: Harper & Row, 1972.

Fisher, Hendrik Johannes. "Food Stylists' Food Image Creation for Print Media and Consumer Interpretation: An Exploratory Investigation." PhD diss., University of Pretoria, 2012. UMI Microform (1595658).

Fisher, M. F. K. *The Art of Eating*. Hoboken, NJ: Wiley, 2004.

———. *Here Let Us Feast: A Book of Banquets—An Epicure's Zestful Visit to the Festive Boards of Ancient & Modern Literature*. New York: Viking, 1946.

Fiumara, Gemma Corradi. *The Metaphoric Process: Connections between Language and Life*. London: Routledge, 1995.

———. *The Other Side of Language: A Philosophy of Listening*. London: Routledge, 1990.

Flandrin, Jean-Louis, and Massimo Montanari, eds. *Food: A Culinary History*. New York: Columbia University Press, 1999.

Fletcher-Watts, Vivienne Joy. "A Study of Deuteronomic and Priestly Legislation with Particular Reference to Clean and Unclean Foods." MA thesis, Andrews University, 1982. UMI Microform (1320840).

Floyd, Richard. "Down to Earth: Moltmann, McFague, and the Search for an Ecological Eschatology." PhD diss., Emory University, 2014. UMI Microform (3639913).

Fosner, Verlon. "Dinner Church: An Urban Proposal." DMin thesis, Assemblies of God Theological Seminary, 2014. UMI Microform (3617565).

Foss, Sonja K. *Rhetorical Criticism: Exploration and Practice*. 5th ed. Long Grove, IL: Waveland, 2018.

Ford, David F., Ben Quash, and Janet M. Soskice, eds. *Fields of Faith: Theology and Religious Studies for the Twenty-First Century*. New York: Cambridge University Press, 2005.

Forrester, Duncan B. *Truthful Action: Explorations in Practical Theology*. Edinburgh: T&T Clark, 2000.

Foucachon, Francis. *Food for Thought: Reflections and Recipes*. 2nd ed. Moscow, ID: Roman Roads Media, 2020.

Fouche, Christopher Edward. "Acquired Tastes: Virtue, Community, and Eating Ethically." PhD diss., University of Florida, 2017. ProQuest (10902796).

Fowl, Stephen E. *Engaging Scripture: A Model for Theological Interpretation*. Malden, MA: Blackwell, 1998.

———, ed. *Theological Interpretation of Scripture: Classic and Contemporary Readings*. Loyola College, MD: Blackwell, 1997.

———. "Scripture." In *The Oxford Handbook of Systematic Theology*, edited by John Webster, Kathryn Tanner, and Iain Torrance, 345–61. New York: Oxford University Press, 2007.

Fowler, Robert M., Edith Blumhofer, and Fernando S. Segovia, eds. *New Paradigms for Bible Study: The Bible in the Third Millennium*. London: T&T Clark, 2004.

Francis, Andrew. "How Then Shall We Eat?" DMin thesis, Princeton Theological Seminary, 2010. UMI Microform (3411332).

———. *What in God's Name Are You Eating: How Can Christians Live and Eat Responsibly in Today's Global Village*. Cambridge: Lutterworth, 2015.

Fujimura, Makoto. *Culture Care: Reconnecting with Beauty for Our Common Life*. Downers Grove, IL: IVP, 2017.

Fuller, Daniel P. *The Unity of the Bible: Unfolding God's Plan for Humanity*. Grand Rapids: Zondervan, 1992.

Fulton Brown, Rachel. "'Taste and See That the Lord Is Sweet' (Ps. 33:9) The Flavor of God in the Monastic West." *The Journal of Religion* 86.2 (2006) 169–204.

Fung, Yu-Lan. *A History of Chinese Philosophy*, Vol. 1, *The Period of the Philosophers*. Translated by Derk Bodde. Princeton: Princeton University Press, 1952.

———. *A Short History of Chinese Philosophy*. Edited by Derk Bodde. New York: Macmillan, 1960.

———. *The Spirit of Chinese Philosophy*. Translated by E. R. Hughes. London: Kegan Paul, Trench, Trubner, 1947.

Gadamer, Hans-Georg. *Philosophical Hermeneutics*. Translated and edited by David E. Linge. Berkeley, CA: University of California Press, 1976.

———. *Truth and Method*. Translated by Garrett Barden and John Cumming. London: Sheed & Ward, 1975.

Garland, David E. *1 Corinthians*. Baker Exegetical Commentary on the New Testament. Grand Rapids: Baker Academic, 2003.

———. *Luke*. Zondervan Exegetical Commentary on the New Testament. Grand Rapids: Zondervan, 2011.

Geary, James. *I Is an Other: The Secret Life of Metaphor and How It Shapes the Way We See the World*. New York: HarperCollins, 2011.

George, Christian. *Sex, Sushi, and Salvation: Thoughts on Intimacy, Community, & Eternity*. Chicago: Moody, 2008.

George, Jinto. "Exploring and Re-Envisioning the Significance of Agrarian Consciousness in Theology with Specific Reference to Kerala." MA thesis, Duquesne University, 2020. ProQuest (27955649).

Georges, Jayson, and Mark D. Baker. *Ministering in Honor-Shame Cultures: Biblical Foundations and Practical Essentials*. Downers Grove, IL: IVP, 2016.

Gerhard, Johann. *On the Nature of Theology and Scripture*. Translated by Richard J. Dinda. Saint Louis, MO: Concordia, 2006.

Gibbs, Raymond W., Jr., ed. *The Cambridge Handbook of Metaphor and Thought*. New York: Cambridge University Press, 2008.

Gignilliat, Mark S. *Reading Scripture Canonically: Theological Instincts for Old Testament Interpretation*. Grand Rapids: Baker Academic, 2019.

Glanzberg, Michael, ed. *The Oxford Handbook of Truth*. New York: Oxford University Press, 2018.

Glaser, Mitch, and Zhava Glaser. *The Fall Feasts of Israel*. Chicago: Moody, 1987.

Godfrey-Smith, Peter. *Theory and Reality: An Introduction to the Philosophy of Science*. 2nd ed. Chicago: University of Chicago Press, 2021.

Goldingay, John. *Models for Scripture*. Grand Rapids: Eerdmans, 1994.

———. *Models for the Interpretation of Scripture*. Grand Rapids: Eerdmans, 1995.

Gomes, Peter J. *The Good Book: Reading the Bible with Mind and Heart*. New York: HarperCollins, 1996.

Gonzalez, Justo L. *The Bible in the Early Church*. Grand Rapids: Eerdmans, 2022.

Gooder, Paula. *The Bible: A Beginner's Guide*. London: Oneworld, 2013.

———. *Body: Biblical Spirituality for the Whole Person*. London: SPCK, 2016.

———. *Everyday God: The Spirit of the Ordinary*. Minneapolis, MN: Fortress, 2015.

Goossaert, Vincent, and David A. Palmer. *The Religious Question in Modern China*. Chicago: University of Chicago Press, 2011.

Gordon, Joseph K. *Divine Scripture in Human Understanding: A Systematic Theology of the Christian Bible*. Notre Dame, IN: University of Notre Dame Press, 2019.

Gorman, Antonia Lee. "The Blood of Goats and Bulls: An Eco-Spiritual Response to the Sacrifice of Creation." PhD diss., Drew University, 2008. UMI Microform (3319118).

Gorman, Michael J. *Participating in Christ: Explorations in Paul's Theology and Spirituality*. Grand Rapids: Baker Academic, 2019.

Gottlieb, Robert, and Anupama Joshi. *Food Justice*. Cambridge: MIT Press, 2013.

Gould, Stephen Jay. *Time's Arrow, Time's Cycle: Myth and Metaphor in the Discovery of Geological Time*. Cambridge: Harvard University Press, 1987.

Graham, Elaine, Heather Walton, and Frances Ward. *Theological Reflection Methods*. 2nd ed. London: SCM, 2019.

Grant, Robert M. *A Short History of the Interpretation of the Bible*. New York: Macmillan, 1963.

Graves, Michael. *The Inspiration and Interpretation of Scripture: What the Early Church Can Teach Us*. Grand Rapids: Eerdmans, 2014.

Green, Chris E. W. *The End Is Music: A Companion to Robert W. Jenson's Theology.* Cascade Companions. Eugene, OR: Cascade, 2018.
Green, Joel B. *Body, Soul, and Human Life: The Nature of Humanity in the Bible.* Ada, OK: Baker Academic, 2008.
Green, Joel B., and Stuart L. Palmer. *In Search of the Soul: Four Views of the Mind-Body Problem.* Downers Grove, IL: IVP, 2005.
Green, Stephen G. *The Holy Scriptures.* Kansas City, MS: Foundry, 2021.
Gregory the Great. *Moralia in Job.* Vol. 1. Translated by James Bliss and Charles Marriott. Jackson, MI: Ex Fontibus, 2012.
Grenfell-Lee, Tallessyn Zawn. "Garden Earth and Church Gardens: Creation, Food, and Ecological Ethics." PhD diss., Boston University, 2016. ProQuest (10113461).
Grimm, Veronika E. *From Feasting to Fasting, the Evolution of a Sin.* London: Routledge, 1996.
Grudem, Wayne. *Systematic Theology: An Introduction to Biblical Doctrine,* 2nd ed. Grand Rapids: Zondervan, 2020.
Grumett, David, and Rachel Muers, eds. *Eating and Believing: Interdisciplinary Perspectives on Vegetarianism and Theology.* London: T&T Clark, 2008.
———. *Theology on the Menu: Asceticism, Meat, and Christian Diet.* London: Routledge, 2010.
Guo, Qiyong, and Tao Cui. "A Study on Pre-Qin Confucian Scholars' Environmental Ethics." In *Contemporary Confucianism in Thought and Action,* edited by Guy Alitto, 41–61. New York: Springer, 2015.
Gustafsson, Ulla, Alizon Draper, Andrea Tonner, and Rebecca O'Connell, eds. *What Is Food? Researching a Topic with Many Meanings.* London: Routledge, 2020.
Guttenplan, Samuel. *Objects of Metaphor.* Oxford: Clarendon, 2005.
Guyer, Paul. *Kant and the Claims of Taste.* 2nd ed. New York: Cambridge University Press, 1997.
Hall, Christopher A. *Reading Scripture with the Church Fathers.* Downers Grove, IL: IVP, 1998.
Hall, David L. "The Way and the Truth." In *A Companion to World Philosophies,* edited by Eliot Deutsch and Ron Bontekoe, 214–24. Malden, MA: Blackwell, 1999.
Hallanger, Nathan J. "Ian G. Barbour." In *The Blackwell Companion to Science and Christianity,* edited by J. B. Stump and Alan G. Padgett, 600–610. Malden, MA: Blackwell, 2012.
Halteman, Matthew C., and Megan Halteman Zwart. "Philosophy as Therapy for Recovering (Unrestrained) Omnivores." In *Philosophy Comes to Dinner: Arguments about the Ethics of Eating,* edited by Andrew Chignell, Terence Cuneo, and Matthew C. Halteman, 129–48. London: Routledge, 2016.
Hamilton, Victor P. *The Book of Genesis, Chapters 1–17.* Grand Rapids: Eerdmans, 1990.
Hammel, Stefan. *Handbook of Therapeutic Storytelling: Stories and Metaphors in Psychotherapy, Child and Family Therapy, Medical Treatment, Coaching and Supervision.* London: Routledge, 2019.
Hankins, John Eric. "Meal, Martyrdom, and Mimesis: The Theology of Jesus at the Last Supper." PhD diss., Southwestern Baptist Theological Seminary, 2007. UMI Microform (3289558).
Happel, Stephen. *Metaphors for God's Time in Science and Religion.* London: Palgrave Macmillan, 2002.

Hart, David Bentley. "'Thine Own of Thine Own': Eucharistic Sacrifice in Orthodox Tradition." In *Rediscovering the Eucharist: Ecumenical Conversations*, edited by Roch A. Kereszty, 142–69. Mahwah, NJ: Paulist, 2003.

Hartley, Gregory P. "Lower Sacraments: Theological Eating in the Fiction of C. S. Lewis." PhD diss., University of South Florida, 2012. UMI Microform (3547600).

Hartley, John E. *Genesis*. New International Biblical Commentary. Peabody, MA: Hendrickson, 2000.

Hartman, Laura Marie. "An Ethics of Consumption: Christianity, Economy, and Ecology." PhD diss., University of Virginia, 2008. UMI Microform (3312142).

Harvey, John Collins. "The Morality of Withdrawing or Withholding Food and Fluid Administered Artificially to the Individual in the Persistent Vegetative State from the Roman Catholic Perspective." PhD diss., St. Mary's Seminary and University, 1988. UMI Microform (8810421).

Hauck-Lawson, Annie S. "Introduction to Special Issue on the Food Voice." *Food, Culture and Society* 7.1 (2004) 24–25.

———. "When Food Is the Voice: A Case Study of a Polish-American Woman." *Journal for the Study of Food and Society* 2.1 (1996) 21–28.

Hauck-Lawson, Annie S., and Jonathan Deutsch, eds. *Gastropolis: Food & New York City*. New York: Columbia University Press, 2009.

Hawkey, James, Ben Quash, and Vernon White, eds. *God's Song and Music's Meanings: Theology, Liturgy, and Musicology in Dialogue*. London: Routledge, 2020.

Hector, Kevin W. *Theology without Metaphysics: God, Language, and the Spirit of Recognition*. New York: Cambridge University Press, 2011.

Heggen, Bruce Allen. "A Theology for Earth: Nature and Grace in the Thought of Joseph Sittler." PhD diss., McGill University, 1995. ProQuest (NN12382).

Heidegger, Martin. *Being and Time*. Translated by John Macquarrie and Edward Robinson. London: Camelot, 1962.

Heim, Erin M. "Paths beyond Tracing Out: The Hermeneutics of Metaphor and Theological Method." In *The Voice of God in the Text of Scripture*, edited by Oliver D. Crisp and Fred Sanders, 112–26. Grand Rapids: Zondervan, 2016.

Heldke, Lisa M. "Foodmaking as a Thoughtful Practice." In *Cooking, Eating, Thinking: Transformative Philosophies of Food*, edited by Deane W. Curtin and Lisa M. Heldke, 203–29. Indianapolis: Indiana University Press, 1992.

Helm, Paul, and Carl R. Trueman, eds. *The Trustworthiness of God: Perspectives on the Nature of Scripture*. Grand Rapids: Eerdmans, 2002.

Helmer, Christine, and Charlene T. Higbe, eds. *The Multivalence of Biblical Texts and Theological Meanings*. Atlanta: Society of Biblical Literature, 2006.

Henneveld, Peter J. "Visualizing the Paschal Mystery: The Feast of Orthodoxy as a *Locus* of a Liturgical Theology of Icons." PhD diss., Catholic University of America, 2019. ProQuest (10937770).

Henry, Carl, F. H. *God, Revelation, and Authority*, Vol. 3, *God Who Speaks and Shows: Fifteen Theses, Part Two*. Waco, TX: Word, 1979.

Herring, Ronald J., ed. *The Oxford Handbook of Food, Politics, and Society*. New York: Oxford University Press, 2015.

Herzog, Frederick, ed. *Theology of the Liberating Word*. Nashville, TN: Abingdon, 1971.

Hesse, Mary B. *Models and Analogies in Science*. Notre Dame, IN: University of Notre Dame Press, 1966.

Hinson, E. Glenn. *Seekers after Mature Faith: A Historical Introduction to the Classics of Christian Devotion.* Nashville, TN: Broadman, 1968.

Hobbes, Thomas. *Leviathan: Or the Matter, Form, and Power of a Commonwealth, Ecclesiastical and Civil.* London: Routledge, 1886.

Hoerr, Caitlin. "'The Word Gave Himself as Food': Female Piety and Food in Italian Renaissance Art." PhD diss., American University, 2015. UMI Microform (1587052).

Hollar, Larry. *Hunger for the Word: Lectionary Reflections on Food and Justice—Year B.* Collegeville, MN: Liturgical, 2005.

Hoover, Alice K. "Spiritual Formation for Holistic Human Health: Connections between Weight Loss and Women's Creativity." PhD diss., United Theological Seminary, 2010. UMI Microform (3504838).

Horton, Michael. *The Christian Faith: A Systematic Theology for Pilgrims on the Way.* Grand Rapids: Zondervan, 2011.

Hughes, Ernest Richard, ed. and trans. *Chinese Philosophy in Classical Times.* London: Dent, 1954.

Hughes, Melanie Dobson. "The Practice of Habits: A Theological Account of Tending to Health." PhD diss., Duke University, 2011. UMI Microform (3474623).

Hunsinger, George. *The Eucharist and Ecumenism: Let Us Keep the Feast.* New York: Cambridge University Press, 2008.

Hwang, Jong-Ryul Leo. "Methodology and Practice of Korean Theology, A Korean Roman Catholic Approach to Doing Theology with *MingJung*." PhD diss., Duquesne University, 2003. UMI Microform (3095233).

Indian Abroad News Service (IANS). "Kitchen Secrets of Confucius, the Great Chinese Philosopher." July 22, 2013. https://food.ndtv.com/opinions/ kitchen-secrets-of-confucius-the-great-chinese-philosopher-693550.

Irenaeus. *Against Heresies.* In *Ante-Nicene Fathers*, Volume 1, edited by Alexander Roberts and James Donaldson, 307–567. Peabody, MA: Hendrickson, 1994.

Jackson, Peter. *Food Words: Essays in Culinary Culture.* London: Bloomsbury Academic, 2015.

Jacobson, Mary Elizabeth. "Increasing Motivation for Weight Loss Utilizing Faith Resources." PhD diss., United Theological Seminary, 2005. UMI Microform (3214845).

Jaeger, Lydia. "Laws of Nature." In *The Blackwell Companion to Science and Christianity*, edited by J. B. Stump and Alan G. Padgett, 453–63. Malden, MA: Blackwell, 2012.

Jang, Shin-Geun. "Constructing a Public Practical Theology: A Trinitarian-Communicative Model of Practical Theology for the Korean Public Church." PhD diss., Princeton Theological Seminary, 2002. UMI Microform (3062344).

Jaques, Jessica. "A Philosophical Reading of Brillat-Savarin's 'The Physiology of Taste.'" *Proceedings of the European Society for Aesthetics* 8, edited by Fabian Dorsch and Dan-Eugen Ratiu, 288–304. Fribourg: ESA, 2016.

Jensen, Lionel M. *Manufacturing Confucianism: Chinese Traditions and Universal Civilization.* Durham, NC: Duke University Press, 1997.

Jensen, Peter F. "God and the Bible." In *The Enduring Authority of the Christian Scriptures*, edited by D. A. Carson, 477–96. Grand Rapids: Eerdmans, 2016.

Jenson, Robert W. *Systematic Theology.* Vol. 1, *The Triune God.* New York: Oxford University Press, 1997.

———. *Systematic Theology.* Vol. 2, *The Works of God.* New York: Oxford University Press, 1999.

Jeremias, Joachim. *The Eucharistic Words of Jesus*. Translated by Norman Perrin. London: SCM, 1966.
Jipp, Joshua W. *Saved by Faith and Hospitality*. Grand Rapids: Eerdmans, 2017.
Johnson, Keith L. *Theology as Discipleship*. Downers Grove, IL: IVP, 2015.
Johnson, Todd E., and Dale Savidge. *Performing the Sacred: Theology and Theatre in Dialogue*. Grand Rapids: Baker Academic, 2009.
Jones, Beth Felker. *Practicing Christian Doctrine: An Introduction to Thinking and Living Theologically*. Grand Rapids: Baker Academic, 2014.
Juel, Donald H. *Shaping the Scriptural Imagination: Truth, Meaning, and the Theological Interpretation of the Bible*. Waco, TX: Baylor University Press, 2011.
Juengst, Sara Covin. *Breaking Bread: The Spiritual Significance of Food*. Louisville, KY: Westminster John Knox, 1992.
Jung, L. Shannon. *Sharing Food: Christian Practices for Enjoyment*. Philadelphia: Fortress, 2006.
Junru, Liu. *Chinese Food*. Cambridge: Cambridge University Press, 2010.
Kaiser, Walter C., Jr. *Recovering the Unity of the Bible: One Continuous Story, Plan, and Purpose*. Grand Rapids: Zondervan, 2009.
Kaizuka, Shigeki. *Confucius*. New York: Macmillan, 1956.
Karris, Robert J. *Eating Your Way through Luke's Gospel*. Collegeville, MN: Liturgical, 2006.
Kaltenmark, Max. *Lao Tzu and Taoism*. Translated by Roger Greaves. Stanford, CA: Stanford University Press, 1969.
Kant, Immanuel. *The Critique of Judgment*. Translated by Werner S. Pluhar. Indianapolis, IN: Hackett, 1987.
Kaplan, David M. *Food Philosophy: An Introduction*. New York: Columbia University Press, 2020.
———. "Introduction." In *The Philosophy of Food*, edited by David M. Kaplan, 1–23. Berkeley, CA: University of California Press, 2012.
———, ed. *The Philosophy of Food*. Berkeley, CA: University of California Press, 2012.
Kass, Leon R. *The Hungry Soul: Eating and the Perfecting of Our Nature*. Chicago: University of Chicago Press, 1999.
Kearney, Richard. "Transfiguring God." In *The Blackwell Companion to Postmodern Theology*, edited by Graham Ward, 369–93. Malden, MA: Blackwell, 2005.
Keener, Craig, and M. Daniel Carroll R., eds. *Global Voices: Reading the Bible in the Majority World*. Peabody, MA: Hendrickson, 2013.
Keller, Tim, and Kathy Keller. *The Songs of Jesus*. New York: Penguin, 2015.
Kempis, Thomas à. *The Imitation of Christ*. San Bernardino, CA: CreateSpace, 2014.
Kennedy, George A., trans. and ed. *Aristotle on Rhetoric: A Theory of Civic Discourse*. New York: Oxford University Press, 1991.
Kennedy, Jonathan Ryan. "*Fan* and *Tsai*: Food, Identity, and Connections in the Market Street Chinatown." PhD diss., Indiana University, 2016. ProQuest (10249424).
Kereszty, Roch. "The Eucharist of the Church and the One Self-Offering of Christ." In *Rediscovering the Eucharist: Ecumenical Conversations*, edited by Roch A. Kereszty, 240–60. Mahwah, NJ: Paulist, 2003.
Keyes, C. D. "An Evaluation of Levinas' Critique of Heidegger." *Research in Phenomenology* 2 (1972) 121–42. http://www.jstor.org/stable/24654228.
Kierkegaard, Søren. *Concluding Unscientific Postscript*. Translated by David F. Swenson. Princeton: Princeton University Press, 1941.

Kilimci, Laris. "How Do Our Food Experiences Influence Our Identity?" Academia.edu. https://www.academia.edu/10638397/How_do_our_food _experiences_influence_ our_identity?email_work_card=view-paper.

Kim, Joon-Woo. "The Idols of Death and the Theology for Life in Korea." PhD diss., Drew University, 1992. UMI Microform (9233186).

Kim, Sangwoo. "Embodied Prayer: The Practice of Prayer as Christian Theology." PhD diss., Duke University, 2016. ProQuest (10154703).

Kim, Sebastian C. H., ed. *Christian Theology in Asia*. New York: Cambridge University Press, 2008.

Kim, Yong Choon. *Oriental Thought: An Introduction to the Philosophical and Religious Thought of Asia*. Springfield, IL: Thomas, 1973.

Kim, Yun Hui. "Christian Ethics of Eating: Food and Self from a Korean Ecofeminist Perspective." PhD diss., Princeton Theological Seminary, 2011. UMI Microform (3489316).

Kiple, Kenneth F., and Kriemhild Conee Onelas, eds. *The Cambridge World History of Food*. New York: Cambridge University Press, 2000.

Klein, William W., Craig L. Blomberg, and Robert L. Hubbard Jr. *Introduction to Biblical Interpretation*. Dallas, TX: Thomas Nelson, 1993.

Koenig, John. *The Feast of the World's Redemption: Eucharistic Origins and Christian Mission*. Harrisburg, PA: Trinity, 2000.

Kohn, Livia. *Introducing Daoism*. London: Routledge, 2009.

Koller, John M. *Oriental Philosophies*. New York: Scribner's Sons, 1970.

Korsmeyer, Carolyn. *Making Sense of Taste: Food and Philosophy*. Ithaca, NY: Cornell University Press, 1999.

Korthals, Michiel. *Before Dinner: Philosophy and Ethics of Food*. Translated by Frans Kooymans. Norwell, MA: Springer, 2004.

Koster, Hillegonda Pietronella. "For the Future of the Earth: Creation and Salvation in the Theologies of Jürgen Moltmann, Catherine Keller, and Kathryn Tanner." PhD diss., University of Chicago, 2011. UMI Microform (3487656).

Kövecses, Zoltan. *Extended Conceptual Metaphor Theory*. New York: Cambridge University Press, 2020.

———. *Metaphor: A Practical Introduction*. 2nd ed. New York: Oxford University Press, 2010.

———. *Metaphor and Emotion: Language, Culture, and Body in Human Feeling*. New York: Cambridge University Press, 2004.

———. *Metaphor in Culture: Universality and Variation*. New York: Cambridge University Press, 2005.

———. *Ten Lectures on Figurative Meaning-Making: The Role of Body and Context*. Boston: Brill, 2020.

———. *Where Metaphors Come From: Reconsidering Context in Metaphor*. New York: Oxford University Press, 2015.

Kramer, Lawrence. *The Hum of the World: A Philosophy of Listening*. Oakland, CA: University of California Press, 2018.

Kreeft, Peter, ed. *Summa of the Summa: The Essential Philosophical Passages of St. Thomas Aquinas' Summa Theologica Edited and Explained for Beginners*. San Francisco: Ignatius, 1990.

BIBLIOGRAPHY

Krug, Karen Lee. "Farm Women's Perspectives on the Agricultural Crisis, Ecological Issues, and United Church of Canada Social Teaching." PhD diss., Victoria University, ProQuest (NN02633).

Kuhn, Thomas. *The Structure of Scientific Revolutions.* 2nd ed. Chicago: University of Chicago Press, 1970.

Kun, Jeanne. *Food from Heaven: The Eucharist in Scripture.* Frederick, MD: Word Among Us, 2007.

Kun, Steve Kin-Yan. "Geoffrey Wainwright's Theology from the Eucharist." PhD diss., Southwestern Baptist Theological Seminary, 2003. UMI Microform (3108662).

Kuva, Patricia Ann. "Women and Food and the Sacred: A Complex Recipe." ThM thesis, St. Stephen's College, 2001. ProQuest (MQ65183).

Ladd, Meleah L. "Liturgical Spirituality in the Kitchen: Glimpsing Domestic Churches through Books with Recipes for Food Practices to Celebrate the Church Year." PhD diss., University of Notre Dame, 2018. ProQuest (13836243).

Lakoff, George. "The Contemporary Theory of Metaphor." In *Metaphor and Thought*, edited by Andrew Ortony, 202–51. 2nd ed. New York: Cambridge University Press, 1993.

Lakoff, George, and Mark Johnson. *Metaphors We Live By.* Chicago: University of Chicago Press, 1980.

———. *Philosophy in the Flesh: The Embodied Mind and Its Challenge to Western Thought.* New York: Basic, 1999.

Laudan, Rachel. *Cuisine and Empire: Cooking and World History.* Berkeley, CA: University of California Press, 2013.

———. "A Plea for Culinary Modernism: Why We Should Love New, Fast, Processed Food." *Gastronomica: The Journal of Food and Culture* 1.1 (2001) 36–44.

Lawley, James, and Penny Tompkins. *Metaphors in Mind: Transformation through Symbolic Modelling.* New York: Crown House, 2000.

Lawrence, Brother. *The Practice of the Presence of God, with Spiritual Maxims.* Grand Rapids: Spire, 1967.

Le Billon, Karen. *French Kids Eat Everything (and Yours Can Too).* Toronto: Collins, 2012.

LeCroy, Timothy R. "The Role of *Corpus* in the Eucharistic Theology of Paschasius Radbertus." PhD diss., Saint Louis University, 2012. UMI Microform (3539809).

Lelwica, Michelle M. "The Politics of Spiritual Hunger: The Intersection of Religion, Gender and Culture in Contemporary American Girls' and Women's Struggles with Food and Their Bodies." PhD diss., Harvard University, 1996. UMI Microform (9631175).

Lepore, Ernest, and Barry C. Smith, eds. *The Oxford Handbook of Philosophy of Language.* New York: Oxford University Press, 2009.

Levering, Matthew. *Engaging the Doctrine of Revelation: The Mediation of the Gospel through Church and Scripture.* Grand Rapids: Baker Academic, 2014.

Levinas, Emmanuel. *Beyond the Verse: Talmudic Readings and Lectures.* Translated by Gary D. Mole. New York: Continuum, 2007.

———. *Totality and Infinity: An Essay on Exteriority.* Translated by Alphonso Lingis. Pittsburgh, PA: Duquesne University Press, 1969.

Lewis, C. S. *The Abolition of Man.* New York: HarperCollins, 1974.

———. *An Experiment in Criticism.* Cambridge: Cambridge University Press, 1961.

Li, Yu-Chin, Tsung-Chih Hu, and Kuo-En Chang. "Identifying Food-Related Word Association and Topic Model Processing Using LDA." *Journal of Library & Information Studies* 16.1 (2018) 23–43.

Libman, Kimberly. "Eating the City: Food Environments, Inequality, and the Everyday Journeys of Eaters in New York and London." PhD diss., City University of New York, 2012. UMI Microform (3508703).

Lieb, Michael, Emma Mason, and Jonathan Roberts, eds. *The Oxford Handbook of the Reception History of the Bible*. New York: Oxford University Press, 2011.

Lih, Lars T. *Bread and Authority in Russia, 1914–1921*. Berkeley, CA: University of California Press, 1990.

Lindbeck, George. *The Nature of Doctrine: Religion and Theology in a Postliberal Age*. 25th anniversary ed. Louisville, KY: Westminster John Knox, 2009.

Lints, Richard. "To Whom Does the Text Belong? Communities of Interpretation and the Interpretation of Communities." In *The Enduring Authority of the Christian Scriptures*, edited by D. A. Carson, 920–47. Grand Rapids: Eerdmans, 2016.

Littlemore, Jeannette. *Metaphors in the Mind: Sources of Variation in Embodied Metaphor*. New York: Cambridge University Press, 2019.

Liu, Gerald C. *Music and the Generosity of God*. London: Palgrave MacMillan, 2017.

Liu, Junru. *Chinese Food*. Cambridge: Cambridge University Press, 2010.

Liu, Wu-Chi. *Confucius, His Life and Time*. New York: Philosophical Library, 1955.

Locke, John. *An Essay Concerning Human Understanding*. London: Tegg and Son, 1836.

Long, D. Stephen. *Divine Economy: Theology and the Market*. London: Routledge, 2000.

Loue, Sana. *The Transformative Power of Metaphor in Therapy*. New York: Springer, 2008.

Louth, Andrew. *Discerning the Mystery: An Essay on the Nature of Theology*. Oxford: Clarendon, 1983.

Louth, Andrew, and Marco Conti, eds. *Genesis 1–2*. Ancient Christian Commentary on Scripture. Downers Grove, IL: IVP, 2001.

Loux, Michael J., and Dean W. Zimmerman, eds. *The Oxford Handbook of Metaphysics*. New York: Oxford University Press, 2005.

Lubac, Henri de. *Medieval Exegesis*, Vol. 1, *The Four Senses of Scripture*. Translated by Mark Sebanc. Grand Rapids: Eerdmans, 1998.

Luša, Đana, and Ružica Jakešević. "The Role of Food in Diplomacy: Communicating and 'Winning Hearts and Minds' through Food." *Media Studies* 8.16 (2017) 99–119.

Luther, Martin. "Preface to Georg Rhau's *Symphoniae iucundae*." In *Luther's Works*, Vol. 53, *Liturgy and Hymns*, edited by Ulrich S. Leopold. Philadelphia: Fortress, 1965.

Mabonzo, Christine Mbeya. "A Liberation Theology of Being *Muntu* from an African Woman's Perspective: A Comparative Study of Thomas Aquinas' Theology of Being and African Worldviews." PhD diss., Claremont Graduate University, 2003. UMI Microform (3091478).

MacCormac, Earl R. *Metaphor and Myth in Science and Religion*. Durham, NC: Duke University Press, 1976.

MacDonald, Nathan. *Not Bread Alone: The Uses of Food in the Old Testament*. Oxford: Oxford University Press, 2008.

———. *What Did the Ancient Israelites Eat? Diet in Biblical Times*. Grand Rapids: Eerdmans, 2008. Kindle.

Madden, Daniel. "Eating So Others May Live: The Commodified Food System and the Implications of How and What We Eat." MA thesis, Villanova University, 2014. UMI Microform (1555463).

BIBLIOGRAPHY

Mādhavānanda, Swāmī. *The Brihadaranyaka Upanishad*. 1950. https://www.wisdomlib.org/hinduism/book/the-brihadaranyaka-upanishad/d/doc117939.html.

Maes, Kenneth C. "Examining Social Determinants of Food Insecurity, Common Mental Disorders, and Motivations among AIDS Care Volunteers in Urban Ethiopia during the 2008 Food Crisis." PhD diss., Emory University, 2010. UMI Microform (3423094).

Magill, Elizabeth Mae. "The Theology and Practice of Sharing Ministry with Those in Need." DMin thesis, Brite Divinity School, 2017. ProQuest (10281957).

Magrassi, Mariano. *Praying the Bible: An Introduction to Lectio Divina*. Collegeville, MN: Order of Saint Benedict, 1998.

Mangalwadi, Vishal. *The Book That Made Your World: How the Bible Created the Soul of Western Civilization*. Nashville, TN: Thomas Nelson, 2011.

Marbut, Teresa. "Restoring a Sacred Understanding of Food: An Ecofeminist Analysis and Spiritual Reflection on What Has Been Lost and Is Being Regained." PhD diss., California Institute of Integral Studies, 2014. UMI Microform (3712652).

Marks, Susan, and Hal Taussig, eds. *Meals in Early Judaism: Social Formation at the Table*. New York: Palgrave Macmillan, 2014.

Marshall, I. Howard. *Beyond the Bible: Moving from Scripture to Theology*. Grand Rapids: Baker Academic, 2004.

Martin, Dale B. *Pedagogy of the Bible: An Analysis and Proposal*. Louisville, KY: Westminster John Knox, 2008.

Mathews, Kenneth A. *Genesis 1—11:26*. The New American Commentary 1A. Nashville, TN: Broadman & Holman, 1996.

Mazzoni, Cristina. *The Women in God's Kitchen: Cooking, Eating, and Spiritual Writing*. New York: The Continuum International Publishing Group, 2005.

McFague, Sallie. *Life Abundant*. Minneapolis, MN: Fortress, 2000.

———. *Metaphorical Theology: Models of God in Religious Language*. Philadelphia: Fortress, 1982.

———. *Models of God: Theology for an Ecological, Nuclear Age*. Philadelphia: Fortress, 1987.

———. *A New Climate for Theology: God, the World, & Global Warming*. Minneapolis, MN: Fortress, 2008.

McFarland, Ian A. "'The Upward Call': The Category of Vocation and the Oddness of Human Nature." In *The Christian Doctrine of Humanity: Explorations in Constructive Dogmatics*, edited by Oliver D. Crisp and Fred Sanders, 217–36. Grand Rapids: Zondervan, 2018.

McFarland, Ian A., David A. S. Fergusson, Karen Kilby, and Iain R. Torrance, eds. *The Cambridge Dictionary of Christianity Theology*. New York: Cambridge University Press, 2011.

McFarlane, Graham. *A Model for Evangelical Theology: Integrating Scripture, Tradition, Reason, Experience, and Community*. Grand Rapids: Baker Academic, 2020.

McGann, Mary E. *The Meal That Reconnects: Eucharistic Eating and the Global Food Crisis*. Collegeville, MN: Liturgical, 2020.

McGee, Harold. *On Food and Cooking: The Science and Lore of the Kitchen*. Rev. ed. New York: Scribner, 2004.

McGlasson, Paul C. *Invitation to Dogmatic Theology: A Canonical Approach*. Grand Rapids: Brazos, 2006.

McGowan, Andrew. *Ancient Christian Worship: Early Church Practices in Social, Historical, and Theological Perspective*. Grand Rapids: Baker Academic, 2014.

———. *Ascetic Eucharists: Food and Drink in Early Christian Ritual Meals*. New York: Oxford University Press, 1999.

McKenzie, Steven L., and Stephen R. Haynes, eds. *To Each Its Own Meaning: An Introduction to Biblical Criticisms and their Application*. Rev. ed. Louisville, KY: Westminster John Knox, 1999.

Meadors, Gary T., ed. *Four Views on Moving beyond the Bible to Theology*. Grand Rapids: Zondervan, 2009.

Meadowcroft, Tim. *The Message of the Word of God: The Glory of God Made Known*. Downers Grove, IL: IVP, 2011.

Meilaender, Gilbert. *Neither Beast Nor God: The Dignity of the Human Person*. New York: Encounter, 2009.

Mencius. *Mencius: An Online Teaching Translation*. Translated by Robert Eno. May 2016. http://ronliskey.com/docs/mengzi.pdf.

Mendez-Montoya, Angel F. "Food Matters: Prolegomena to a Eucharistic Discourse." PhD diss., University of Virginia, 2007. UMI Microform (3263506).

———. *The Theology of Food: Eating and the Eucharist*. Hoboken, NJ: Wiley-Blackwell, 2009.

Merrill, Eugene H. *Everlasting Dominion: A Theology of the Old Testament*. Nashville, TN: Broadman & Holman, 2006.

Mickelsen, A. Berkeley, and Alvera M. Mickelsen. *Understanding Scripture: How to Read and Study the Bible*. Rev. ed. Peabody, MA: Hendrickson, 1992.

Migliore, Daniel L. *Faith Seeking Understanding: An Introduction to Christian Theology*. 3rd ed. Grand Rapids: Eerdmans, 2014.

Milbank, John. *Being Reconciled: Ontology and Pardon*. London: Routledge, 2003.

———. *Theology and Social Theory: Beyond Secular Reason*. 2nd ed. Malden, MA: Blackwell, 2006.

Milbank, John, and Catherine Pickstock. *Truth in Aquinas*. London: Routledge, 2001.

Milbank, John, Catherine Pickstock, and Graham Ward, eds. *Radical Orthodoxy: A New Theology*. London: Routledge, 1999.

Millar, J. Gary. *Changed into His Likeness: A Biblical Theology of Personal Transformation*. Downers Grove, IL: IVP, 2021.

Mills, Ryan D. "No Longer Strangers or Aliens: Exiled Bodies, Bonhoeffer's Theology of Holy Communion, and Celebrating Eucharist among Exiles." PhD diss., Dubuque Theological Seminary, 2016. ProQuest (10582925).

Moberly, R. W. L. *The Bible in a Disenchanted Age: The Enduring Possibility of Christian Faith*. Grand Rapids: Baker Academic, 2018.

———. *The Bible, Theology, and Faith: A Study of Abraham and Jesus*. New York: Cambridge University Press, 2004.

Moltmann, Jürgen. *The Crucified God: The Cross of Christ as the Foundation and Criticism of Christian Theology*. Minneapolis, MN: Fortress, 1993.

Montanari, Massimo. *Food Is Culture*. New York: Columbia University Press, 2006.

Moore, Andrew, and Michael Scott, eds. *Realism and Religion: Philosophical and Theological Perspectives*. Burlington, VT: Ashgate, 2007.

Moore, Stephen D. *The Bible in Theory: Critical and Postcritical Essays*. Atlanta: Society of Biblical Literature, 2010.

BIBLIOGRAPHY

Moore-Keish, Martha L. "'*Do* This in Remembrance of Me': A Ritual Approach to Reformed Eucharistic Theology." PhD diss., Emory University, 2000. UMI Microform (9993475).

Mootz, Francis J., III, and George H. Taylor, eds. *Gadamer and Ricoeur: Critical Horizons for Contemporary Hermeneutics*. New York: Continuum, 2011.

Moreland, J. P., and Scott B. Rae. *Body & Soul: Human Nature & the Crisis in Ethics*. Downers Grove, IL: IVP, 2000.

Morrison, John Douglas. *Has God Said? Scripture, the Word of God, and the Crisis of Theological Authority*. Eugene, OR: Pickwick, 2006.

Moser, Paul K., ed. *The Oxford Handbook of Epistemology*. New York: Oxford University Press, 2002.

Moskala, Jiri. "The Laws of Clean and Unclean Animals of Leviticus 11: Their Nature, Theology, and Rationale (An Intertextual Study)." PhD diss., Andrews University, 1998. UMI Microform (9917743).

Motyer, J. Alec. *The Prophecy of Isaiah: An Introduction and Commentary*. Downers Grove, IL: IVP, 1993.

Moughtin-Mumby, Sharon. *Sexual and Marital Metaphors in Hosea, Jeremiah, Isaiah, and Ezekiel*. New York: Oxford University Press, 2008.

Muers, Rachel. *Eating and Believing: Interdisciplinary Perspectives on Vegetarianism and Theology*. London: T&T Clark, 2008.

Munger, Christine Luna. "Five Ordinary Movements for Practical Theological Spiritual Formation." PhD diss., St. Thomas University, 2014. UMI Microform (3668211).

Murphy, Francesca Aran, ed. *The Oxford Handbook of Christology*. New York: Oxford University Press, 2015.

Murphy, Nancey. *Bodies and Souls, or Spirited Bodies?* New York: Cambridge University Press, 2006.

Nagel, Ernest. *The Structure of Science: Problems in the Logic of Scientific Explanation*. New York: Harcourt, Brace, 1961.

Nancarrow, Paul S. "The Eucharistic Universe: Toward a Sacramental Theology of Nature." PhD diss., Vanderbilt University, 2000. UMI Microform (9996268).

Neel, Douglas E., and Joel A. Pugh. *The Food and Feasts of Jesus: Inside the World of First-Century Fare, with Menus and Recipes*. Lanham, MD: Rowman & Littlefield, 2012.

Nesteruk, Alexei V. *Light from the East: Theology, Science, and the Eastern Orthodox Tradition*. Minneapolis, MN: Fortress, 2003.

Nichols, Stephen J., and Eric T. Brandt. *Ancient Word, Changing Worlds: The Doctrine of Scripture in a Modern Age*. Wheaton, IL: Crossway, 2009.

Niebuhr, Reinhold. *The Nature and Destiny of Man: A Christian Interpretation*. New York: Scribner's Sons, 1949.

Nishioka, Yoshiyuki Billy. "Rice and Bread: Metaphorical Construction of Reality—Towards a New Approach to World View." PhD diss., Fuller Theological Seminary, 1997. UMI Microform (9726206).

Noble, Denis. *Dance to the Tune of Life: Biological Relativity*. New York: Cambridge University Press, 2017.

———. *The Music of Life: Biology beyond the Genome*. New York: Oxford University Press, 2006.

Nolland, John. *Luke 9:21—18:34*. Word Biblical Commentary 35B. Dallas, TX: Word, 1993.

Norman, Corrie E. "Sin and Food." In *Encyclopedia of Food and Culture*, edited by Solomon H. Katz and William Woys Weaver, 3: 286–88. New York: Scribner's Sons, 2003.

Nyssa, Gregory of. *The Life of Moses*. Translated by Abraham J. Malherbe and Everett Ferguson. New York: Paulist, 1978.
Oden, Thomas C. *Classic Christianity: A Systematic Theology*. New York: HarperCollins, 1992.
———. *The Living God—Systematic Theology*, Vol. 1. Peabody, MA: Hendrickson, 2001.
Oh, Jea S. "*Salim*, Process of Life: An Asian Postcolonial Ecofeminist Theology." PhD diss., Drew University, 2010. UMI Microform (3420010).
O'Keefe, John, and R. R. Reno. *Sanctified Vision: An Introduction to Early Christian Interpretation of the Bible*. Baltimore, MD: Johns Hopkins University Press, 2005.
Olson, Carl. *Religious Studies: The Key Concepts*. London: Routledge, 2011.
Olson-Bang, Erica. "The God Who Loves Strangers: An Ethical Theology of Hospitality." PhD diss., Fordham University, 2012. UMI Microform (3563409).
Origen. *Against Celsus*. In *Ante-Nicene Fathers*, Vol. 4, edited by Alexander Roberts and James Donaldson, 395–669. Peabody, MA: Hendrickson, 2004.
———. *De Principiis*. In *Ante-Nicene Fathers*, Vol. 4, edited by Alexander Roberts and James Donaldson, 239–382. Peabody, MA: Hendrickson, 2004.
———. *The Philocalia*. Translated by George Lewis. Toledo, OH: Veritatis Splendor, 2019.
Ortony, Andrew, ed. *Metaphor and Thought*. 2nd ed. New York: Cambridge University Press, 1993.
———. "Metaphor, Language, and Thought." In *Metaphor and Thought*, edited by Andrew Ortony, 1–16. 2nd ed. New York: Cambridge University Press, 1993.
Osborne, Grant R. *The Hermeneutical Spiral: A Comprehensive Introduction to Biblical Interpretation*. Rev. ed. Downers Grove, IL: IVP, 2006.
Oswalt, John N. *The Book of Isaiah: Chapters 44–66*. Grand Rapids: Eerdmans, 1998.
Ovey, Michael J. *The Feasts of Repentance: From Luke-Acts to Systematic and Pastoral Theology*. Downers Grove, IL: IVP, 2019.
Packer, J. I. "Faith." In *Baker's Dictionary of Theology*, edited by Everett F. Harrison, Geoffrey W. Bromiley, and Carl F. H. Henry, 208–11. Grand Rapids: Baker, 1960.
———. *Engaging the Written Word of God*. Peabody, MA: Hendrickson, 1999.
———. *Truth & Power: The Place of Scripture in the Christian Life*. Downers Grove, IL: IVP, 1996.
Paddison, Angus. *Scripture: A Very Theological Proposal*. London: T&T Clark, 2009.
Palamas, Gregory. *The Triads*. Translated by Nicholas Gendle. New York: Paulist, 1983.
Palmer, David A. "The Body: Health, Nation, and Transcendence." In *Chinese Religious Life*, edited by David A. Palmer, Glenn Shive, and Philip L. Wickeri, 87–106. Oxford: Oxford University Press, 2011.
Patalinghug, Leo. *Epic Food Fight: A Bite-Sized History of Salvation*. Cincinnati, OH: Servant, 2014.
Patterson, Charmayne E. "Give Us This Day Our Daily Bread: The African American Megachurch and Prosperity Theology." PhD diss., Georgia State University, 2007. UMI Microform (3278594).
Patterson, Sue. *Realist Christian Theology in a Postmodern Age*. New York: Cambridge University Press, 2002.
Payette, Alex. "Contemporary Confucian Revival: Reflecting on the Nation, the State and Modernity." In *Concepts and Methods for the Study of Chinese Religions I: State of the Field and Disciplinary Approaches*, edited by Andre Laliberte and Stefania Travagnin, 45–66. Boston: de Gruyter, 2019.

Peacocke, Arthur. *Creation and the World of Science: The Re-shaping of Belief.* New York: Oxford University Press, 2004.

———. *Intimations of Reality: Critical Realism in Science and Religion.* Notre Dame, IN: University of Notre Dame Press, 1984.

———. *Paths from Science towards God: The End of All Our Exploring.* New York: Oneworld, 2001.

Peckham, John C. *Canonical Theology: The Biblical Canon, Sola Scriptura, and Theological Method.* Grand Rapids: Eerdmans, 2016.

Peden, Ivan H. M. "The Poor Are Always with Us: A Description of a Sample of Non-Poor Laity's Perceptions of the Poor and Ministry to the Poor." DMin diss., Princeton Theological Seminary, 2000. UMI Microform (9989066).

Penniman, John David. "*Lacte Christiano Educatus*: The Symbolic Power of Nourishment in Early Christianity." PhD diss., Fordham University, 2015. UMI Microform (3715393).

Pepper, Stephen C. *World Hypotheses: A Study in Evidence.* Berkeley, CA: University of California Press, 1942.

Perdue, Leo G. *Wisdom in Revolt: Metaphorical Theology in the Book of Job.* Decatur, GA: Sheffield Academic, 1991.

Perkins, Elaine, ed. *Food Microbiology: Fundamentals, Challenges, and Health Implications.* New York: Nova, 2016.

Perullo, Nicola. *Taste as Experience: The Philosophy and Aesthetics of Food.* New York: Columbia University Press, 2016.

Peterson, Eugene H. *Christ Plays in Ten Thousand Places: A Conversation in Spiritual Theology.* Grand Rapids: Eerdmans, 2005.

———. *Eat This Book: A Conversation in the Art of Spiritual Reading.* Grand Rapids: Eerdmans, 2006.

———. *The Jesus Way: A Conversation on the Ways That Jesus Is the Way.* Grand Rapids: Eerdmans, 2007.

———. *A Long Obedience in the Same Direction: Discipleship in an Instant Society.* 2nd ed. Downers Grove, IL: IVP, 2000.

Phan, Peter C. *The Cambridge Companion to the Trinity.* New York: Cambridge University Press, 2011.

Pickowicz, Nate. *How to Eat Your Bible: A Simple Approach to Learning and Loving the Word of God.* Chicago: Moody, 2021.

Pierson, Arthur T. *The Bible and Spiritual Criticism.* Grand Rapids: Baker, 1970.

Pilcher, Jeffrey M. *Food in World History.* 2nd ed. London: Routledge, 2017.

———, ed. *The Oxford Handbook of Food History.* New York: Oxford University Press, 2012.

Pinker, Steven. *The Stuff of Thought: Language as a Window into Human Nature.* New York: Penguin, 2007.

Pinnock, Clark. *The Scripture Principle: Reclaiming the Full Authority of the Bible.* 2nd ed. Grand Rapids: Baker, 2006.

Piper, John, and David Mathis, eds. *With Calvin in the Theater of God: The Glory of Christ and Everyday Life.* Wheaton, IL: Crossway, 2010.

Plakias, Alexandra. *Thinking through Food: A Philosophical Introduction.* Peterborough, ON: Broadview, 2019.

Plato. *Plato: Complete Works.* Edited by John M. Cooper and D. S. Hutchinson. Indianapolis: Hackett, 1997.

———. *Gorgias*. In *Plato: Complete Works*, translated by Benjamin Jowett, 172–268. Copenhagen: Titan Read Classics, 2015. Kindle.

———. *Phaedo*. In *Plato: Complete Works*, translated by Benjamin Jowett, 693–827. Copenhagen: Titan Read Classics, 2015. Kindle.

———. *The Republic*. In *Plato: Complete Works*, translated by Benjamin Jowett, 1011–1372. Copenhagen: Titan Read Classics, 2015. Kindle.

———. *Symposium*. In *Plato: Complete Works*, translated by Benjamin Jowett, 931–1010. Copenhagen: Titan Read Classics, 2015. Kindle.

———. *Timaeus*. In *Plato: Complete Works*, translated by Benjamin Jowett, 2365–2440. Copenhagen: Titan Read Classics, 2015. Kindle.

Pollan, Michael. *Cooked: A Natural History of Transformation*. New York: Penguin, 2013.

———. *Food Rules: An Eater's Manual*. New York: Penguin, 2009.

———. *In Defense of Food: An Eater's Manifesto*. New York: Penguin, 2008.

———. *The Omnivore's Dilemma: A Natural History of Four Meals*. New York: Penguin, 2006.

Popper, Karl. *The Logic of Scientific Discovery*. London: Routledge, 2002.

Porter, Stanley E., ed. *Dictionary of Biblical Criticism and Interpretation*. London: Routledge, 2007.

———. "Hermeneutics, Biblical Interpretation, and Theology: Hunch, Holy Spirit, or Hard Work?" In *Beyond the Bible: Moving from Scripture to Theology*, edited by I. Howard Marshall, 97–128. Grand Rapids: Baker Academic, 2004.

Porter, Stanley E., and Jason C. Robinson. *Hermeneutics: An Introduction to Interpretive Theory*. Grand Rapids: Eerdmans, 2011.

Posadas, Jeremy D. "The Body of Christ Worships in the Era of Biopower: Towards a Liturgical Somatics." PhD diss., Emory University, 2012. UMI Microform (3555503).

Prandi, Michele. *The Building Blocks of Meaning: Ideas for a Philosophical Grammar*. Philadelphia: John Benjamins, 2004.

———. *Conceptual Conflicts in Metaphors and Figurative Language*. London: Routledge, 2017.

Price, H. H. *Belief*. London: George Allen & Unwin, 1969.

Prickett, Stephen. "The Bible as a Holy Book." In *Companion Encyclopedia of Theology*, edited by Peter Byrne and Leslie Houlden, 142–59. London: Routledge, 1995.

Probyn, Elspeth. *Carnal Appetites: FoodSexIdentities*. London: Routledge, 2000.

Progoff, Ira, trans. *The Cloud of Unknowing*. New York: Dell, 1983.

Prothero, Stephen. *God Is Not One: The Eight Rival Religions That Run the World—and Why Their Differences Matter*. New York: HarperCollins, 2010.

Putman, Rhyne R. *In Defense of Doctrine: Evangelicalism, Theology, and Scripture*. Minneapolis, MN: Fortress, 2015.

———. *The Method of Christian Theology: A Basic Introduction*. Nashville, TN: B&H, 2021.

Putti, Joseph. *Theology as Hermeneutics: Paul Ricoeur's Theory of Text Interpretation and Method in Theology*. San Francisco: International Scholars Publications, 1994.

Quintilian. *The Institutio Oratoria, Books VII–IX*. Translated by H. E. Butler. Boston: Harvard University Press, 1959.

Rad, Gerhard von. *Genesis: A Commentary*. Rev. ed. Philadelphia: Westminster, 1972.

Radner, Ephraim. *A Time to Keep: Theology, Mortality, and the Shape of a Human Life*. Waco, TX: Baylor University Press, 2016.

Rahner, Karl. *Foundations of Christian Faith: An Introduction to the Idea of Christianity.* Translated by William V. Dych. New York: Crossroad, 1984.

Ralph, Margaret Nutting. *Does the Bible Tell Me So?* Lanham, MD: Rowman & Littlefield, 2019.

Ramage, Matthew J. "Towards a Theology of Scripture: Joseph Ratzinger's 'Method C' Hermeneutic and *Sacra Doctrina* on the Afterlife in the Old Testament." PhD diss., Ave Maria University, 2009. UMI Microform (3615137).

Ramsey, Ian T. *Models and Mystery.* New York: Oxford University Press, 1964.

———. *Models for Divine Activity.* London: SCM, 1973.

Rea, Michael C. "Authority and Truth." In *The Enduring Authority of the Christian Scriptures*, edited by D. A. Carson, 872–98. Grand Rapids: Eerdmans, 2016.

Reasoner, Mark. *Five Models of Scripture.* Grand Rapids: Eerdmans, 2021.

Reed, Stephen Alan. "Food in the Psalms." PhD diss., Claremont Graduate School, 1987. UMI Microform (8705185).

Reno, R. R. *Genesis.* Grand Rapids: Brazos, 2010.

Reyes Fee, Maria Eugenia. "The Art of Theaster Gates and a Theology of Hospitality." PhD diss., Fuller Theological Seminary, 2019. ProQuest (13895617).

Reynolds, Philip Lyndon. *Food and the Body: Some Peculiar Questions in High Medieval Theology.* Boston: Brill, 1999.

Richards, I. A. *The Philosophy of Rhetoric.* New York: Oxford University Press, 1965.

Ricoeur, Paul. *Freud and Philosophy: An Essay on Interpretation.* Translated by Denis Savage. New Haven, CT: Yale University Press, 1970.

———. *Oneself as Another.* Translated by Kathleen Blamey. Chicago: University of Chicago Press, 1992.

———. *The Rule of Metaphor: The Creation of Meaning in Language.* Translated by Robert Czerny, Kathleen McLaughlin, and John Costello. London: Routledge Classics, 2003.

———. *The Rule of Metaphor: Multi-disciplinary Studies of the Creation of Meaning in Language.* Translated by Robert Czerny. Toronto: University of Toronto Press, 1975.

Ritchie, Sarah Lane. *Divine Action and the Human Mind.* New York: Cambridge University Press, 2019.

Roesner, David. *Musicality in Theatre: Music as Model, Method, and Metaphor in Theatre-Making.* Farnham, UK: Ashgate, 2014.

Rogerson, J. W., and Judith M. Lieu, eds. *The Oxford Handbook of Biblical Studies.* New York: Oxford University Press, 2006.

Rohr, Richard. *Things Hidden: Scripture as Spirituality.* Cincinnati, OH: St. Anthony Messenger, 2008.

Roop, Eugene F. *Genesis.* Believers Church Bible Commentary. Scottdale, PA; Herald, 1987.

Russell, Letty M. *Just Hospitality: God's Welcome in a World of Difference.* Louisville, KY: Westminster John Knox, 2009.

Russell, Robert John. *Cosmology: From Alpha to Omega—The Creative Mutual Interaction of Theology and Science.* Minneapolis, MN: Fortress, 2008.

Russell, Robert John, Nancey Murphy, and Arthur R. Peacocke, eds. *Chaos and Complexity: Scientific Perspectives on Divine Action.* 2nd ed. Vatican City State: Vatican Observatory, 2000.

Rutledge, Fleming. *The Crucifixion: Understanding the Death of Christ.* Grand Rapids: Eerdmans, 2015.

Ryken, Leland, James C. Wilhoit, and Tremper Longman III, eds. *Dictionary of Biblical Imagery: An Encyclopedic Exploration of the Images, Symbols, Motifs, Metaphors, Figures of Speech, and Literary Patterns of the Bible*. Downers Grove, IL: IVP, 1998.

Sacks, Sheldon, ed. *On Metaphor*. Chicago: University of Chicago Press, 1979.

Sanders, John, ed. *Atonement and Violence: A Theological Conversation*. Nashville, TN: Abingdon, 2006.

———. *The God Who Risks: A Theology of Providence*. Downers Grove, IL: IVP, 1998.

Sanders, Noah. *Born-Again Dirt: Farming to the Glory of God*. Goodwater, AL: Rora Valley, 2014.

Sanderson, Irene. *Food Fortification: Technology and Quality Control*. New Orleans, LA: White Press Academic, 2018.

Santos, Michael J. "From Eden to Garden: Liberationist Sources for Ethical Food Production." MA thesis, Villanova University, 2015. UMI Microform (1586834).

Sarisky, Darren. *Reading the Bible Theologically*. New York: Cambridge University Press, 2019.

Satlow, Michael L. *How the Bible Became Holy*. New Haven, CT: Yale University Press, 2014.

Saucy, Robert. *Scripture: Its Power, Authority, and Relevance*. Nashville, TN: Thomas Nelson, 2001.

Scheeben, Matthias Joseph. *Handbook of Catholic Dogmatics*, Book 5, *Soteriology, Part One: The Person of Christ the Redeemer*. Steubenville, OH: Emmaus Academic, 2020.

Schmitt, Eleonore. "Food in the Bible." In *Encyclopedia of Food and Culture*, edited by Solmon H. Katz and William Woys Weaver, 1:197–201. New York: Scribner's Sons, 2003.

Schneider, Stephen. "Good, Clean, Fair: The Rhetoric of the Slow Food Movement." *College English* 70.4 (2008) 384–402.

Schon, Donald A. *Displacement of Concepts*. London: Routledge, 1963.

Schut, Michael, ed. *Food and Faith: Justice, Joy, and Daily Bread*. Harrisburg, PA: Morehouse, 2010.

Scorgie, Glen G., ed. *Dictionary of Christian Spirituality*. Grand Rapids: Zondervan, 2011.

Scoville, Judith N. "Toward a Theological Ethic of the Land: Environmental Ethics in the Context of American Agriculture." PhD diss., Graduate Theological Union, 1995. UMI Microform (9610060).

Searle, John. *Speech Acts: An Essay in the Philosophy of Language*. London: Cambridge University Press, 1969.

Seitz, Christopher R. *Colossians*. Brazos Theological Commentary on the Bible. Grand Rapids: Baker, 2014.

Shahar, Meir, and Robert P. Weller. "Introduction: Gods and Society in China." In *Unruly Gods: Divinity and Society in China*, edited by Meir Shahar and Robert P. Weller, 1–36. Honolulu: University of Hawai'i Press, 1996.

Shatzer, Jacob. *Transhumanism and the Image of God*. Downers Grove, IL: IVP, 2019.

Shaver, Stephen R. "Metaphors of Eucharistic Presence: A Cognitive Linguistics Approach to an Ecumenical Theology of Bread, Wine, and the Body and Blood of Christ." PhD diss., Graduate Theological Union, 2017. ProQuest (10741782).

Shen, Michael Li-Tak. *Canaan to Corinth: Paul's Doctrine of God and the Issue of Food Offered to Idols in 1 Corinthians 8:1—11:1*. New York: Lang, 2010.

BIBLIOGRAPHY

———. "Paul's Doctrine of God and the Issue of Food Offered to Idols in 1 Corinthians 8:1—11:1." PhD diss., Dallas Theological Seminary, 2003. UMI Microform (3103849).

Sherley-Price, Leo. *Confucius and Christ: A Christian Estimate of Confucius*. London: Dacre, 1951.

Sherlock, Charles. *The Doctrine of Humanity: Contours of Christian Theology*. Downers Grove, IL: IVP Academic, 1997.

Shryock, John K. *The Origin and Development of the State Cult of Confucius: An Introductory Study*. New York: Paragon, 1966.

Shuman, Joel James, and L. Roger Owens, eds. *Wendell Berry and Religion: Heaven's Earthly Life*. Lexington, KY: University Press of Kentucky, 2009.

Silvers, Matthew Ryan. "Tables of Peace: Constructing a Theology of an Interreligious Welcome Table." DMin thesis, Brite Divinity School, 2017. ProQuest (10685222).

Simatupang, Florian M. P. "A Renewal Theology of the Eucharist: The Sacramental Process of *Search-Encounter-Transformation*." PhD diss., Regent University, 2021. ProQuest (28323713).

Simmons, Leanne Sue. "Taking Back the Body: Eating Disorders, Feminist Theological Ethics and Christic Gynodicy." PhD diss., Princeton Theological Seminary, 2001. UMI Microform (3006837).

Simon, Arthur. *Bread for the World*. Grand Rapids: Eerdmans, 1975.

Skubal, Susanne. *Word of Mouth: Food and Fiction after Freud*. London: Routledge, 2002.

Sloman, Aaron. *The Computer Revolution in Philosophy: Philosophy, Science, and Models of Mind*. New York: Harvester, 1978.

Smedes, Taede A. "Arthur Peacocke." In *The Blackwell Companion to Science and Christianity* edited by J. B. Stump and Alan G. Padgett, 589–99. Malden, MA: Blackwell, 2012.

Smith, Dennis E. "Food and Dining in Early Christianity." In *A Companion to Food in the Ancient World*, edited by John Wilkins and Robin Nadeau, 357–64. Malden, MA: Wiley & Sons, 2015.

———. *From Symposium to Eucharist: The Banquet in the Early Christian World*. Minneapolis, MN: Fortress, 2003.

Smith, D. Howard. *Confucius*. London: Maurice Temple Smith, 1973.

Smith, James K. A. *Speech and Theology: Language and the Logic of Incarnation*. London: Routledge, 2002.

Smith, Wilfred Cantwell. *What Is Scripture? A Comparative Approach*. London: SCM, 1993.

Soskice, Janet Martin. *The Kindness of God: Metaphor, Gender, and Religious Language*. New York: Oxford University Press, 2007.

———. *Metaphor and Religious Language*. Oxford: Clarendon, 1985.

Soza, Joel R. *Food and God: A Theological Approach to Eating, Diet, and Weight Control*. Eugene, OR: Wipf and Stock, 2016.

Spanogle, Jeffrey F. "Participation and Union: The Holiness Command in Leviticus and Its Eschatological Purpose." PhD diss., Trinity International University, 2016. ProQuest (10259319).

Spellman, Ched. *Toward a Canon-Conscious Reading of the Bible: Exploring the History and Hermeneutics of the Canon*. Sheffield, UK: Sheffield Phoenix, 2020.

Sproul, R. C. *Knowing Scripture*. Rev. ed. Downers Grove, IL: IVP, 2009.

Stallman, Robert C. "Divine Hospitality in the Pentateuch: A Metaphorical Perspective on God as Host." PhD diss., Westminster Theological Seminary, 1999. UMI Microform (9930628).

Standage, Tom. *An Edible History of Humanity*. London: Bloomsbury, 2009.

Standridge, Jordan. "Seven Metaphors for God's Word." *The Cripplegate*, January 31, 2017. https://thecripplegate.com/seven-metaphors-for-gods-word.

Stanton-Roark, Nicholas. "Politics and the Eucharist." ThM thesis, Anderson University, 2015. ProQuest (10115704).

Stausberg, Michael, and Steven Engler, eds. *The Oxford Handbook of the Study of Religion*. Oxford: Oxford University Press, 2016.

———, eds. *The Routledge Handbook of Research Methods in the Study of Religion*. London: Routledge, 2011.

Steenberg, Matthew C. *Of God and Man: Theology as Anthropology from Irenaeus to Athanasius*. London: T&T Clark, 2009.

Stenmark, Lisa L. "Feminist Philosophies of Science: Towards a Prophetic Epistemology." In *The Blackwell Companion to Science and Christianity*, edited by J. B. Stump and Alan G. Padgett, 82–92. Malden, MA: Blackwell, 2012.

Stephenson, Loren Rae. "When Reading Was Food for the Soul: The Nourishment Trope for the Concept of Literary Value, Antiquity to the Thirteenth Century." PhD diss., Indiana University of Pennsylvania, 2022. ProQuest (28969050).

Stern, David E. "Remembering and Redemption." In *Rediscovering the Eucharist: Ecumenical Conversations*, edited by Roch A. Kereszty, 1–15. Mahwah, NJ: Paulist, 2003.

Stiles Williams, Jennifer R. "Theater and the Church: A Theatrical Theology of Discipleship, Public Theology and Social Resistance." DMin thesis, Drew University, 2021. ProQuest (28644801).

Still, Elias C., III. "Divisions over Leaders and Food Offered to Idols: The Parallel Thematic Structures of 1 Corinthians 4:6–21 and 8:1—11:1." *Tyndale Bulletin* 55.1 (2004) 17–41.

———. "The Meaning and Uses of ΕΙΔΩΛΟΘΥΤΟΝ in First Century Non-Pauline Literature and 1 Cor 8:1—11:1: Toward Resolution of the Debate." *Trinity Journal* 23.2 (2002) 225–34.

———. "Paul's Aims Regarding εἰδωλοθυτα: A New Proposal for Interpreting 1 Corinthians 8:1—11:1." *Novum Testamentum* 44.4 (2002) 333–43.

———. "The Rationale behind the Pauline Instructions on Food Offered to Idols: A Study of the Relationship between 1 Corinthians 4:6–21 and 8:1—11:1." PhD diss., The Southern Baptist Theological Seminary, 2000. UMI Microform (3008647).

Stone, Howard W., and James O. Duke. *How to Think Theologically*. 3rd ed. Minneapolis, MN: Fortress, 2013.

Stone, Rachel Marie. *Eat with Joy: Redeeming God's Gift of Food*. Downers Grove, IL: IVP, 2013.

Stratton, Stanley Brian. "Coherence, Consonance, and Conversation: The Interaction of Theology and Natural Science in the Quest for a Unified World-View." PhD diss., Princeton Theological Seminary, 1997. UMI Microform (9730193).

Stronstad, Roger. *Spirit, Scripture and Theology: A Pentecostal Perspective*. Baguio City, Philippines: Asia Pacific Theological Seminary Press, 1995.

Stuart, Douglas. *Hosea-Jonah*. Word Biblical Commentary 31. Waco, TX: Word, 1987.

BIBLIOGRAPHY

Stuckey, Barb. *Taste What You're Missing: The Passionate Eater's Guide to Why Good Food Tastes Good*. New York: Free, 2012.

Sullivan-Dunbar, Sandra Jeanne. "'I Was Hungry and You Gave Me Food': Agape, Justice and Special Relations Seen through the Lens of Dependent Care." PhD diss., University of Chicago, 2010. UMI Microform (3432831).

Sumner, Darren. "Theory and Metaphor in Calvin's Doctrine of the Atonement." In *The Princeton Theological Review* 13.2 (2007) 49–60.

Sutton, David E. *Remembrance of Repasts: An Anthropology of Food and Memory*. Oxford: Berg, 2001.

Sweeney, Kevin W. "Hunger Is the Best Sauce." In *The Philosophy of Food*, edited by David M. Kaplan, 52–68. Berkeley, CA: University of California Press, 2012.

Symons, Michael. "Epicurus, the Foodies' Philosopher." In *Food & Philosophy: Eat, Think and Be Merry*, edited by Fritz Allhoff and Dave Monroe, 13–30. Malden, MA: Blackwell, 2007.

———. "Sacrifice." In *Encyclopedia of Food and Culture*, edited by Solomon H. Katz and William Woys Weaver, 3:223–24. New York: Scribner's Sons, 2003.

Tanner, Kathryn. *Christ the Key*. New York: Cambridge University Press, 2010.

Taylor, Charles. *A Secular Age*. Cambridge: Harvard University Press, 2007.

Teiser, Stephen F. "The Spirits of Chinese Religion." In *Religions of China in Practice*, edited by Donald S. Lopez Jr., 3–37. Princeton: Princeton University Press, 1996.

Telfer, Elizabeth. *Food for Thought: Philosophy and Food*. London: Routledge, 1996.

Tertullian. *Against Marcion*. In *Ante-Nicene Fathers*, Vol. 3, edited by Alexander Roberts and James Donaldson, 269–475. Peabody, MA: Hendrickson, 2004.

———. *Against Praxeas*. In *Ante-Nicene Fathers*, Vol. 3, edited by Alexander Roberts and James Donaldson, 597–632. Peabody, MA: Hendrickson, 2004.

Thiselton, Anthony C. *Approaching Philosophy of Religion: An Introduction to Key Thinkers, Concepts, Methods, & Debates*. Downers Grove, IL: IVP, 2018.

———. *Approaching the Study of Theology: An Introduction to Key Thinkers, Concepts, Methods and Debates*. Downers Grove, IL: IVP, 2018.

———. *Hermeneutics: An Introduction*. Grand Rapids: Eerdmans, 2009.

———. *The Hermeneutics of Doctrine*. Grand Rapids: Eerdmans, 2007.

———. "Knowledge, Myth, and Corporate Memory." In *Believing in the Church: The Corporate Nature of Faith*. A Report by The Doctrine Commission of the Church of England. Wilton, CT: The Central Board of Finance of the Church of England, 1982.

———. *New Horizons in Hermeneutics: The Theory and Practice of Transforming Biblical Reading*. Grand Rapids. Zondervan, 1992.

———. *Systematic Theology*. Grand Rapids: Eerdmans, 2015.

———. *The Thiselton Companion to Christian Theology*. Grand Rapids: Eerdmans, 2015.

———. *Thiselton on Hermeneutics: Collected Works with New Essays*. Burlington, VT: Ashgate, 2006.

———. *The Two Horizons: New Testament Hermeneutics and Philosophical Description with Special Reference to Heidegger, Bultmann, Gadamer, and Wittgenstein*. Grand Rapids: Eerdmans, 1980.

Thomas, Owen C. *Introduction to Theology*. Harrisburg, PA: Morehouse, 1983.

Thompson, Marjorie J. *Soul Feast: An Invitation to the Christian Spiritual Life*. Louisville, KY: Westminster John Knox, 2005.

Thompson, Mark D. *A Clear and Present Word: The Clarity of Scripture*. New Studies in Biblical Theology 21. Downers Grove, IL: IVP, 2006.

———. *The Doctrine of Scripture: An Introduction*. Wheaton, IL: Crossway, 2022.

———. "The Generous Gift of a Gracious Father: Toward a Theological Account of the Clarity of Scripture." In *The Enduring Authority of the Christian Scriptures*, edited by D. A. Carson, 615–43. Grand Rapids: Eerdmans, 2016.

Thorsen, Donald A. D. *The Wesleyan Quadrilateral: Scripture, Tradition, Reason, and Experience as a Model of Evangelical Theology*. Indianapolis, IN: Light and Life Communications, 1997.

Tierney, R. Kenji, and Emiko Ohnuki-Tierney. "Anthropology of Food." In *The Oxford Handbook of Food History*, edited by Jeffrey M. Pilcher, 117–34. New York: Oxford University Press, 2012.

Tillich, Paul. *Systematic Theology*. 3 vols. Chicago: University of Chicago Press, 1951–63.

Tongue, Denis H. "Hope." In *Baker's Dictionary of Theology*, edited by Everett F. Harrison, Geoffrey W. Bromiley, and Carl F. H. Henry, 271. Grand Rapids: Baker, 1960.

Topley, Marjorie. "Cosmic Antagonisms: A Mother-Child Syndrome." In *Religion and Ritual in Chinese Society*, edited by Arthur P. Wolf, 233–49. Stanford, CA: Stanford University Press, 1974.

Toppin, Shirlyn. "'Soul Food' Theology: Pastoral Care and Practice through the Sharing of Meals: A Womanist Reflection." *Black Theology: An International Journal* 4.1 (2006) 44–69.

Tornau, Christian. "Saint Augustine." *The Stanford Encyclopedia of Philosophy* (Summer 2020), edited by Edward N. Zalta. https://plato.stanford.edu/archives/sum2020/entries/augustine.

Torrance, T. F. *Atonement: The Person and Work of Christ*. Downers Grove, IL: IVP, 2009.

———. *Divine Meaning: Studies in Patristic Hermeneutics*. Edinburgh: T&T Clark, 1995.

———. *The Trinitarian Faith: The Evangelical Theology of the Ancient Catholic Church*. 2nd ed. London: T&T Clark, 1997.

Toulmin, Stephen. *The Philosophy of Science*. New York: Hutchinson House, 1953.

Toussaint-Samat, Maguelonne. *A History of Food*. 2nd ed. Translated by Anthea Bell. Malden, MA: Wiley-Blackwell, 2009.

Tozer, A. W. *The Pursuit of God*. Chicago: Moody, 2006.

Traina, Robert A. *Methodical Bible Study: A New Approach to Hermeneutics*. New York: Biblical Seminary in New York, 1952.

Treier, Daniel J. *Introducing Theological Interpretation of Scripture: Recovering a Christian Practice*. Grand Rapids: Baker Academic, 2008.

Truong, Tu Thien Van. "*Menh Troi*: Toward a Vietnamese Theology of Mission." PhD diss., Graduate Theological Union, 2009. UMI Microform (3367962).

Tsai, Yen-zen. "Food Fellowship and the Making of a Chinese Church: Cases from Contemporary China and Taiwan." In *Concepts and Methods for the Study of Chinese Religions III: Key Concepts in Practice*, edited by Paul R. Katz and Stefania Travagnin, 65–90. Boston: de Gruyter, 2019.

Turbayne, Colin Murray. *The Myth of Metaphor*. Rev. ed. Columbia, SC: University of South Carolina Press, 1971.

Turretin, Francis. *Institutes of Elenctic Theology*, Vol. 1, *First through Tenth Topics*. Translated by George Musgrave Giger. Phillipsburg, NJ: P & R, 1997.

Vaihinger, Hans. *The Philosophy of 'As If': A System of the Theoretical, Practical and Religious Fictions of Mankind*. Translated by C. K. Ogden. London: Routledge and Kegan Paul, 1911.

Vanderslice, Kendall. *We Will Feast: Rethinking Dinner, Worship, and the Community of God*. Grand Rapids: Eerdmans, 2019.

Van Hecke, P., ed. *Metaphor in the Hebrew Bible*. Biblioteca Ephemerium Theologicarum Lovaniensium 187. Dudley, MA: Leuven University Press, 2005.

Vanhoozer, Kevin J. *Biblical Narrative in the Philosophy of Paul Ricoeur: A Study in Hermeneutics and Theology*. New York: Cambridge University Press, 1990.

———, ed. *The Cambridge Companion to Postmodern Theology*. New York: Cambridge University Press, 2003.

———, ed. *Dictionary for Theological Interpretation of the Bible*. Grand Rapids: Baker, 2005.

———. *Doers and Hearers: A Pastor's Guide to Making Disciples through Scripture and Doctrine*. Bellingham, WA: Lexham, 2019.

———. *The Drama of Doctrine: A Canonical Linguistic Approach to Christian Theology*. Louisville, KY: Westminster John Knox, 2005.

———. *Faith Speaking Understanding: Performing the Drama of Doctrine*. Louisville, KY: Westminster John Knox, 2014.

———. *First Theology: God, Scripture, and Hermeneutics*. Downers Grove, IL: IVP, 2002.

———. *Is There a Meaning in This Text? The Bible, the Reader, and the Morality of Literary Knowledge*. Grand Rapids: Zondervan, 1998.

———. "May We Go beyond What Is Written after All? The Pattern of Theological Authority and the Problem of Doctrinal Development." In *The Enduring Authority of the Christian Scriptures*, edited by D. A. Carson, 747–92. Grand Rapids: Eerdmans, 2016.

———. *Remythologizing Theology: Divine Action, Passion, and Authorship*. New York: Cambridge University Press, 2010.

———. "The Semantics of Biblical Literature: Truth and Scripture's Diverse Literary Forms." In *Hermeneutics, Authority, and Canon*, edited by D. A. Carson and John D. Woodbridge, 53–104. Grand Rapids: Zondervan, 1986.

Vanhoozer, Kevin J., and Daniel J. Treier. *Theology and the Mirror of Scripture: A Mere Evangelical Account*. Studies in Christian Doctrine and Scripture. Downers Grove, IL: IVP, 2015.

Van Huyssteen, Wentzel. *Theology and the Justification of Faith: Constructing Theories in Systematic Theology*. Translated by H. F. Snijders. Grand Rapids: Eerdmans, 1989.

Verene, Donald P. *The Science of Cookery and the Art of Eating Well: Philosophical and Historical Reflections on Food and Dining in Culture*. Stuttgart: Ibidem, 2018.

Vervaeke, John, Christopher Mastropietro, and Filip Miscevic. *Zombies in Western Culture: A Twenty-First Century Crisis*. Cambridge: Open Book, 2017.

Vico, Giambattista. *The New Science of Giambattista Vico*. 3rd ed. Translated by Thomas Goddard Bergin and Max Harold Fisch. Ithaca, NY: Cornell University Press, 1948.

Visser, Margaret. *The Rituals of Dinner: The Origins, Evolution, Eccentricities, and Meaning of Table Manners*. Toronto: HarperPerennial Canada, 2000.

Von Feuchtersleben, Ernst F. *The Dietetics of the Soul*. New York: Francis, 1854.

Wainwright, William J. *The Oxford Handbook of Philosophy of Religion*. New York: Oxford University Press, 2005.

Waldman, Gary. *Introduction to Light: The Physics of Light, Vision, and Color*. Mineola, NY: Dover, 1983.

Walls, Andrew F. *The Cross-Cultural Process in Christian History*. Maryknoll, NY: Orbis, 2002.

Walton, John H. *Genesis*. The NIV Application Commentary. Grand Rapids: Zondervan, 2001.
Wang, Gung-Hsing. *The Chinese Mind*. New York: John Day, 1946.
Ward, Timothy. *Words of Life: Scripture as the Living and Active Word of God*. Downers Grove, IL: IVP, 2009.
Ware, Kallistos. *The Orthodox Way*. Crestwood, NY: St. Vladimir's Seminary Press, 1993.
Warfield, B. B. *The Inspiration and Authority of the Bible*. Phillipsburg, NJ: P & R, 1980.
Warren, Meredith J. C. *My Flesh Is Meat Indeed: A Nonsacramental Reading of John 6:51–58*. Minneapolis, MN: Fortress, 2015.
Warren, Tish Harrison. *Liturgy of the Ordinary: Sacred Practices in Everyday Life*. Downers Grove, IL: IVP, 2016.
Washburn, Marilyn Roberts. "The Contributions of Jürgen Moltmann's Theology to a Theology of Health and Healing." PhD diss., Emory University, 1992. UMI Microform (9300569).
Waterhouse, Steven. *Not by Bread Alone: An Outlined Guide to Bible Doctrine*. Amarillo, TX: Westcliff, 2007.
Waters, Alice, Bob Carrau, and Cristina Mueller. *We Are What We Eat: A Slow Food Manifesto*. New York: Penguin, 2021.
Waters, Guy P. *The Lord's Supper as the Sign and Meal of the New Covenant*. Short Studies in Biblical Theology. Wheaton, IL: Crossway, 2019.
Watson, Francis. *Text and Truth: Redefining Biblical Theology*. Grand Rapids: Eerdmans, 1997.
Webb, Stephen H. *Good Eating*. Ada, MI: Brazos, 2001.
Webster, Jane S. *Ingesting Jesus: Eating and Drinking in the Gospel of John*. Atlanta: Society of Biblical Literature, 2003.
Webster, John, ed. *The Cambridge Companion to Karl Barth*. Cambridge: Cambridge University Press, 2000.
———. *The Domain of the Word: Scripture and Theological Reason*. London: T&T Clark, 2012.
———. *Holy Scripture: A Dogmatic Sketch*. Cambridge: Cambridge University Press, 2003.
———. *Word and Church: Essays in Church Dogmatics*. New York: Continuum, 2006.
Webster, John, and Kathryn Tanner, and Iain Torrance, eds. *The Oxford Handbook of Systematic Theology*. New York: Oxford University Press, 2007.
Weeks, Noel. *The Sufficiency of Scripture*. Carlisle, PA: Banner of Truth Trust, 1988.
Weingarten, Susan. "Review of *Not Bread Alone: The Uses of Food in the Old Testament*." *Gastronomica: The Journal of Food and Culture* 11.2 (2011) 115–16.
Weller, Robert P. "Chinese Cosmology and the Environment." In *Chinese Religious Life*, edited by David A. Palmer, Glenn Shive, and Philip L. Wickeri, 124–38. Oxford: Oxford University Press, 2011.
Wenham, Gordon J. *Genesis 1–15*. Word Biblical Commentary 1. Waco, TX: Word, 1987.
Wenham, John. *Christ and the Bible*. 3rd ed. Reprint, Eugene, OR: Wipf and Stock, 2009.
Wertz, Spencer K. *Food & Philosophy: Selected Essays*. Fort Worth, TX: TCU, 2016.
Westacott, Emrys. "The Slave Boy Experiment in Plato's *Meno*." ThoughtCo. January 28, 2019. https://www.thoughtco.com/slave-boy-experiment-in-platos-meno-2670668.
Westermann, Claus. *Genesis 1–11: A Continental Commentary*. Translated by John J. Scullion. Minneapolis, MN: Fortress, 1994.

Wheaton, Gerry. *The Role of Jewish Feasts in John's Gospel*. New York: Cambridge University Press, 2015.
Wheelwright, Philip. *Metaphor and Reality*. Bloomington, IN: Indiana University Press, 1962.
Whidden, David L., III. *Christ the Light: The Theology of Light and Illumination in Thomas Aquinas*. Minneapolis, MN: Fortress, 2014.
White, Sean A. "Southern Baptist and British Baptist Contributions to a Theology of the Lord's Supper since 1948: Beyond a Theology of the Elements toward a Sacramental Theology of Enactment." PhD diss., Union Theological Seminary, 2007. UMI Microform (3258662).
Whitehead, Alfred North. *Process and Reality*. New York: Free, 1979.
Wilczek, Frank. *Fundamentals: Ten Keys to Reality*. New York: Penguin, 2021.
Wilhelm, Richard. *Confucius and Confucianism*. Translated by George H. Danton and Annina Periam Danton. New York: Harcourt Brace Jovanovich, 1931.
Wilkins, John M., and Shaun Hill. *Food in the Ancient World*. Malden, MA: Blackwell, 2006.
Wilkins, John M., and Robin Nadeau, eds. *A Companion to Food in the Ancient World*. Malden, MA: Wiley & Sons, 2015.
Williams, A. N. *The Architecture of Theology: Structure, System, and Ratio*. Oxford: Oxford University Press, 2011.
Williams, Carol A. "*The True Comfort of a Christian, or Food for a Distressed Soul*: David Dickerson's Overlooked Work." *Reformation & Renaissance Review: Journal of the Society for Reformation Studies* 9.2 (2007) 173–210.
Williams, Rowan. *Being Human: Bodies, Minds, Persons*. Grand Rapids: Eerdmans, 2018.
Williamson, Paul R. *Sealed with an Oath: Covenant in God's Unfolding Purpose*. Downers Grove, IL: IVP, 2007.
Willis, Dustin, and Brandon Clements. *The Simplest Way to Change the World: Biblical Hospitality as a Way of Life*. Chicago: Moody, 2017.
Willoughby, Brittany D. "Biting the Apple: Sin, Policy, and Sin in the United States." MA thesis, Georgetown University, 2011. UMI Microform (1502960).
Wilson, Bee. *Consider the Fork: A History of How We Cook and Eat*. New York: Basic, 2012.
———. *First Bite: How We Learn to Eat*. New York: Basic, 2015.
———. *The Way We Eat Now: How the Food Revolution Has Transformed Our Lives, Our Bodies, and Our World*. New York: Hachette, 2019.
Wilson, Carol Bakker. "For I Was Hungry and You Gave Me Food: Pragmatics of Food Access in the Gospel of Matthew." PhD diss., Brite Divinity School, 2012. UMI Microform (3558634).
Wilson, Douglas. "The Sacred Script in the Theater of God." In *With Calvin in the Theater of God: The Glory of Christ and Everyday Life*, edited by John Piper and David Mathis, 83–96. Wheaton, IL: Crossway, 2010.
Wirzba, Norman. *Food and Faith: A Theology of Eating*. Cambridge: Cambridge University Press, 2011.
———. *The Paradise of God: Renewing Religion in an Ecological Age*. New York: Oxford University Press, 2003.
Witherspoon-Brown, Monty. "Soul Food Theology: The Proclamation of Health and Wellness." DMin thesis, Drew University, 2016. ProQuest (10105361).
Wolf, Arthur P. "Gods, Ghosts, and Ancestors." In *Religion and Ritual in Chinese Society*, edited by Arthur P. Wolf, 131–82. Stanford, CA: Stanford University Press, 1974.

Wolterstorff, Nicholas. *Divine Discourse: Philosophical Reflections on the Claim That God Speaks*. New York: Cambridge University Press, 1995.
Wong, Eva. *The Shambhala Guide to Taoism*. Boston: Shambhala, 1997.
Woofenden, Anna. *This Is God's Table: Finding Church beyond the Walls*. Harrisonburg, VA: Herald, 2020.
Work, Telford. *Living and Active: Scripture in the Economy of Salvation*. Grand Rapids: Eerdmans, 2002.
Worth, Sarah E. *Taste: A Philosophy of Food*. London: Reaktion, 2021.
Wright, N. T. *Scripture and the Authority of God: How to Read the Bible Today*. New York: HarperCollins, 2005.
Wright, N. T., Simon Gathercole, and Robert B. Stewart, *What Did the Cross Accomplish? A Conversation about the Atonement*. Louisville, KY: Westminster John Knox, 2021.
Wright, William M., IV, and Francis Martin. *Encountering the Living God in Scripture: Theological and Philosophical Principles for Interpretation*. Grand Rapids: Baker Academic, 2019.
Wu, Kijin James. "A Protestant Theological Inquiry into a Classical Confucian Idea of Offering Sacrifices to Ancestors (*Jizu*)." PhD diss, Boston University, 2008. UMI Microform (3293784).
Wurgaft, Benjamin Aldes. *Meat Planet: Artificial Flesh and the Future of Food*. Oakland, CA: University of California Press, 2019.
Yang, Y. C. *China's Religious Heritage*. New York: Abingdon-Cokesbury, 1943.
Yao, Xinzhong. *An Introduction to Confucianism*. Cambridge: Cambridge University Press, 2000.
Yeo, Khiok-Khng. "Rhetorical Interaction in 1 Corinthians 8 and 10: Potential Implications for a Chinese, Cross-Cultural Hermeneutic." PhD diss., Northwestern University, 1992. UMI Microform (9309491).
Yeung, See Yin Celine. "Received by Christ: A Reworking of the Reformed Theology of the Lord's Supper." PhD diss., Princeton Theological Seminary, 2020. ProQuest (27993772).
Young, Frances M. *Biblical Exegesis and the Formation of Christian Culture*. New York: Cambridge University Press, 1997.
Young, Robin Darling. "The Eucharist as Sacrifice according to Clement of Alexandria." In *Rediscovering the Eucharist: Ecumenical Conversations*, edited by Roch A. Kereszty, 63–91. Mahwah, NJ: Paulist, 2003.
Yutang, Lin. *The Wisdom of Confucius*. New York: Modern Library, 1938.
Zager, Daniel, ed. *Music and Theology: Essays in Honor of Robin A. Leaver*. Lanham, MD: Scarecrow, 2007.
Zeller, Benjamin E., Marie W. Dallam, Reid Neilson, Nora L. Rubel, and Martha Finch, eds. *Religion, Food, and Eating in North America*. New York: Columbia University Press, 2014.

Scripture Index

OLD TESTAMENT

Genesis
1–17	191
1–11:26	198
1–2	197
1:3	54
1:17	45
1:29	126, 140
1:30	114
2:16–17	163
2:8	162
3:1–19	115, 126, 163
3:19	126
9:3	140
25:27–34	161
26:30–31	128–29
31:54	129
32:13–21	129
33:8–11	129
43:34	91

Exodus
3:8	132
3:17	132
12	126
13:5	132
13:9	86
16:32–35	86
18:12	129
24:11	129
33:3	132
35:13	126

Leviticus
2:13	130
10	77
11	200
20:24	132

Numbers
13:27	132
14:8	132
16:13–14	132
18:19	130
23:19	63

Deuteronomy
1:1—21:9	138, 184
4:28	88
5:32	77
6:3	132
8:3	86, 88, 105, 116
8:10	172
11:9	132
26:9	132
26:15	132
27:3	132
30:14	126, 146, 152
30:15	116
30:19	116
31:20	132
32:21	88

Joshua

1:8	129
5:6	132
9:3–15	129

1 Samuel

1:4–5	91
3:7	90
3:21	90
7:6	171
9:23	91
16:23	79

1 Kings

19:4–8	171

2 Chronicles

13:5	130

Ezra

8:21–23	171

Nehemiah

8:10	91
8:12	91

Esther

4:16	171
9:19	91
9:22	91

Job

1:4	97
23:12	171
29:3	109

Psalms

1:2	129
4:7	54
19:1–6	45
19:8	109
19:10	87
22:1	90
23:5	126
31:5	90
33:9	189
34:8	xvii, 87, 93, 118, 126, 175
35:10	54
36:7–8	152, 172
36:8	126
36:9	52
43:3	109
50:12–15	114
51:12	125
67:6	126
78:24–25	126
81:10	126, 135
81:16	126
104:4	15
111:5	129
112:8	143
119:11	125
119:103	87, 140
119:105	49, 52, 85, 109
126:3	xv
136:25	88
145:15–16	114

Proverbs

3:8	88
6:23	109
9:4–6	125
9:5–6	88, 126
10:11	89
13:14	89
14:27	89
16:22	89
24:13–14	89
25:21	150
27:17	xvi
30:8–9	166

Isaiah

4:4	15
5:13	88, 97
25:6–9	132
40–55	88

SCRIPTURE INDEX

42:18–25	88
44–46	87, 201
48:1–8	88
48:14	88
50:4	88
50:8	88
55	88, 90
55:1–4	125
55:1–3	87
55:2–3	88
55:1	97, 147, 151
55:3	87, 130
55:11	117, 134–35

Jeremiah

1–25	185
2:13	140, 152, 163
11:5	132
15:16	xvii, 86
23:29	85
31:31–36	114
32:22	132
32:40	130

Ezekiel

1–19	87, 178
2:8—3:3	87
20:6	132
20:15	132
34:2	95
37:26	130

Daniel

10:3	171

Hosea

3:4	88
10:8	90

Amos

8:11–13	151
8:11–12	88

NEW TESTAMENT

Matthew

4:1–2	171
4:4	56, 85–86, 89–90, 105, 108
4:7	90
4:10	90
5:14–16	74, 83
5:13	130
5:14	74
6:11	134, 172
6:16	171
8:11–12	167
8:11	151
9:10–13	129
9:10–11	150
9:11	90
10:14	90
11:19	150
11:25	121
13:3–23	135
15:5–8	90
15:14	117
16:6	93
16:12	93
16:24	166
18:3	121
19:14	175
22:37–40	145
24:35	134
25:1–13	152
25:31–46	163
25:44–45	163
25:35	147
26	126
26:26–29	126, 158
26:26	162
26:29	133

Mark

2:15–17	129
2:16	90, 150
4:27	162
6:11	90
8:34	166

Mark (cont.)
9:50	130
12:31	148
14:22–25	158
14:24	114

Luke
1:53	126, 152
2:7	89
2:12	89
2:16	89
5:27–32	91
5:29–32	129
5:29	150
5:30	90
6:31	150
6:39	117
7:36–50	91, 129
9:21—18:34	91–92, 200
9:10–17	129
10:38–42	91
10:39	91
10:42	79, 147
13:18–21	144
14:1–14	91
14:13	125
15:1–2	150
18:16	175
22:19–20	158
22:19	158
24:13–35	91
24:27	42, 89

John
1:1–5	46
1:14	141
3:15–16	163
3:3	164
3:16	126
3:17	147
4:15	162
4:34	89, 141, 144, 166
5:39–40	89, 127, 159
5:19	89
5:30	89
5:36	89
5:39	121
5:40	152
6:25–59	162, 168
6:60–70	158
6:38–45	105
6:51–58	211
6:53–58	127
6:35–38	149
6:50–51	126
6:33	89
6:35	89, 126–27
6:38	89
6:41	89
6:48	89
6:50	89, 163
6:51	89, 133, 151
6:56	168
6:63	131
6:68	90, 91, 128, 144, 151–52, 163
7:38–39	160, 162
7:39	168
8:31–32	143
8:12	46
8:28	89
8:51	90
8:52	90
10:17–18	91
10:28	167
12:32	151
12:49	89
12:50	89
13:14	91
14:15–23	90
14:10	89
14:12	91
15:5	137
15:10	90
15:13	91
15:17	90
17:7–8	105
21	91
21:15–17	91, 151
21:18–19	151

SCRIPTURE INDEX

Acts

2:45–46	147
4:12	126
6	92, 130
6:2–4	92
6:1	126, 147
6:2	147
6:4	130, 147
8	42
10	103
10:9–16	150
10:9–15	127
14:15–17	45
14:17	152
16:31	135
17:25	125
17:28	71, 124, 146
17:16–29	45
19:29–31	51

Romans

5:4–5	144
5:8	145
10:8	126, 146, 152
10:13	135
10:17	79
11:22	125, 140
12:1	104, 128, 163
12:20	150
14:17	161

1 Corinthians

1:26–29	125
2:10–13	131
2:14–16	167
2:13–14	160
2:12	132
3:1–3	92
3:2	107, 139
3:3	92
4:6–21	207
4:9	51
6:13–14	140
8:1—11:1	205, 206, 207
8	161, 213
8:8	161
10	213
11:23–34	126
11:23–30	158
11:24	162
11:27	158
13:4–7	82
13:4	148
13:13	74
15:17	145

2 Corinthians

1:3–11	144
3:3	133
3:18	101, 146
11:23–33	122

Galatians

2:11–21	127
3:27–28	150
6:14–15	163

Ephesians

1:6	153
1:13	167
2:8–9	135
3:16	131
3:18–19	131
3:20	80
4:14	143
4:24	167
5:18	178
6:12	72

Philippians

2:13	146
3:19	161

Colossians

1:23	143
4:6	130

1 Thessalonians

2:13	135

1 Timothy

2:4	125, 152
4:1	138
4:6	89, 94, 138, 161
6:16	46

2 Timothy

1:13–14	130
1:13	94
2:15	60
3:16	47, 55, 86
3:17	117

Titus

1:2	63

Hebrews

4:12–13	85
4:12	49, 60
4:15	143
5:12–14	92
6:4–5	167
6:5	131
6:18	63
10:16–17	114
10:25	149
11:16	137
12:16	161
13:8–9	143
13:9	93
13:20	130

James

1:22–26	78
1:6	143
1:21	135
1:22	60
1:23	85

2:15–17	147
2:17–25	78
2:20	141
2:26	78

1 Peter

1:23	85
2:20–22	163
2:2	106, 108, 139
2:3	131
3:18	126
5:2	107

2 Peter

1:16–18	47
1:20–21	56
1:19	46, 109
1:21	47, 160

1 John

1:1–3	47
1:5	46, 54, 57
1:7	77
2:8–11	46
2:2	126
3:15–16	163
3:17	147

Revelation

7:9	127, 132, 151
10	100, 108
10:1–4	99
10:8–11	111
10:9–11	98
10:9–10	89
19:6–9	133, 144
19:9	127, 151
21:23	72
22:2	127

Subject Index

accessibility, 13, 15, 34, 62, 66, 70, 73, 76, 84, 90, 96, 98, 105, 107, 109, 118, 121, 124–26, 145–46, 151, 161, 170
addiction, 122, 169, 172
anthropology (theological), 53, 71–72, 124, 174, 185, 188, 207, 208–9
Aquinas, Thomas. *See* Thomas Aquinas.
Aristotle, xiii, xxi–xxiii, 1–7, 34, 66, 178, 194
Athanasius, xiii, xxvi, 94–95, 108–9, 120, 178, 182, 207
authority (of Scripture), xix, xx, xxv, 22, 30–31, 42–43, 46–48, 50–51, 55, 57–59, 62–63, 67, 75, 84, 110, 112–15, 121, 128, 159–60, 177, 179, 182–83, 186, 192–93, 197, 200, 202, 204–5, 209–11, 213

Balthasar, Hans Urs von, 41, 53–54, 179, 184
Barbour, Ian G., xxiv, 11, 16–20, 27–28, 30–31, 33, 35–36, 179, 191
Barth, Karl, 21, 86, 131, 136–37, 179, 181, 211
beauty, 2, 60–61, 79, 152, 178, 189
Belasco, Warren, xxii, 119–20, 125, 180
Black, Max, xxiv, 6–7, 11–12
Boisvert, Raymond, xxii, 69, 79, 137, 181
Bread of Life, 89, 90, 100, 126–27, 152, 169

Calvin, John, 22, 25, 53–54, 91–92, 183, 202, 208, 212

canon, xxv, 37, 42–44, 46, 48, 63, 177, 188, 190, 198, 202, 206, 210
children, xv, 9, 17, 23, 26, 28, 83, 92, 121, 125, 139, 163, 172, 175, 187
clarity (of Scripture), xx, 46, 48–49, 55, 61–62, 64, 110, 118–19, 121, 123, 208–9
coherence, 19, 27–28, 33, 78, 177, 207
community, xv, 21, 32, 36, 39, 43–44, 48, 58, 65–66, 72–73, 75, 79, 81, 83, 93, 101–3, 122–23, 125, 128, 132–33, 136–37, 147–51, 153, 156, 164, 170, 175, 177, 184, 187, 189–90, 198, 210
complexity, 24, 33, 40, 67, 71, 84, 185, 204
Confucius, 113, 184–86, 188, 193–94, 197, 208, 211–13
corporate memory, 38–39, 65, 175, 208
covenant, 45, 61, 78, 87–89, 93, 103, 114, 128–30, 132–33, 145–47, 149–50, 153, 175, 180, 211, 212
Creator-creature distinction, 71, 124, 161
criteria, xiii, xx, xxvi, 1, 16, 18–19, 21, 24, 27–30, 36, 38, 50, 109, 153–54, 156–58, 173
culture, xiii, 5, 8–10, 30, 34, 36, 43–44, 51, 65–67, 68–70, 81, 83–84, 86, 104, 113, 121–24, 126–27, 132, 143, 149, 155, 164–65, 168–70, 172, 175, 177, 180–81, 183–84, 186–90, 192–93, 195–96, 199–200, 205, 208, 210–11, 213

SUBJECT INDEX

death, xxii, 51, 60, 63, 66, 70, 86, 88–89, 90–91, 93, 103, 115–17, 119–20, 124–27, 136, 140, 142, 145, 151–52, 163, 165–67, 168–69, 195, 204

dependence, 21, 71, 77–78, 80, 83, 102, 108, 124, 127, 134, 138, 148, 152, 159, 163, 168, 171–72, 175

diversity, 17, 19, 33, 39, 57, 70, 123–24, 132, 151, 149, 175, 210

doxology, 152

Dulles, Avery, 27, 29, 32, 35–36, 187

ecclesiology, 71–72, 124, 128, 160, 188

embodiment, 35, 39, 41, 69, 74, 78–79, 83–84, 86, 99, 101–2, 104, 108, 111–12, 123, 131, 134, 140–42, 145, 175, 195–97

"empty space," 73–74, 84, 133, 182

enablement, 61, 71, 77, 81, 83, 111–12, 115, 118, 134–35, 138, 160

enjoyment, 40, 54–55, 60–61, 68, 73, 94, 108, 110, 118, 125, 128, 147, 152, 194

eternal life, 59, 89, 91, 126–28, 143–44, 151–52, 158–59, 163, 167

Eucharist, 89, 140, 158, 162, 178, 184, 186–88, 192, 194–96, 198–200, 205–7, 213

evangelical, xvi, xxv, xix, 24, 28, 30, 38, 50, 55, 86, 131, 136–37, 162, 177, 179–80, 184, 186–87, 198, 203, 209–10

exercise, 39, 42, 58, 92, 109, 117, 119, 122, 131, 133–34, 137–38, 141–42, 144–45, 159, 164, 166, 170–71, 175

experience, xxi, xxiv, 8, 10, 15–17, 19, 21–22, 25–29, 31–33, 37, 39, 50–51, 54, 65, 79, 81, 84, 95, 98, 101, 104, 112, 128, 142, 146, 149, 167, 182, 186, 195, 198, 202, 209

faith, xix, xxii, xxv, 12, 15–16, 19, 21, 27–32, 61–62, 65, 71, 74–75, 77–79, 83–85, 87, 89, 72, 93–96, 98, 106, 104, 113, 115, 117–18, 124, 126, 129, 134–42, 147, 152, 161

faithfulness, xiii, xv, 12, 27–31, 36, 38, 50, 52–54, 84, 109–10, 137–38, 153–54, 156–58, 166, 171, 173

fast-food, 104, 168, 172

fasting, 171–72, 180, 188, 191

Feeley-Harnik, Gillian, 86–89, 128, 146, 188

Feinberg, John, xiii, xx–xxi, xxv, xxvi, 27, 33, 38, 45–49, 50–52, 54, 55, 58, 63, 68, 72, 74, 80, 98, 100, 105–11, 114–16, 119–20, 160, 173–74, 188

fittingness, xiii, 3, 30, 32–34, 36, 38, 50, 55, 65, 84, 109–10, 121, 153–54, 156–58, 173

Fiumara, Gemma Corradi, xxi, 2, 4–6, 9–10, 21, 23, 38, 155, 188

fruitfulness, xiii, 19, 21, 27, 30, 34–36, 50, 70–72, 74, 84, 109, 124, 134, 153–54, 156–58, 173

gift, 61, 75, 89, 103, 126, 134, 140, 166–67, 172, 207, 209

grace, xvii, 13, 21, 77, 79, 93, 126, 133–35, 152–53, 184, 192

Gregory the Great, xiii, xxvi, 92, 94, 97–98, 108–9, 122, 191

growth, 67, 104–5, 107–8, 122–23, 138–40, 142, 149, 168, 174, 177, 187

habits, 44, 64, 78, 81, 101, 122, 140, 143, 168–69, 193

Heldke, Lisa, xxii, 69, 79, 181, 185, 192

hermeneutics, xx, xxiii–xxiv, 18, 24–25, 27, 29–30, 33, 39–41, 51, 75–76, 82, 93, 139, 164–65, 174, 177, 179, 181–82, 184, 189, 192, 200–201, 203–4, 206, 208–10, 213. *See also* interpretation.

Hobbes, Thomas, 5, 154–55, 183, 193

Holy Spirit, ix, 14–15, 19, 42, 44, 46–49, 56–57, 73, 83, 92, 100–101, 107, 111–12, 131, 144–45, 159–62, 167–68, 170, 203

hope, 47, 72, 74, 79–80, 82–83, 91, 88, 101, 123, 132–33, 143–44, 185, 209

SUBJECT INDEX

hospitality, xvi, xxi, 5, 8–9, 21, 79, 103, 129–31, 147, 151, 162, 167, 181, 194, 201, 204, 207, 212

hunger, 69, 86, 94–95, 106, 114, 119–20, 125–26, 138, 145, 151–52, 175, 178, 193, 196, 208

identity, 72, 89, 129, 132–33, 168, 178, 188, 194–95

imagination, 12, 15, 18, 38, 43–44, 61, 63–64, 77, 80, 99, 101, 110, 111, 119, 128, 143, 179, 182, 194

improvisation, 39–40, 43–44, 57, 75–77, 134, 185

inerrancy, 46–48, 55, 62–64, 84, 110, 119, 120–21

Ingesting Jesus, 89–91, 151, 158, 211

inspiration, iv, 22, 44, 46–47, 55–57, 64, 84, 110–12, 121, 160, 177, 181, 188, 190, 211

interpretation, iv, x, xiii, xvi, xx, xxiv–xxv, 2, 5, 13, 17, 22, 26, 29, 37–39, 51, 59, 65, 67, 72, 75–76, 97, 123–24, 131, 156, 173–74, 177, 179–81, 187–90, 194–95, 197, 200–201, 203–4, 209–10, 213. *See also* hermeneutics.

intimacy, 99, 102–3, 112, 136–37, 142, 146, 164, 168, 190

judgment, 5, 22, 31, 44, 50, 52, 60, 68–69, 86, 88, 93, 95, 115–16, 120, 133, 154, 163, 194

Kaplan, David, xxii, 128, 137, 182, 194, 208

Lakoff and Johnson, xiii, xxi, 5–6, 8–10, 22, 34, 86, 196

life, xv, xvii, xx–xxii, xxvi, 2, 7–11, 15, 17–19, 22–23, 26, 28, 35, 39–41, 45–47, 49, 55–57, 59, 60–64, 66–68, 70–72, 76–84, 86–94, 98, 100–108, 110, 113, 115–17, 119–20, 122, 124–28, 131, 133–35, 137–38, 140, 142–44, 145–47, 149–51, 152, 158–65, 167–70, 172, 174–75, 179–83, 187–91, 195, 197–98, 200–204, 206, 208–9, 211–12

light, xiii, xx–xxi, xxvi, 21–23, 27, 34–35, 38, 45–52, 54–55, 57–62, 64, 68–72, 74, 77–81, 83–86, 89–90, 105, 109–10, 112, 115, 117–21, 123–27, 130–32, 134–35, 138, 141–46, 150–55, 157, 164, 173, 184–85, 188, 200, 210, 212

love, xiii, 8, 14, 22–23, 28, 32–33, 61, 65, 73–74, 79, 82–83, 85, 90–91, 94, 101–2, 104, 108, 115–16, 131, 140, 144–49, 150–51, 152–53, 166, 172, 182–84, 187, 196, 201

Locke, John, 5, 154–55, 197

Marriage Supper of the Lamb, xxvi, 127, 144, 151–52

Martin, Dale, xx, xxv, xix, 37, 156, 198

McFague, Sallie, xxiii, xxiv, 10, 21, 22–27, 31, 33, 35, 37, 79, 80, 84–85, 155–56, 173, 189, 198

meat, 86, 92, 97, 107, 139, 143, 169, 188, 191, 211, 213

merit, 77, 134–35, 148, 174

metabolism, xxi, 111, 123, 144

metaphor, x–xi, xiii, xx–xxiii, 1–13, 17, 20–29, 30–38, 43–45, 47–48, 50–51, 53–54, 65–69, 74, 79–80, 84–87, 89–91, 98, 101, 106, 110, 120, 127, 154–57, 170, 173, 177–79, 181–86, 188, 190–92, 195–98, 200–210, 212

milk, 87, 92, 106–7, 132, 139, 149

mundane, 73, 81, 84, 104–5, 108, 122, 139–40, 144, 161, 175

mundanity, 73, 81, 84, 104–5, 108, 122, 139–40, 144, 161, 175

musical score, xiii, xx–xxi, xxvi, 22, 38–41, 43–44, 50–54, 56–68, 70–73, 75–85, 109, 115–19, 121–22, 124, 126, 134–35, 138, 141–42, 144–46, 153–54, 157, 164, 173

mystery, 9, 13–15, 33–34, 53, 71, 155–57, 170, 182, 192, 197, 204

SUBJECT INDEX

necessity (of Scripture), xx, 55, 59–60, 62–64, 83–84, 91, 101, 105, 108, 110, 115–16, 119, 121, 125, 134, 152, 171
nourishment, xxii, 95, 98, 102–3, 115–17, 119, 125, 137, 141, 202, 207

Origen, xiii, xxvi, 52, 94–96, 98, 108–9, 117, 119, 131, 170, 201

parable, 26, 73
participation, 42, 44, 58, 69, 78, 100, 102, 125, 134–35, 140, 147, 186, 206
Passover, 86, 126, 175
Peacocke, Arthur, 15, 19, 20–21, 34–35, 202, 204, 206
performance, 38–39, 41–42, 44, 51, 57, 61, 63, 65–68, 75, 77–81, 84, 117, 119, 121–22, 125, 134, 141–44
Peterson, Eugene, xiii, xix, xx, 3, 5, 10, 37–38, 65, 89, 98–99, 100–101, 108–9, 111, 117–18, 127, 135–36, 140–41, 160, 202
Plato, 64, 69, 202–3, 211
prayer, 37, 68, 83, 92, 99, 101, 108, 119, 127, 134, 156, 172, 195
preaching, 74–75, 107–8, 129, 174, 182
Putman, Rhyne, xvi, xix, xxv, 5, 22, 28, 30–31, 38–39, 50, 65, 67–68, 174, 203

Quintilian, 4–5, 7, 34, 203

Ramsey, Ian T., 13–17, 19–20, 25, 30, 32–33, 156–57, 204
regularity, 88, 104, 122–23, 144, 146–48
revelation, 8, 14–15, 27, 29, 31–32, 35–37, 45–49, 52, 54, 60, 99, 111, 116, 127, 181, 187–88, 192, 196
Richards, I. A., xxiii, 5, 6–8, 11, 155, 204

salt, 130–31, 180
salvation, 20, 22, 25, 47, 53, 61, 72, 79, 90, 92–93, 101, 103, 106, 125–27, 131, 134–35, 138, 140, 143, 152, 163–64, 167, 170, 179, 190, 195, 201, 213

science, xxiv, xxvi, 5, 7–9, 12–14, 16, 18–20, 22, 24, 26, 32–33, 35, 59, 121, 136, 155, 164–65, 177, 179, 182, 185–86, 190–93, 197–98, 200, 202, 204, 206–7, 209
score. *See* musical score.
script. *See* theatrical script.
"Scripture is food," vii, x, xiii, xx, xxvi, 37–38, 85, 93–94, 104, 123, 130, 151, 153–54, 157–59, 165, 169, 172–73, 175
social imaginary, 127, 175
sola scriptura, xxv, 30, 42, 50–51, 202
Soskice, Janet M., xxiii, 1–2, 5–6, 11–12, 20, 23, 25–26, 28–33, 35, 156, 189, 206
soteriology, 20, 71, 124–25, 205
speech-act theory, 44–45, 50
Spurgeon, Charles, 175
starvation, 66, 140, 152
sufficiency (of Scripture), xx, 28, 46, 48–49, 55, 61–62, 64, 71, 77, 83–84, 110, 116–18, 134, 137, 211
sustenance, 81, 89, 103, 105, 118, 134, 143, 152, 163, 168
swallowing God's Word, 87, 89, 97, 99, 118, 134, 135–38, 140–42, 146, 151–52, 167

taste, xxi, xvii, 69, 82, 87, 89, 90, 92, 96, 99–100, 103, 106, 118, 126, 128, 131, 133, 138, 167, 175, 182, 188, 191, 189, 193, 195, 202, 208, 213
terror, 60, 115
theater, 41, 51, 53–54, 56–60, 63–64, 66–68, 71–73, 75–79, 80–83, 115, 119, 125–26, 135, 137, 142–45, 150–51, 185, 202, 207, 212
theatrical script, xiii, xx–xxi, xxvi, 41–45, 50–54, 56–68, 70–73, 75–85, 112, 115–19, 121–22, 124, 131, 135, 138, 141–42, 144–46, 153–54, 157, 164, 173
theo-drama, xiii, xx–xxi, xxvi, 41–42, 44, 51, 53–54, 56, 66, 72, 78, 80, 173, 179

theology, xiii, xxiii, xxiv–xxvi, 5, 10, 13–15, 18–19, 21, 22–33, 35, 37–38, 44, 50–51, 54–55, 66, 71–72, 75–76, 79–80, 84–86, 94, 98, 100, 102, 109–10, 124, 127–28, 131, 136–40, 143, 150, 155–56, 162, 168–69, 171, 173–75, 177–84, 186–99, 200–203, 205–8, 209–10, 211–12,

Thiselton, Anthony, xiii, xx–xxi, xxiv, xxvi, 38–41, 43, 50, 54, 65, 75–76, 82, 173, 208

Thomas Aquinas, ix, 6, 21, 55, 195, 197, 199, 212

tradition, xi, 7, 15, 20, 22, 25, 27–29, 31–32, 36–37, 40, 42, 48, 52–55, 59, 61, 65–66, 72, 75, 84–85, 94, 109, 114–15, 117, 128, 140, 160, 171, 179, 181, 183–84, 192–93, 198, 200, 209

transformation, 112, 126, 159, 164, 183, 196, 199, 203, 206

truth, ix, xx, xxiii–xxiv, 5–6, 14, 18, 23–24, 25–27, 30, 32–33, 38, 41, 43, 45, 47, 49, 51, 58–59, 60, 62, 63–64, 69–70, 76, 78–79, 83, 96–97, 100, 116, 119–23, 132, 134, 138–39, 142–43, 152, 155, 164–67, 181–83, 189, 190–91, 194, 199, 201, 204, 210–11

urgency, 60, 86, 95, 98, 110, 115, 117, 119, 125, 145, 150–51, 164

Vanhoozer, Kevin, xiii, xx, xxi, 37–38, 41–45, 50–51, 53–57, 63–67, 73–76, 78, 80–82, 110–11, 114–15, 128, 168–69, 173, 177, 210

violence, xxi, 5, 8–9, 21, 79, 99, 131, 156, 162, 181, 205

visceral, xiii, xx, 108–9, 117, 120, 125, 140, 146, 150, 153, 163

Wirzba, Norman, xiii, xxii, 71, 98, 100, 102–4, 108–9, 115, 126, 134, 140, 147–48, 152, 180, 212

Word of God, ix, xi, xix, xxv–vi, 5, 22, 54, 86, 90, 92, 100, 112, 121, 131–32, 138–39, 141–42, 161, 167, 179–80, 199–202, 211

www.ingramcontent.com/pod-product-compliance
Lightning Source LLC
Chambersburg PA
CBHW051053230426
43667CB00013B/2273